SNOWBALL
IN A
BLIZZARD

About the Author

Steven Hatch is Assistant Professor of Medicine at the University of Massachusetts Medical School. He is also a practicing physician, clinical consultant, and medical student educator. Prior to his medical training, Hatch worked as a science writer for the Boston University School of Medicine.

SNOWBALL IN A BLIZZARD

The Tricky Problem of Uncertainty in Medicine

Steven Hatch

ATLANTIC BOOKS
London

First published in the United States in 2016 by Basic Books,
an imprint of the Perseus Books Group.

First published in Great Britain in 2016 by Atlantic Books,
an imprint of Atlantic Books Ltd.

This paperback edition published in Great Britain in 2017 by Atlantic Books.

10 9 8 7 6 5 4 3 2 1

A CIP catalogue record for this book is available from the British Library.

Paperback ISBN: 978 1 78239 989 6
E-book ISBN: 978 1 78239 988 9

Printed in Great Britain by Clays Ltd, St Ives plc

Atlantic Books
An Imprint of Atlantic Books Ltd
Ormond House
26–27 Boswell Street
London
WC1N 3JZ

www.atlantic-books.co.uk

For my Mother and Father

sorry, Pops, wish I coulda got it done sooner

Contents

Confusion + Science = Answers*

*Answers may require years of studying (real studying, not humanities studying) to be understood and will be expressed in terms of probability rather than absolute certainty.

—C. G. P. GREY

The diagnostic enterprise hinges on an optimistic notion that disease is part of a natural world that only awaits our understanding. But even if this is true, nature gives up its secrets grudgingly, and our finite senses are in some ways ill-suited to extracting them.

—GARY GREENBERG

Author's Note to the International Edition

THIS BOOK IS A SURVEY OF THE LANDSCAPE OF UNCERTAINTY IN MODERN medicine. My goal is to give the reader a sense of the challenges that can be found in all areas of medicine, which means that I cover a broad swath of topics ranging from cancer to women's health to cardiovascular disease to infectious disease and others besides. It is a wide overview, although I do not try to sacrifice depth in the process.

Because I practice medicine in the States, my preoccupations naturally involve the culture and philosophy of American medicine. The financing of medicine in the UK allows for a more rational allocation of resources, which minimizes or eliminates altogether some of the more perverse incentives that make US per capita spending on health nearly double that of almost every other highly industrialized country (even though the outcomes are no better, and are probably worse). That said, overdiagnosis and overtreatment are very real phenomena not just in the US but throughout the developed world, including the UK. They result from the collision between ever-advancing technologies and the uncertainties inherent in any automated system that purports to inform us about the world. We also tend to have a collective, partially misplaced faith that such technologies tidily solve all diagnostic and treatment dilemmas.

Indeed, it is the British medical establishment that has been in the vanguard of identifying and discussing the problems unleashed by uncertainty in medicine. Dr. Iona Heath, a London physician who recently retired from the NHS, has over the past several years written a series of eloquent essays focused on overdiagnosis and overtreatment, and the *British Medical Journal* has been one of the most receptive forums in the profession for considering the consequences of too much medicine.

In terms of wider medicine, disease is disease, and the physiology of a heart attack is no different in Leeds as it is in Las Vegas. However, Lyme disease, which I discuss in chapter five, remains mostly an American pathology—"pathology" both in the sense of what the odd little bacterium *Borrelia* does to its human host, as well as the profound anxiety that the condition produces, along with the consequent misunderstandings between patients and doctors. But ticks live everywhere in the world, and the diseases they transmit to humans with their bites are beginning to be appreciated in the UK and Europe just as in the US. Moreover, the kind of organized anti-rationalism that the believers in so-called chronic Lyme practice in the US has parallels in the UK. Previously it came mainly in the form of opposition to vaccination, but we are seeing the Lyme controversy surface in the UK as well, with the group Lyme Disease Action UK serving as a possible analogue to the Stateside pseudoscience-based organization ILADS that I discuss in that chapter.

The health system in the UK brings some of its own problems, given the top-down management of the National Health Service as well as its tight budgetary constraints. Communication is a topic I take up at the conclusion of the book and is at the heart of broaching uncertainty in medicine. It is also the number one issue that results in complaints to the UK Parliamentary and Health Service Ombudsman. The notion of "ICU rounds," which I explain in detail, may come as something of a surprise to British readers, but the practice has caught on here in the US, in no small part because of the huge benefits to be had with improved communication between the medical staff and patients and their families. There is much to suggest that what thoughts I have on redefining the role between doctor and patient may be even more important in the UK than the US.

As noted in the Acknowledgements, I am grateful to many colleagues who have provided their insights in areas beyond any clinical expertise I possess. If I have made any penetrating or illuminating observations in this book, the entirety of credit should go to them. But any inaccuracies, misrepresentations of fact, or failures of communication are due to me and me alone.

Newton, Massachusetts, and
Monrovia, Liberia, February 2016

Foreword

It is cold and raining outside the hospital—typical for this time of year. Rounds are about to start in the Intensive Care Unit. It's going to be a long day, as the unit is full. There are many tests that will need to be ordered and reviewed, many treatment options to consider, and many conversations with patients and family members that will need to take place. The charge nurse calls for the team to gather: the lead attending physician, the nurses, the pharmacist, the social worker, a medical resident. The difficult business of tending to patients on the edge of life is beginning its daily cycle.

The first stop is the room of a seventy-year-old woman who came to the emergency room with abdominal pain. Her symptoms began a little more than a day before she called the ambulance and got progressively worse during that time. By the time she came to the ER the night before, she was pale, and her skin was cool and clammy. Her blood pressure was low, which is why she was sent to the ICU.

Now, twelve hours later, her pressure continues to remain low, and she has been given special medications called "pressors" to boost it. She is awake but drowsy, and she doesn't respond much to questions. The team sweeps in and gathers around the bedside, looking over the paper chart, logging in to the portable laptop computer to review the labs, shuffling around to accommodate the group in the small space.

The patient's daughter and husband sit nearby. They are not asked to leave.

The medical resident summarizes the case for the team. Since coming in to the hospital, the patient has been given fluids and antibiotics. The resident explains that the on-call radiologist performed an abdominal ultrasound the previous evening.

"Why didn't we get a CAT scan?" the attending physician asks.

"Her creatinine was 1.4," the resident responds. "They wouldn't give her the contrast."

"So what did it show?"

"Normal bowel gas pattern, liver looked okay, not much else."

"Do we know why her kidney function is so low?"

"No, we don't," says the resident, who then offers a few thoughts as to what might be the cause and how it might be worked up. "I think if she doesn't improve, then we should call radiology and push for the CAT scan."

"We could throw her into ATN," the patient's nurse observes. "And it may not help us with the diagnosis."

None of this technical language is translated for the family, and the team doesn't stop to unpack the subtleties of the diagnostic dilemma. This is rounding as it's been done for generations in medicine: a highly specialized, fast-paced discussion to consider what is going on and what more needs to be done to restore a patient to health. What makes these rounds unusual is that this discussion is taking place directly in front of the family. There is no attempt to make it anything other than what it is, so the family has a direct window on how the team "really" functions. And although they have understood little of the jargon being bandied about, they heard the phrase "no, we don't" quite clearly and understood exactly what *that* meant.

The discussion continues for several more minutes. They examine the patient, itemize the various issues involved in her care, and formulate a detailed plan for the day. At the end, as the team readies itself for the next patient, the attending physician turns to the husband and daughter and explains, this time in the language of laypeople, the plan, which mainly revolves around finding the cause of the pain and the low blood pressure. Finally, he asks if they have any questions.

"So, you don't know why she's sick?" the daughter asks.

"Right now, I'm not sure."

"And you think it's a good idea to get this CAT scan, or not?"

"At the moment, I'm not sure. I want some more tests to return before I decide on that. Normally the CAT scan in this case is the best test we could order, but with her that carries some real risk, mainly because of the fact that the contrast we use can damage the kidneys, sometimes irreversibly."

"Do you think she needs antibiotics?"

"Yes. Of that, I'm pretty sure, at least until we have some other explanation that would clearly indicate we can safely stop them."

And with that, the team leaves.

What this family just witnessed was a discussion in which they heard the phrases "we don't know" and "I'm not sure" more than once. To some laypeople, that may smack of clinical incompetence or cluelessness, but actually such phrases are common currency in medical rounds. Nothing about this example is particularly unusual. Patients with unknown conditions and diagnostic dilemmas like hers are medicine's daily bread. Yet, far from creating anxiety and distress, the husband and the daughter are *satisfied* with the care she is receiving, and the frank admissions of uncertainty leave them *more* confident in the team than they would be if they had not been allowed to observe rounds in its unadorned state.

The example is fictitious.

But this ICU, where doctors and nurses and other health professionals openly confess to uncertainty, in plain sight of patients and families, is real.

INTRODUCTION

> There are known knowns; there are things we know that
> we know. There are known unknowns, that is to say, there
> are things that we know we don't know. But there are also
> unknown unknowns; there are things we do not know we
> don't know.
>
> —SECRETARY OF STATE DONALD RUMSFELD, 2002

*H*ow do we know that medicines work? How do we know that a blood test can unlock the mysteries of the body or that eating a particular diet may allow us to live longer? For instance, everyone knows with the kind of certainty that the earth revolves around the sun that smoking causes lung cancer, even though many of us have witnessed firsthand smokers who lived to old age as well as nonsmokers cut down by the disease. So why are we so confident of the harms of smoking? What allows public health officials to take to the airwaves and make that pronouncement with such certainty? Certainty brings a sense of comfort, but we do not often consider how we arrived at it.

Many of us take for granted that we live in an age of medicine where, to put it quite simply, we know what we are doing. We can read about common treatments for ailments that afflicted people in previous centuries and think to ourselves *I'm sure glad I didn't live in that time.* We look back at the confidence that doctors had in bloodletting, purgatives, and poultices of dung with horror; we see the faith of healers around the world in herbal remedies that we know are no match for our knowledge of biochemical molecular mechanics, which forms the basis of what we now call rational drug design.

If you had to ask someone who knew a little of the history of medicine about when it became modern, they'd say the transformation took place over about fifty years spanning the late nineteenth and early twentieth centuries. They would cite early precedents that indicated change was soon to come, like the creation of that ubiquitous tool of medicine, the stethoscope (1816), the dawn of modern anesthesia at Massachusetts General Hospital (1846), John Snow's detective work on cholera in London that basically founded modern epidemiology (1854), and so on. But the development of biochemistry by the 1880s, with its increasingly sophisticated ability to identify, purify, and even synthesize physiologically active compounds, really marked the turning point for medicine as a scientific discipline. This was followed in quick succession by the discovery of X-rays in 1895 and the development of the EKG in the early 1900s, which we still use today almost exactly as we did then. Everything that came before these advances was largely quackery, and everything after, largely rational.

This is, of course, an imagined generalization, as well as an oversimplification, but I don't think it stretches credulity to suggest that many people harbor some kind of notion like this about medicine. During the twentieth century, they would say, medicine could finally stand alongside its "harder" brethren of physics and chemistry and claim to be modern without a trace of irony. The reason we would allow ourselves to be subject to the ravages of some phenomenally toxic treatments for, say, pancreatic or bone marrow cancer, and regard equally toxic treatments doled out in 1750 for dropsy as something just short of manslaughter, is because we *know* that the cancer treatments can prolong life. We have science to shed light on the situation, and science not only separates the wheat from the chaff, but it invents new treatments by its intimate knowledge of the body at the molecular level, and not by running off into the forest gathering nuts and leaves helter-skelter, administering them to patients in an equally random manner.

Make no mistake, this depiction of medicine has much truth behind it. The advent of biochemistry really *did* allow for much more highly effective treatments, and early radiology set the stage for a quantum leap in the quality of diagnoses over the next several decades. Moreover, this period saw the rise of regulatory agencies that forced drug manufacturers to market their products based only on narrow indications for the diseases they could prove to treat, and state laws gave physicians and apothecaries rigorously trained in the sciences an almost complete monopoly on the business of healing. In the eighteenth century, pretty much anyone, anywhere in the West, no matter their level of education and scientific training, could hang up a shingle, call themselves "doctor," and treat patients in whatever way they saw fit. Yet in the age of modern medicine, about the past hundred years, if one did this without possessing the proper credentials, one would likely face jail time.

Since the beginning of this modern period of medicine, the advances have come with ever-increasing speed, in nearly every aspect of practice: breakthroughs in microbiology, in pharmacology, in surgery. In his signature work, *The Greatest Benefit to Mankind,* the eminent historian Roy Porter attempts to compress the entire history of medicine into a single volume.* The first half of the book, fully 350 pages of dense text, is devoted to the first 5,000 years of the profession, including chapters on early Chinese and Indian medicine. The second half of the book, by contrast, covers just the past *200.* It is an unmistakable message: *some* stuff was interesting in medical antiquity, but it was mostly a minor attraction until somewhere after 1800, and the show really got going the century after that.

This characterization can be found in popular culture as well. A few years ago the BBC aired a medical drama for two seasons. Known as *Casualty 1907* and *Casualty 1909* and marketed outside the UK under the title *London Hospital,* the show was a carefully constructed imagining of what life was like as modern medicine was taking shape in earnest. As much as the show was meant to entertain, it also clearly envisioned itself as a form of dramatic history lesson, in effect asking its viewers to think about how much has changed, but also what has not. We see, for instance, a rigid sexual hierarchy that has since been (mostly) obliterated, with male surgeons and physicians dashing about in dapper Edwardian dress, giving unambiguous orders to female nurses clad in demure floor-length dresses, color coded to their level of rank. We follow the patients' stories as they lie in large public wards instead of private rooms, many of them dying of

---

* A fantastic book. An abysmally boring, stuffy title.

diseases that we now dispatch with a spritz of penicillin. On the surface, it's a very antiquated environment.*

But those familiar with the inside of a hospital will find some of the similarities to today's health-care facilities uncanny: the aseptic technique of the OR, with gowned, gloved, and masked personnel, is practiced; infectious outbreaks, despite the inability of the staff to use antibiotics because they weren't yet discovered, are monitored and rapidly quarantined; and a variety of what was then experimental scientific gadgetry is employed, the clear forerunners to our high-tech medical subspecialties such as radiology. Their technology wasn't as sophisticated as ours, but these doctors and nurses, and the medical system they inhabit, is recognizably modern. They *know* what they are doing, at least in broad outlines. Moreover, they know what they know and they know what they don't, and that there is more to be discovered in the years to come. You can almost sense they are aware that modern doctors and nurses will be looking back at their work, knowing it was unsophisticated at one level but also aware that such work was on a trajectory. *We are like you,* these characters whisper. *We have solved the puzzle about* how *to know. It's a matter of details from here on out.*

Those characters, although invented in a contemporary writer's head, are saying something true about early modern medicine. We really *can* draw a straight line between us and them; their tools were crude, but we approach patient care and think about pathology in fundamentally the same way. The arrow of medical and scientific progress is quite real.

I work as a physician and was educated in this scientific method in the manner of tens of thousands of my brothers and sisters over the past century. We were trained in places like Iowa, Addis Ababa, London, Tokyo, and Mumbai. We speak a common language and have similar ways of thinking such that I can travel to Monrovia in the heart of West Africa, get off the airplane, go straight to the hospital and evaluate a patient there, offer drugs from their stockroom with which I am familiar, and teach nascent doctors about disease, in much the same way that I do in Worcester, Massachusetts. And I know that what we provide with our

---

* While I was writing this book, an American TV show called *The Knick* aired on the network Cinemax, which was similar in its preoccupations.

so-called Western approach can have a much more significant impact on the diseases people face in all of those places compared to the offerings of those who still traffic in folk remedies.

Yet, like all characterizations rooted in a powerful truth, our pride in our modernity has the potential to blind us to our own shortcomings and leave us overconfident in our abilities.

This book is in large part about those shortcomings and the resulting overconfidence it can produce. The term we'll give to this phenomenon is *uncertainty.* In the coming pages, we'll carefully consider uncertainty—specifically, the uncertainty that permeates the theory and practice of modern medicine. The book's premise is simple: namely, that doctors do not often "know" what they are doing with the same kind of mathematical precision that we associate with rocket scientists or chemical engineers. A diagnosis is, much more often than not, a conjecture, and a prognosis is typically less certain than *that.* There is a good deal more haziness in the world of medicine than most people—those both outside *and* inside that world—understand. The consequences of those misunderstandings can be perilous for physician and patient alike.

Uncertainty lies at the heart of what physicians do on a daily basis. Sometimes they are entirely aware of it, and sometimes they fail to appreciate it. Sometimes it prominently features in discussions between doctor and patient. And sometimes it is completely misunderstood. The purpose of this book is to show the reader not only *that* this is so, but *how* it is so as well.

Many of the original thinkers on probability and uncertainty were card playing and gambling types living in the eighteenth and nineteenth centuries. This isn't accidental, as these pastimes predispose one to bend one's thinking toward the statistical. It would take medicine a few centuries to catch on in earnest, but the groundwork for incorporating uncertainty into medicine was being laid during this heyday of the Enlightenment. Today, the early deeds of these medical pioneers are typically intoned with great solemnity at some occasion involving pomp and circumstance such as a White Coat ceremony or a medical school graduation. Interestingly, such evocations of the past are done for almost precisely the wrong reasons, with the protagonists being falsely depicted as bringers of truth and light to otherwise ignoramical colleagues. In Chapter 6, we'll see one of the most famous examples of a great medical hero who is typically portrayed as a towering genius, only he misunderstood the meaning of the very discovery he was credited with making.

Much of this book will discuss uncertainty by emphasizing the underestimated imperfection of results. My goal will be to show that these results, whether those of an individual blood test or those of a 10,000-person study five years in the making, need to be approached with varying levels of caution. I will try to highlight some areas in which doctors or patients or both have gotten themselves into trouble by neglecting uncertainty when they interpret results, not realizing that a positive test may sometimes be negative in reality or that a new miracle drug may not be so miraculous.

In the coming pages, I will attempt to survey the landscape of uncertainty in the diagnosis and treatment of human disease. One central assumption I make is that uncertainty, at least for the foreseeable future, is an irreducible feature of modern medicine and that understanding uncertainty is a vastly better strategy than ignoring it. My aim here is to explain those areas in which medical problem solving is most profoundly misunderstood, precisely because such misunderstandings can have, at the extreme, lethal consequences. This is as true for the physician who blithely and injudiciously prescribes a course of antibiotics for an elderly patient with a touch of a cough, who subsequently develops severe antibiotic-associated *Clostridium difficile* colitis, as it is for the family members of a patient in the ICU who keep pressing the medical team to perform invasive, high-risk tests that aren't likely to help with their loved one's outcome. This is as true for the policy makers and "disease advocates" who recommend screening tests that sometimes aren't very accurate as it is for the politicians who may take unscientific, and ultimately harmful, positions in the pursuit of currying favor with a special interest group. In short, I intended to make this book a practical exercise, a consideration of the consequences of uncertainty in medicine.

You might be wondering right now how uncertainty takes shape—that is, what does it actually *mean* to say that doctors are either uncertain about what they are doing or are overly confident because they haven't taken enough uncertainty into account? To better acquaint ourselves with how uncertainty manifests itself, let's consider one of the most well-known doctor-patient scenarios in medicine: the "cancer prognosis" talk. After all, when newly diagnosed cancer patients sit down with their oncologists, they ask a reasonable question: *how long do I have to live?* Most of us would expect to hear a dispassionate prediction from the physician as they stare the patient squarely, if sympathetically, in the eyes: *I'm sorry, but you have 8 months* . . . or *you have 2 years* or some other hard number that will coldly and scientifically state the simple truth.

What moment in the physician-patient encounter could be more well-known? This conversation forms the basis of plot lines in TV dramas and movies. Many or most patients and their family members rightly assume that, given the staggering array of blood tests and body scans that are performed in the aftermath of a new cancer diagnosis, all of that information can be reviewed by an oncologist and lead to a fairly accurate prediction of survival time. Nobody thinks that oncologists can predict someone's remaining time to the day or the week, but most assume that their predictions are accurate to within at least a few weeks' time.

In fact, oncologists almost *never* make these kinds of predictions because, as a rule, they're not very good at them. Only as death approaches closely do oncologists become reasonably decent at prognosticating survival length—and even then, the evidence that they predict survival time accurately is mixed at best. One review found that, even among terminally ill patients whose median survival is only four weeks, doctors were correct to within a week of survival in only 25 percent of cases, and in another 25 percent their predictions were wrong by more than four weeks! This review paper looked only at patients who were clearly at the end of their lives, and pretty much anyone, whether they possess a doctorate in medicine or not, can look at such patients and make a prediction with the same level of accuracy. So oncologists are keenly aware that guessing the life span of a patient with virtually any cancer, unless they are presenting at a very advanced stage, is an exercise in folly.

What oncologists *can* do with much greater accuracy is talk about the behavior of *groups* of people who have a given cancer that present at a given stage. Based on data collected about cancer patients over the past four decades, they can talk about the *odds* of survival. For example, we know that a patient who has localized bladder cancer has about a 70 percent chance of being alive at five years. We know this because cancer is a disease that is tracked by the federal government—physicians are required to submit each case to a national database we'll explore later—so that number is fairly precise. But oncologists saying to patients that they have a 70 percent chance of survival at five years is a very different thing than predicting they have about four years left of life, as some patients with bladder cancer will decline very quickly, and others will live for many years to come. Such discussions necessarily entail an honest admission by clinicians that they cannot look into the crystal ball, and such statements are only meant for patients and families to consider the odds, weighing the risks and benefits as they move forward and make decisions about their care because cancer treatment can often make patients very sick and reduce their quality of life.

Even here, however, the acknowledgment that a patient is subject to laws governed by probability rather than certainty can sometimes prove misleading. If a patient has squamous cell cancer of the lung, a very common kind of cancer, and the cancer is staged accurately, a doctor's statement that the patient has a 40 percent two-year survival with aggressive treatment is likely to be very accurate. This is because thousands of people each year develop this disease, and data from such a large cohort is less subject to the vicissitudes of random statistical fluctuations. Thus, researchers can know with reasonable precision how many people are likely to survive in a given time span.

But take a more unusual cancer, such as chondrosarcoma. This disease, a cancer of cartilage cells, is quite uncommon: only about four hundred people are diagnosed with the disease each year in the United States. Moreover, chondrosarcoma strikes people at various stages in life, and the cancer can appear at different parts in the body. It may turn out that an overall 40 percent survival is simply because the average of the past two years was 10 percent followed by 70 percent. Thus, the rarity of a given disease can cause even confident statements conceding inherent uncertainty to be untrustworthy! This is uncertainty in action. But it can be found everywhere in medicine, not just cancer diagnosis or prognosis. My goal here is to introduce you to some of the most important medical topics today in which uncertainty plays a starring role.

Snowball in a Blizzard

I chose the title *Snowball in a Blizzard* in part because it provides a useful metaphor for uncertainty. Picture a game in which we are testing you on your ability to recognize snowballs thrown through the air by some person, say, one hundred feet away, in the midst of a raging blizzard. You don't how many snowballs we're going to throw nor how often nor how fast or slow. You just have to look out into the whiteness and decide whether you see randomness or you have identified something as worthy of attention.

It should not be too hard for readers to picture the difficulty in the task. In the first chapter, we'll see an example where a scientist fiendishly performed almost exactly this experiment, except instead of using snowballs, he used schizophrenics while sane individuals served as the blizzard, and he tried to see whether psychiatrists were, as people would generally assume, good at spotting the "snowballs." (Though, to be clear, he didn't throw the patients through the air but rather had them present to psychiatric hospitals for admission.)

Snowball in a Blizzard, then, underscores that uncertainty is a structural component of data interpretation and is not merely some occasional and accidental feature of the system. Sometimes the uncertainty lies in diagnosis: *Does this test really mean that I have this disease?* Sometimes it pertains to treatment: *If I take this drug, am I really going to benefit from it?* Sometimes it concerns environmental risks: *Is it really okay for me to have coffee while I'm pregnant?* Rarely are the answers to these questions a simple unqualified yes or no. Uncertainty is nearly always part of the discussion; the only real question is, to what extent?

Moreover, *Snowball in a Blizzard* has a special resonance in medicine, for it is a well-known phrase among one group of doctors, a sort of inside joke they have indicating their keen appreciation of the complexities of data interpretation. I learned of it many years ago when I was a medical student at the University of Cincinnati, when I was rotating on the radiology service. One day we attended a lunch sponsored by the department, intended to be an overview for any of us who might be interested in pursuing radiology as a career. One of the speakers was finishing up his fellowship in pediatric radiology, and he had just accepted a position at a suburban hospital outside Philadelphia. "I'll be doing mostly general radiology, a little bit of everything," he said, but quickly added, "though I'm not going to do mammography. They have other folks for that. And I'm perfectly happy to avoid mammography anyway."

"Why would you want to avoid mammography?" someone asked.

"Because it's like trying to find a snowball in a blizzard," he immediately replied.

The phrase hit me like a thunderbolt. I came to learn that the witticism wasn't his originally but was a bit of grim humor passed around by radiologists as a commentary on the difficulties of detecting breast cancer— the "snowball"—in the "blizzard" of otherwise healthy breast tissue. (We will have much to say about mammograms in the coming pages.) Many radiologists, this doctor noted, have found themselves facing lawsuits for having missed tumors in women who went on to develop cancer.

Thus, "snowball in a blizzard" compresses all of the challenges of uncertainty into one pithy phrase. In doing so, it also expresses something peculiar about medicine that is not quite the same as the uncertainty discussed in other recent books, such as Nate Silver's *The Signal and the Noise* or Nicholas Nassim Taleb's *The Black Swan.* Those books have tackled, for instance, the problems associated with guessing which baseball team or political candidate will win, what will happen with the stock market, or when the next big earthquake will hit California. These are unknown future events, and the bare thesis of these books might be thought of as *predicting the future is not impossible, but it's more difficult than you think.* Yet, when radiologists make cracks about finding snowballs in blizzards, they are implying not only that the future is uncertain but that knowing what's going on *right now* and directly in front of one's nose can be equally uncertain!

Finally, it is fortuitous that the phrase "snowball in a blizzard" is used specifically with reference to mammography, for not only does it describe the technical challenges involved in accurate readings of mammograms, it also serves as a metonym about the contentious debate that has evolved around the practice. The biggest killer in the Western world is, by far, cardiovascular disease, and yet it is mammography that is arguably the most hotly debated medical technology in public health policy, particularly in the United States and the United Kingdom. Much has been written about mammography and the dimensions of the public discussion; my goal in a later chapter will be to apply a small amount of mathematical rigor to the debate to clarify the logic that guided the public health authorities when they issued new guidelines several years ago.

The Spectrum of Certainty

I will turn throughout the book to the notion of the spectrum of certainty—just *how much* we know about a given subject—and then make comparisons with other health matters. It is a compass by which one can

Benefit						Harm
high confidence		reasonable confidence	pure speculation	reasonable confidence		high confidence
strong evidence	moderate evidence	weak evidence	no evidence or contradictory evidence	weak evidence	moderate evidence	strong evidence

Figure I.1. Spectrum of certainty.

navigate the landscape of doctorspeak and the weighty decisions doctors or health authorities sometimes ask patients and family members to make. For instance, we know with a great deal of certainty that a sedentary lifestyle combined with a high-calorie, high-fat diet puts an individual at high risk of a variety of unpleasant medical problems. But do we know whether eating dark chocolate once each day will help prevent Alzheimer's dementia? As I will show in Chapter 7, the answer is, not so much. But let's sketch out the spectrum and then step back and see how it can be useful.

At the left end of the spectrum, we encounter the idealized form of medical knowledge, where we have a high level of confidence that we really do know something, that this something indicates clear-cut benefits, and that our knowledge will not be subject to massive revision.* Most people, and many doctors, believe this is the state of much current

---

* Readers shouldn't infer any political implications from this left-right-center scheme; it's totally arbitrary, whatever my political views.

medical knowledge, although I am a bit less sanguine that this is so. To be clear, I harbor no doubts whatsoever that red blood cells transport oxygen, for instance, or that HIV causes AIDS or that antibiotics improve a patient's chances of surviving bacterial pneumonia. But there are a good many other aspects of medicine that remain in murkier territory.

The center-left side of the spectrum is what most would consider *reasonable* but not absolute confidence. Do drugs for diabetes save lives? Depending on the drug, the answer is yes—but several diabetes medications come with some pretty serious side effects such that we can't assure *every* patient that taking them will be beneficial. Many diagnostic technologies occupy this part of the spectrum, as we'll discuss in the first few chapters. This part of the spectrum is still a pretty good place to find oneself, but there is room for improvement.

As we approach the middle of the spectrum, we enter the realm of pure speculation, where evidence is either completely contradictory or lacking altogether. For instance, at present there is much research devoted to the impact of the gut microbiome—that is, the many billions of bacteria that live inside our intestines and the DNA that they possess—on human behavior and mental state. Researchers have a sense that *something* is going on, though exactly *what* it is and how this may translate into drugs that might alter our perception of the world and how we interact with it is anyone's guess. (That hasn't stopped rampant speculation on the Internet about "mood altering" food regimens, however, an example of the profit to be made in creating the illusion of certainty. This is a problem that extends beyond the hawkers of fad diets: in Chapters 6 and 7, we'll look at what happens when multinational conglomerates do essentially the same thing.)

As we start to move toward the right side of the spectrum, we begin to have greater confidence in our knowledge, but this time our increasing certainty is of the *harms* of some drug or innovation or diagnostic approach. Perhaps the most provocative argument I will make in this book is that the practice of using mammograms to screen otherwise healthy women under the age of fifty is on the center-right spectrum of certainty and that there is a minimal to moderate amount of evidence that, as currently performed, mammography in this population carries overall net harm.

Finally, the right side of the spectrum is where we're quite confident that some practice is harmful. For example, avoiding antibiotics is a bad idea when one has clear signs of a probable bacterial infection. But it's also a bad idea to take antibiotics, especially for prolonged periods, when there is no evidence of bacterial infection. Occasionally, some groups have a vested interest in sowing seeds of confusion and having people believe that some medical knowledge is in the middle of the spectrum when in fact it is out toward the right end, as it is in this case. Chapter 5, which looks at the treatment of Lyme disease, will explore one such group in depth.

The spectrum of certainty is a crucial tool to help make sense out of the sometimes overwhelming information with which a patient or family member can be bombarded when trying to understand a health issue. My argument is that uncertainty is the great unspoken secret of medicine and that by ignoring this fundamental uncertainty we are doing real harm to ourselves. However, I don't make this argument in a linear fashion. False certainty can lead us as doctors and patients to misinterpret data and thus make bad choices; each chapter, in some way, adds evidence to this argument. But I cover a lot of ground and investigate many different disciplines. That's by design so that you can see just how pervasive uncertainty really can be. By utilizing the idea of the spectrum of certainty, readers can envision the broader claims of the book without having to "reinvent the wheel," as it were, as they read each new chapter, struggling to connect each divergent story, hearing only the static and not the signal.

A working notion of the spectrum of certainty also allows one to move past the binary construction of doctors either knowing everything or doctors knowing nothing at all (more on this latter view anon). It also provides readers with some perspective on how best one can probe a health-care provider, allowing one to ask the deceivingly simple question about what is or isn't known about a subject. Finally, it provides a framework by which we can apply some mathematical precision to a topic. For example, in Chapter 1 we'll look at the prostate specific antigen (PSA) test, a screening tool for prostate cancer; when one attempts to quantify the exact benefits of the PSA test, the often fierce debates over the past ten to twenty years about its value seem fairly ridiculous.

Consider the Donald Rumsfeld quote that began the introduction. "There are known knowns, there are known unknowns, and there are unknown unknowns"—his quip came as part of a tart reply to a reporter who had the temerity to question whether the Bush administration should have anticipated the chaos that engulfed Iraq after the US armed forces deposed Saddam Hussein in 2002. His point, a rather dressed-up version of the observation "shit happens," was meant to convey the impossibility of knowing with certainty how a post-Hussein world would work. Whatever else one may think of Rumsfeld, the administration he served, or the planning and prosecution of the Iraq War, he left us with one of the more crisp and useful observations of the nature of epistemology: sometimes one is certain of the state of the world, sometimes one can have a clue about it, and sometimes one is utterly flummoxed by what's really out there.

This book is primarily concerned about the middle region of the spectrum of certainty: the known unknowns in medicine. Moreover, this book asserts something that may be a surprise to both patients and doctors alike: *most* of medicine functions in the world of known unknowns—as well as the unknown unknowns! That is, doctors often may know the general outlines of a problem but may not know, or even be able to know, with total certainty the specific problem in a given patient at a given time. This book is an attempt to describe that aspect of medicine where the light of knowledge is dim and the mind can play tricks on itself, diagnosing things that turn out not to be there or creating mass hysteria over relatively trivial and distant threats such as exotic, tropical viruses while simultaneously ignoring the public menace of the double cheeseburger, a significantly more lethal object in the Western world.

The writer Michael Pollan wryly informed the readers of his book *In Defense of Food* that his opening seven words—"eat food, not too much, mostly plants"—were the boiled-down advice of his entire tome, and the chapters themselves were merely clarification and elaboration of that advice. In medicine, too, we have an answer to the seemingly ferociously daunting question, how do I stay healthy? We've known the answer with increasing scientific certainty for several decades now, and it mirrors the straightforwardness of Pollan's advice in the same number of words:

Exercise more,
Eat less, and
Do not smoke.

This is the far left of the spectrum of certainty, and not much else can be found out there except one or two items that we'll take up during the course of this book. Unless you have some relatively unusual disease such as lupus or primary biliary cirrhosis that is often genetically determined or requires special medications, this is really all you need to know about maintaining your health. That is because most people in the West die from cardiovascular disease and diabetes (which is why you should eat modestly and exercise) or emphysema and lung cancer (which is why you shouldn't smoke). Everything else is, largely, commentary. Of course, there are important health stories that deserve coverage, but one could make a strong case that these seven words should begin and end *every* news item that deals with medicine and health. So, for those reading books on the economy class model, I just gave away the secrets to healthy living at the outset, and you can feel free to read no further.

The Road Map

Broadly speaking, there are three major portions of this book. The early chapters deal with problems relating to uncertainty in *diagnosis*—that is, when do we know that someone has a disease? Chapter 1, "*Primum Non Nocere*" (an ancient Latin dictum meaning "first, do no harm" that continues to be regarded as a bedrock value of medicine to this day) looks at the conundrum of overdiagnosis. With increasingly sensitive ways of detecting disease by means of technological advances in radiology and biochemistry, we are able to find diseases earlier in their course and thus have a greater impact on mortality. But it's become clear over the past generation that there is a price to be paid for this, and it has come in our finding "disease" that turns out *not* to be disease in the conventional sense of the term—namely, some biologic process that would lead to illness or death if left unattended. For instance, we'll see how doctors have found more and more cases of cancer, even though finding these cancers earlier hasn't ended up saving any lives, which must mean that the cancers they've found aren't the kind of cancers that actually kill people.

The problem is that we can only know such nondisease diseases exist at a population level; when confronted with an individual patient, it is impossible to know with much certainty that some treatment will carry the expected benefit. Since all treatments carry risks, this means that we are quite probably harming some patients as a consequence of overdiagnosis.

The second chapter, "The Perils of Predictive Value," briefly recounts the tale of the physicist and author Leonard Mlodinow when he received a shocking diagnosis of a terminal illness as part of a standard insurance exam. Only the diagnosis was wrong, and we will investigate just how wrong it was. Mlodinow's story is a cautionary tale in the perils of what are known as "false-positive" tests, which is exactly what it sounds like— tests that appear to indicate disease but do so wrongly because no test is 100 percent perfect. The consequences of false-positive tests—and what treatments doctors might suggest as a consequence of those tests—can range from mild anxiety to outright bodily mutilation.

For reasons that I will discuss, false positives are a frequent problem in screening tests, and as such Mlodinow's story helps illustrate the core issue in the third chapter, "Snowball in a Blizzard," which looks at the thorny issue of mammography. Although mammograms continue to be regarded as one of the most important ways in which women can have an enormous positive impact on their health, the data suggest a more nuanced reality. In large part this is because the technology can detect breast cancer before it becomes clinically apparent, but uncertainty creates false positives, and women whose mammograms are falsely positive can suffer serious harm. Thus, ascertaining the true value of mammography involves weighing these two opposing variables. I will demonstrate, by looking at some sample data, the relative size of the benefit, as well as the risk.

The middle chapters of the book are mainly concerned with uncertainty in *treatment*. Chapter 4, "The Pressures of Managing Pressure," looks at recent guidelines for treating hypertension and how uncertainty divided expert consensus in a fairly dramatic manner. Chapter 5, "Lyme's False Prophets," investigates a different set of expert-driven recommendations, which formed a kind of mirror image of the hypertension guidelines: although the expert consensus about Lyme diagnosis and treatment is absolute, the popular perception is that there is great controversy. "Lyme's False Prophets" looks at how this public confusion arose through the Internet, various advocacy groups, and at least one powerful politician.

Chapter 6, "The Origins of Knowledge and the Seeds of Uncertainty," considers how uncertainty forms a structural component of drug trials. I will explore two of the biggest blockbuster classes of drugs of the modern age: lipid-lowering statin drugs such as Lipitor and the antidepressant class of drugs known as SSRIs, such as Prozac. In both cases, I'll put them under a microscope to see what we do and don't know about what these drugs can offer to patients and consider the impact that uncertainty has on the term "effectiveness" in relation to drugs. Chapter 7, "The Correlation/Causation Problem," evaluates ways other than drug trials that we learn about (or fail to know about) a drug's usefulness. That is, although drug trials produce as a rule the most ironclad data about how good a drug can be, there are other methods for assessing a drug's effectiveness, and these methods are subject to their own kinds of uncertainty. I'll consider some of the major challenges involved in interpreting "retrospective" data.

Finally, I will briefly look at the role media plays in shaping our attitudes about medicine either by emphasizing or disregarding uncertainty. We live in an age of unfettered access to all sorts of media, and yet whether one is watching a local television newscast or reading the latest online health report, a good number of stories follow broadly similar patterns, frequently leaving consumers overestimating medicine's miraculousness on the one hand or overscared by the system on the other. But I'll also examine one crusader for health media and his organization's vision for how the media can provide a more balanced picture of what modern medicine has to offer without too much fuss, if they would only listen.

After we've gone on this tour, I'll consider ways in which the average person might benefit from an increased understanding about these concepts because the topics driving health care today will surely be different not long after the publication of this book. Lastly, in the Appendix, I will explain in a very nontechnical way some of the mathematical concepts that underpin the discipline of biostatistics, using some of the studies we have looked at as models for understanding such concepts without using equations.

Uncertainty pervades medicine: surgeons as well as psychiatrists must cope with its presence, whether they are aware of it or not. Problems that arise from uncertainty can be found in the hospital corridors, the pathology lab, the nursing home, and in urgent telephone calls from sick and worried patients. Nearly all exercises in clinical judgment involve incorporating uncertainty into equations of medical reasoning—a variable that, like Einstein's cosmological constant, cannot be stamped out no matter how much brainpower is brought to bear. By developing an appreciation for uncertainty, we can get at the heart of many of today's medical mysteries. By bringing uncertainty into open discussion, we can assess the real value of mammograms, recognize the hype of so many medical reports, sense when to push a physician for more testing, or resist a physician's enthusiasm when other tests or treatments are being offered.

Ultimately, appreciating the subtleties and parameters of uncertainty allows patients and family members to be empowered. I am writing this book to help people understand uncertainty to help them navigate the swift currents and roiling waters of modern medicine. I cannot promise to translate the often inscrutable language of physicians and the medical research that is their touchstone, but I can attempt to give people a tool by which real communication can take place.

Nobody Knows Anything

It may be unsettling to a reader thus far unaccustomed to these concepts to be told that uncertainty is central to modern medicine. A sense of despair can set in when discussions of probability and statistics take center stage in the doctor-patient interaction. Frank admissions of uncertainty can often be met with irritation, because the idea that a test doesn't provide an unassailable answer that describes a crystal-clear reality is so foreign to many people. Some may have the emotional urge to conclude, after reading thus far, that these tests are pretty much worthless and that, in the immortal words of screenwriter William Goldman, "nobody knows anything."

But this book is not a jeremiad. The nihilism of "nobody knows anything," although emotionally satisfying on a certain level, is just that: an emotional response, a spasm of frustration with a health-care system that is mightily complicated enough, to say nothing of expensive, bureaucratic, and frequently impersonal. Only by stripping away the layers of misunderstanding about what medicine is and how it works can patients and families begin to be their own best advocates. Uncertainty is far from the only area in which misconceptions exist, but I would argue it is a critical area, and grasping it might just help people avoid some of the more unpleasant shocks that medicine is capable of delivering.

Indeed, the *point* of highlighting all these various instances of the limits of our medical knowledge is to demonstrate that these can be teaching moments—occasions where we can illustrate what's at stake in a medical decision and how we think about a problem. Are the stakes high or low? Are the repercussions of a decision significant or trivial? And is the evidence supporting a given decision overwhelming, minimal, or somewhere in between? By opening up about uncertainty, we are championing patient autonomy, rather than arrogantly flicking it away as an irritating feel-good ideal.

This book is *hopeful* in its outlook, which I ask readers to keep in mind if they find themselves thinking in the early chapters how deeply flawed our medical practices truly are, and how foolish our certainties. My goal is to offer you a vision: *read this book and you will learn something to improve your life and deepen your understanding of the process of medicine.* I want readers to see how embracing uncertainty allows for more humane treatment, less anxiety, and better care. But to do that we will need to confront some sobering realities of our modern medical system. It may require the periodic deep breath and the awareness that acquainting yourself with this medical machine can occasionally make for bleak reading. Have faith, for there are rewards in knowing and understanding. There is a tangible and powerful light at the end of the tunnel.

Narrative and Uncertainty

Why do people—physician and patient alike—have such difficulties coping with concepts as probability and uncertainty? The answers can be found in the disciplines of evolution and psychology and are largely beyond the scope of this book, but the power of stories, and the influence of narratives on our thinking, is critically important. We think about ourselves, and of the universe around us, in absolute terms of cause and effect. We don't regard our lives as being subject to mere chance; we assume that the variables are within our control and that our successes can be attributed to our strengths and our failures to our weaknesses. Medicine, too, is a story of sorts, and we resist the notion that chance plays a key role in the endeavor.

But this just isn't so. It is a trick of the mind, and it impedes us from understanding the modern world. Daniel Kahneman, a Nobel laureate in economics, refers to this as the "narrative fallacy," writing that it inevitably arises "from our continuous attempt to make sense of the world," adding that "the explanatory stories that people find compelling are simple; are concrete rather than abstract . . . and focus on a few striking events that happened rather than on the countless events that failed to happen." In medicine—both at the personal and at the policy level—succumbing to the narrative fallacy can be disastrous.

Take a look at nearly any news story on medicine, and you will see this devotion to narrative in full view. Invariably, a story on a new diabetes drug or a fancy new surgical technique or an unfortunate reaction to a medication will begin with the saga of one (or more) patients. All too frequently statistics aren't even mentioned: Is this patient's story common or rare? Is the story applicable to the many or the few? When these rather important details are sidestepped, the misunderstandings can be profound, with the result that patients and families often feel betrayed when the state-of-the-art technology fails to deliver.

I think the reason people have so much difficulty coping with uncertainty is that these powerful narratives, from which the narrative fallacy arises, are both hidden and in plain sight. You can almost pluck these narratives out of the air as they swirl around us. They are found in the e-mails that circulate through cyberspace, where links to health news items are shared by colleagues and friends; they lurk in the television dramas that portray doctors working at the cutting edge; and they can be heard in the chit-chat of weekend dinner parties, with people exchanging concerns and fears, both real and imagined, about various public health scares. Nowhere in these exchanges can you find people explicitly stating them, for they would seem laughable oversimplifications. Yet I would argue that they are there nonetheless, and they have a major influence on our thinking.

A variety of mutually reinforcing narratives are upended by a discussion about overdiagnosis. *Technology is beneficial* is one message (with the implication that it is *always* so), and this overlaps with *images reveal everything* and *expert doctors radiate confidence*. These are entries in the "medicine is good" category, and they explain in part the enduring goodwill of the vast majority of the public toward physicians and why they remain among the most respected of professions.

Then there is the dark side of these narratives, which fall under the "medicine is bad" heading, and although they are often held by people completely hostile to the basic principles of modern medicine, they aren't held only by antiscientific cranks. These messages include *technology is cold* and *the pharmaceutical industry tries to keep people sick for profit* and *doctors are too often* too *sure of themselves*. These medicine narratives lead to the kind of distrust that has allowed, for instance, the spread of so-called alternative medicine, which is mostly harmless as long as patients are healthy but can sometimes lead to delays in treatment for people with serious illnesses.

At some level, the "medicine is good" and the "medicine is bad" narratives are *both* right. I am not implying I believe in an anything-goes cultural relativism, but rather that, because our knowledge is based on uncertainty, medicine cannot essentially be *only* one thing or another. You can find specific stories to support both of these worldviews. Want to be appalled by doctors who suck at the teat of the pharmaceutical industry through bloated consulting fees and influence peddling that is corruption in all but name only? Spend some time investigating some of the more unsavory aspects of modern psychiatry.* Want to see the triumph of modern medicine as it conquers death? Learn about the development of electrocardiography or the history of antibiotics and what they've each done for patients in the past hundred or so years.

---

* Sorry, psychiatry: you're far from the only specialty with such problems, but you may be the worst. And, to be clear, by "psychiatry" I am referring not (solely) to *psychiatrists,* i.e., the specialists trained in psychiatry, but the *practice,* in whatever form, of psychiatry, which includes a hefty amount of primary care physicians doling out atypical antipsychotics and the like.

Thus, any of these narratives can be "true" in particular situations. My point is that they're so powerful that they can be capable of having all of us, doctors and patients alike, ignore *evidence* that suggests that in a given situation those narratives are wrong. The drug industry may be driven by profits (see: psychiatry, modern practice of), but the vaccines they make really are safe and lifesaving—indeed, astonishingly so—and perform vastly better than virtually any other pharmaceutical product. Yet there is a persistent and irrational belief, even among some highly sophisticated and well-informed people, that vaccines are associated with a variety of harms, particularly autism. The tenacity with which people cling to views such as these, or the obliviousness of those people to the strong evidence that such views are simply wrong, is due in large measure to the power of these narratives that color our thinking.

This book argues that, to find our way forward and extricate ourselves from being victims of these sometimes overly simplistic narratives, we must look past the slogans and instead directly wrestle with the data. I don't offer an analysis of all the narratives that underlie each of the stories I will tell in the coming pages, but they are there nonetheless, coloring and shaping our attitudes about new medical developments in addition to long-standing medical practices. These narratives, like the science and medicine they try to make sense of, are not inherently good or bad; they are tools by which we can either improve our wellness, or butcher ourselves—sometimes to death—in the name of health.

PRIMUM NON NOCERE: THE MOTIVATIONS AND HAZARDS OF OVERDIAGNOSIS

Many people are overconfident, prone to place too much faith in their intuitions . . . when people believe a conclusion is true, they are also very likely to believe arguments that appear to support it, even when those arguments are unsound.

—DANIEL KAHNEMAN

Stripped of all its complexities, the process of medicine consists of two basic activities. The first activity concerns diagnosis: the identification of some condition, some malady that afflicts the body. The second activity—done with some hope and luck in addition to some science—is treatment: the attempted eradication of disease, or at least the relief of symptoms, through the prescription of medicines or the correction of anatomy via surgery. Doctors, and the folk healers who preceded them, have been engaged in this two-pronged approach for millennia.

The emphasis on careful diagnosis characterizes the vocation of medicine even from antiquity: it is why we still regard Hippocrates, who lived more than 2,000 years ago, as our profession's paterfamilias. Although our medicine has changed radically since the time of the ancient Greeks, we can still see the faint outlines of their diagnostic approach to this day. For instance, medical students routinely learn to observe a characteristically odd shape to fingernails known as "clubbing"; its identification suggests a variety of chronic diseases ranging from emphysema to cancer, and Hippocrates himself is credited with the earliest known clinical descriptions of the phenomenon. To this day, some of the old-timers will still use the term "Hippocratic nails" to describe clubbing.

The process of diagnosis until very recently consisted mainly of talking to patients about their symptoms and examining them—that is, investigating their bodies for the physical signs associated with disease. But we have witnessed a quantum leap over the past generation or so, and the act of diagnosis today would have blown the mind of a doctor from one hundred years ago. What doctors possess now to not only identify but precisely locate a disease is astonishing. MRIs and CT scans allow us to peek under the hood, so to speak, and look all the way through the body as if we had sliced it up, sometimes finding small pockets of infection or cancer that would have been difficult bordering on impossible to find before their advent. Blood tests can distinguish among dozens of viruses and bacteria, identify whether some infections occurred in the past or are happening in the present, report our electrolyte levels, locate the exact spot of a genetic mutation out of 3 billion "letters" of DNA, and do all of this within days, if not hours. Cameras can now be used to visualize seemingly any part of the body on a television screen, even to the point where we can swallow a pill with a tiny camera and in less than a day drop off a cartridge with an image file of a colonoscopy.

As we launch into this first stop on our tour of uncertainty, one point requires some emphasis at the outset: this is *amazing*. We are living in a golden age of diagnosis. There are entire categories of disease of which we have only recently become aware—conditions that we had mistakenly lumped into others, lacking the technology to distinguish them. As we improve in our ability to discover diseases and find ever-better tests by which we can diagnose such diseases, the likelihood that doctors will make life better for their patients increases exponentially. These new technologies are absolutely indispensable to that process.

That said, the changes wrought by what we might call the great diagnostic shift is only beginning to be understood. There has been a slow recognition that not all of these changes have been beneficial. The precision with which we can make diagnoses is profound, but precision is not the same thing as certainty. One of the main problems with diagnosis today is that these new technologies are so sensitive, so able to find diseases, and in such early stages of development, that they leave us too confident that we've identified disease when we probably haven't. This process of finding-disease-that-isn't-disease is called overdiagnosis, and it is possibly the most important real-world consequence of our misguided faith in certainty.

The best place to start to illustrate this, ironically, is by investigating a profession that still barely uses all of this new diagnostic technology: psychiatry. I'll begin by looking at one of the more infamous chapters in the history of that profession and considering how that might be related to CTs and MRIs and blood tests and all the rest.

Error Machines

Between 1969 and 1972, a group of eight patients had presented to a variety of psychiatric hospitals across the United States with a remarkably similar complaint. They all said they were hearing voices. This is hardly uncommon in psychiatric institutions, but in each case the voices said the same three words: "empty," "hollow," and "thud."

Many of these eight patients worked in the field of mental health: four were either psychologists or psychiatrists, and a fifth was a graduate student in psychology. The remaining three included another doctor (a pediatrician), a painter, and a housewife. None of them had any prior history of psychiatric problems, and none of them behaved strangely during their initial evaluations. Following the initial assessments, seven of these eight patients were admitted with the diagnosis of paranoid schizophrenia, while the eighth was diagnosed with manic-depressive psychosis.

What made this cohort of patients singularly interesting to the profession of psychiatry, and why they are known to posterity, is that in addition to having precisely the same auditory hallucination at different times and in different places, they shared one other feature: they were all completely sane. These eight "patients" were, in fact, volunteers for a brilliant and devious study conducted on the *psychiatrists*, and more broadly on the staff at the psychiatric facilities where the evaluations took place. The results were published in 1973 in one of the most unusual papers ever to grace the pages of *Science*, then as now one of the greatest scientific journals in the world.

The research question of the author, Dr. David Rosenhan, was elegant in its simplicity: Could highly trained mental health professionals detect a sane patient in an insane place? The answer was a resounding no. The details of what has since been come to be called the Rosenhan experiment make for somewhat uncomfortable reading and can be found without difficulty on the Internet. The results, written in a fluid prose style easily comprehensible to nonscientists, should be humbling to the profession of psychiatry. More than forty years after the publication of this seminal experiment, I am still not sure if that is the case.

The key to the experiment relied on the distinction between a psychiatric symptom in a sane person and the clinical definition of insanity. For the experiment, the participants were otherwise normal people presenting with one single, transient, unusual symptom. They all reported experiencing an isolated auditory hallucination, and although such a symptom is associated with mental illness, a lone hallucination is not equivalent to schizophrenia. Many people experience transitory hallucinations without having a total psychiatric breakdown. What is required for a diagnosis like schizophrenia is evidence of a person's complete inability to function in the world as a consequence of the hallucinations and the inability to stop or control such hallucinations to the point where that person is overwhelmed. The pseudopatients—which included Rosenhan himself—were all instructed to behave as they normally do in life, which prior to their admission had raised no alarm to anyone. The only psychiatric diagnosis that could reasonably be made fell far short of schizophrenia or manic depression.

Their sanity made no difference. Despite the paucity of evidence that they suffered from deeper pathology, not only did all of the participants end up with the most global and profound labels of mental illness, they were held for astonishingly long times to manage these conditions. The average length of hospitalization was nineteen days, with the shortest lasting seven days and the longest a dumbfounding fifty-two. Moreover, it was hardly the psychiatrists alone who failed to notice the sanity of the participants, as the nurses and attendants treated the patients in the same manner. Indeed, a review of the nursing records showed that they interpreted specific behaviors as evidence of pathology, even though such behavior would raise no suspicions outside a mental hospital. "Patient engaged in writing behavior" was one of the observations made when one pseudopatient was simply taking notes on his surroundings for later review, a line that has since been quoted hundreds of times in the medical literature and by patient advocates skeptical of modern psychiatry's benefits.

By contrast, the insane—that is, the true psychiatric patients—were surprisingly good at spotting sanity. During the first three hospitalizations, 35 of 118 patients voiced varying degrees of suspicion that the participants were either journalists, professors, or some other kind of sane person "checking up on the hospital." Despite reassurances that they "had been sick before but were fine now," some of the actual patients persisted in their belief that the pseudopatients had no history of psychiatric problems for the entire length of the hospitalizations in question. In some ways, the number is even more remarkable, because the 35 "diagnoses" offered by the psychiatric patients came unbidden, in contrast to those of the psychiatry staff who were charged with the responsibility of making a diagnosis. "The fact that the patients often recognized normality when staff did not raises important questions," Rosenhan commented in what can only be regarded as a major understatement.

Yet the most fiendish portion of the Rosenhan experiment came after these pseudopatients were discharged. Rosenhan presented the results to the staff at a prestigious psychiatric research and teaching hospital and was greeted with widespread disbelief. Surely, the staff argued, such a miscarriage of medicine would not occur at our institution. So Rosenhan tipped his hand and informed them that over the course of the next three months, one or more pseudopatients would be admitted to their hospital. He provided the staff with questionnaires to assess their assessments, so to speak, of the level of sanity or insanity of the admitted patients. During the experimental period, 193 patients were admitted. Of these, 41 were considered to be pseudopatients by at least one staff member, and 23 were labeled pseudopatients by the psychiatrists. Nineteen patients in all were identified as pseudopatients by at least two mental health professionals. In reality, none of the 193 admissions were pseudopatients— or as Rosenhan sardonically noted, if they were, they weren't involved in his research.

Viewed in sum, the Rosenhan experiment appears to be a case study in the limitations in psychiatric diagnosis and the effects of institutionalization on the mentally ill. "It could be a mistake, and a very unfortunate one, to consider that what happened to us derived from malice or stupidity on the part of the staff," he wrote in conclusion. "Where they failed, as they sometimes did painfully, it would be more accurate to attribute those failures to the environment in which they, too, found themselves than to personal callousness."

The meaning of the Rosenhan experiment is still hotly debated to the present day. Does it demonstrate that psychiatry is hopelessly mired in subjective impressions, where once a label is applied, it sticks beyond all reason, to the point that prolonged sane behavior cannot even be recognized for what it is? Or was the experiment jerry-rigged to arrive at this conclusion in the first place? Among the criticisms of the research was that, instead of testing the ability of the psychiatrists to diagnose insanity, it was actually just testing the ability of the patients to lie. One analysis offered the following counterfactual: if a person could steal a few pints of blood, swallow it, and later present to an emergency room vomiting up the blood without explaining what happened, the subsequent diagnosis of a stomach ulcer wouldn't mean that the staff didn't know how to diagnose that condition.

My goal here is not to take a strong side in this dispute, although on the whole I do find Dr. Rosenhan's critique compelling and think the data does indeed support his thesis. Regardless, I wish to point out that the legacy of the Rosenhan experiment is almost universally understood through the lens of *psychiatry* and what it means for that profession, and nobody ever considers the wider implications it may have for the rest of medicine. Psychiatrists are often, if only politely and subtly, dismissed by their colleagues for engaging in what is seen as a quasimedieval enterprise. Internists, surgeons, and obstetricians can all employ tests that provide binary or quantifiable results. Their ability to diagnose conditions is vastly superior to the crude tools of psychiatry, the reasoning goes. Why should they be surprised that someone showed psychiatrists, however bright they are, don't know what they're doing?

But I would argue the experiment's results can in fact be applied well beyond the realm of psychiatry—they can be generalized to *all* doctors when they consider *all* diagnoses. And there is a growing body of research showing that nonpsychiatric doctors can be just as flawed in their judgments as insanity doctors who are unable to see sane people standing right in front of them. Rosenhan thought he was doing an experiment on diagnosis in psychiatry, but at a deeper level he was performing an experiment on diagnosis itself, and it wasn't psychiatrists per se who failed in this regard, it was doctors. The fact that very few physicians outside of psychiatry who have read this research think it applies to them speaks more to the provincialism of these specialties than to anything else. As we shall see, there is increasing evidence that not only are all physicians prone to the same kinds of cognitive errors witnessed in the Rosenhan experiment, but there is a good chance physicians are doing harm as a result.

This book is primarily concerned with data. As I will try to show in the chapters to come, most data in the realm of medicine is inherently fuzzy—tests are almost never 100 percent positive or 100 percent negative, and there are real-world consequences related to just how certain one can be that a test's result matches the underlying reality. We are only very rarely at the far end of the spectrum of certainty, where we can be extremely confident of our diagnoses and the benefits of our treatments. Some diseases require only a single test whose results can be interpreted with high degrees of certainty, but many others require a careful consideration of several pieces of information, at least some of which can be contradictory.

The human brain making a diagnosis can be thought of as another illustration of this principle. The psychiatrists in the Rosenhan experiment made two kinds of diagnostic errors. First, they diagnosed insanity in patients who were not insane: we call that kind of diagnosis a "false positive." Likewise, when tipped off that pseudopatients would be wandering the halls of their institutions, the psychiatrists suddenly saw sanity in patients with genuine mental illness, and that is known as a "false negative." As I will discuss in the chapters dealing with mammography and Lyme disease, these two concepts of false-positive and false-negative errors are critically important to seeing how uncertainty affects doctors and patients alike. The error rates associated with false-positive and false-negative diagnoses can be quantified. Thus, doctors who process this data and offer a diagnosis can be thought of as "diagnosis machines," and, like all tests, these diagnosis machines are subject to overcalls and undercalls.

This chapter, then, looks at human cognition, but it does so with the perspective that we are, in some sense, error machines whose characteristics can be mathematically described in similar ways to all the other tests in medicine. To do so, we will need to consider cognitive biases, the "how" of our mental errors, as well as our motivations for doing so—the "why" of them. This is only a brief detour, as there are many fine books written about the subject of cognition. In particular, the experimental psychologist Daniel Kahneman's book *Thinking Fast and Slow*, whose quote began the chapter, and to which we will return shortly, takes on this topic specifically.

Why did the psychiatrists in the Rosenhan experiment fail so profoundly? Were they merely negligent? Or was there some biological principle at work that predisposed them to miss the obvious? I would argue for the latter. Consider the following story about one of the pseudopatients who truthfully reported the state of his emotional life to a psychiatrist during his initial evaluation. He said he was close with his mother as a child and distant from his father, but as he grew older he found himself becoming closer to his father and more distant from his mother. He was happily married but reported having occasional spats, and had children who on rare occasion had been spanked (keeping in mind this was in the early 1970s when spanking was a less frowned-upon child-rearing method than it is today). In short, whatever the powerful psychological issues that drove his perception of his relationships, none of this story seems particularly disturbing and could describe any number of perfectly sane people we know, including us.

In the psychiatrist's mind, however, the story was a demonstration of the severe pathology lurking underneath:

> This white 39-year-old male . . . manifests a long history of considerable ambivalence in close relationships, which begins in early childhood. A warm relationship with his mother cools during his adolescence. A distant relationship with his father is described as becoming very intense. *Affective stability is absent*. His *attempts to control emotionality* with his wife and children are punctuated by angry outbursts and, in the case of the children, spankings. And while he says that he has several good friends, *one senses considerable ambivalence embedded in those relationships* also. (my emphasis)

One can't claim that the psychiatrist's misdiagnosis was due to being distracted during the evaluation: this note suggests that the doctor paid careful attention to his history. For instance, the note points to the fact of the pseudopatient's changing relationship to his parents as being psychologically significant. But everyone has a rich inner psychological life filled with emotional conflicts worthy of exploration, whether in the setting of psychotherapy or not. In this case, this fact was interpreted as a complete absence of "affective stability," which is psychiatryspeak for an inability to form solid, lasting relationships with people. Routine conflicts with his wife—it would be pathological not to have occasional disputes in the course of a marriage—indicated a controlling personality. Finally, the fact that he had friends should have been a powerful piece of evidence suggesting he was living a healthy life, but instead the psychiatrist used this fact to conclude nearly the complete opposite, by sensing "considerable ambivalence" of the patient toward his friends.

The process by which a psychiatrist manages to involute a person's mundane-but-healthy relationships into deep psychopathology requiring prolonged hospitalization is known as the confirmation bias. It is powerful, and everyone is capable of suffering from it. Confirmation bias occurs when we misinterpret incoming information because we have a strongly held hypothesis that makes us want to see things as they are not. Ultimately, confirmation bias takes the form of circular reasoning. A thirty-nine-year-old man discussing occasional conflicts in his personal life? That's a sign of an unstable personality. How do we know he is personally unstable? Because he presented to a psychiatric institution complaining of auditory hallucinations. But how do we know that he has paranoid schizophrenia rather than having suffered from an isolated sensory event? Well, just look at the conflict in his interpersonal relationships! The mistake seems so obvious from our perch as spectators, but in the case of the Rosenhan experiment, we were in on the fix from the start. How well would we have fared had we been in their shoes?

Confirmation bias can be subtle, and it is far from the only cognitive error to which doctors—that is, human beings—can be prone. Psychological theorists are not fully settled on the question of why we make so many of these errors in data interpretation, but over the past generation a group of psychologists has sought to explain our systematic tendency toward various cognitive errors through the lens of evolution. They have proposed a model known as error management theory, which incorporates uncertainty right at its heart. As humans moving through a world constantly bombarded by data, we are forced to make hypotheses about our environments and to act on them for survival, despite our inability to be completely certain our hypotheses are correct. Is it safe to go outside? Is a storm coming? Is this other human an enemy, a friend, or neither? When we face questions such as these, we are in the milieu of uncertainty, and our responses to these questions can sometimes have life-or-death consequences. Error management theory posits that, through evolution, we have developed into creatures with a predilection for specific cognitive biases. Over thousands of generations, the theory goes, it paid off for us to look at the world in a skewed way. There is an evolutionary advantage in misinterpreting our environment to an extent.

Why might it be advantageous to us to make repeated mental mistakes? Consider the following scenario: You are living in a forest tens of thousands of years ago, at the dawn of modern humanity, when our ancestors were more or less the same as we are in a physiological and anatomical sense. As you move through this forest seeking food, you are aware that the forest floor has all manner of objects. Many of them are just sticks, but some of them are poisonous snakes. Most of the time there is enough visual information for you to separate the sticks from the snakes, but what happens when the two blur together? What do you do when, say, it is twilight, and some small rodent of which you were unaware had scurried away and in doing so made a stick roll over so that it can't be easily distinguished from a moving snake?*

Error management theory suggests that we can make two errors of interpretation in this context. We can overdiagnose the situation by regarding the stick as a snake, and flee—that's a false-positive error. Likewise, we can underdiagnose the situation regarding a harmful snake as a stick, which is a false-negative error. It should be clear that these two misinterpretations of environment, although equal in the degree of the cognitive error, have very different real-world consequences. If we think a

---

* The snake/stick hypothetical is the creation of Professor Martie Haselton of UCLA; see bibliography for further information.

stick is a poisonous snake, we flee from a harmless object at little overall cost (unless, of course, we run headlong into a real snake). If, however, we ignore the threat of the real snake, we can die. These two cognitive errors, therefore, are asymmetric: if you started out with tribes of people divided equally between those predisposed to snake overdiagnosis and snake underdiagnosis, you would eventually see more snake overdiagnosers in subsequent generations simply because the snake underdiagnosers would eliminate themselves from the gene pool from lethal bites. Error management theory argues that we are hardwired by evolution to misinterpret our surroundings, and that we are much more likely to overread a situation than we are to do the opposite, seeing patterns in data where in fact there is nothing but noise. We not only look for the snowballs in blizzards, we instinctively see ones that aren't there. It is how we are built.

In medicine, this means we have a powerful tendency to overdiagnose disease. We see patterns of data that suggest to us that patients have disease when in fact they do not. And because of rapid advances in diagnostic technology, we have been doing more overdiagnosis in medicine than ever before.

The Rise of Pseudodisease

As part of a series wrapping up 2013 in news, National Public Radio in the USA highlighted some stories they regarded as the "best good news" of the year. Since news is typically about things gone wrong, and good news stories aren't inherently predisposed to flashy headlines ("Something Works!"), the report noted that too much news could make you think humans can't do anything right. To provide some pick-me-up perspective, they offered the three following examples: it is safer to fly now than ever before, life in sub-Saharan Africa is getting a lot better, and death from cancer is decreasing. "A person in their mid-50s has a chance of dying from cancer that's 20 percent lower than a person of the same age in 1990, 1991," said Dr. Otis Brawley, the chief medical officer of the American Cancer Society. He specifically cited the drops in the death rates of breast and colorectal cancer as being exemplary.

While factually accurate, the cancer entry might have been better served had a big asterisk been placed alongside it, insofar as one can place an asterisk on the radio.* Nestled as it was between two other items whose improvement came about almost exclusively through technology, a layperson could reasonably conclude that the "cancer is down" message is due to medicine's ongoing march of progress via breakthrough scientific achievements. Yet the reality is a good deal more complicated, and our progress with respect to cancer is, at best, more of a mixed bag. For instance, lung cancer death rates are declining, but this is due almost completely to the reduction in smoking. It's unquestionably a public health triumph, but the science of it was worked out nearly sixty years ago and isn't due to any fancy technology. (If anything, the fact that it took so long for us to see our lung cancer mortality fall should be cause for mild embarrassment rather than celebration.) Not only is the drop in the lung cancer death rate not attributable to any scientific game changers, but as we have adopted more sophisticated technology as we screen for cancers, we've had to cope with effects more appropriately described as subtly sinister than unambiguously beneficial.

Cancer in the early twenty-first century has had some unquestionable successes, at least some of which are due to the kind of genuine laboratory wizardry that grace websites and newspaper front pages all over the world.† But what is left unsaid in the stream of happy analysis is that medicine's ability to recognize cancer is starting to show the same problems we witnessed in the psychiatrists of the Rosenhan experiment: we are seeing diseases that aren't really there. Note that I say "diseases" and not "cancers"—more on that shortly.

---

* To be clear, Dr. Brawley has frequently attempted to raise public awareness about the problems associated with overdiagnosis. I include his quote here because it serves as a useful instance in understanding how overdiagnosis can lead to statistical versions of optical illusions.

† Arguably, the most important advance in cancer treatment in the past generation has been the development of the drug imatinib, which goes by the trade name Gleevec, for chronic myelogenous leukemia, or CML. Gleevec has largely turned CML from a fatal disease to a chronic one, and consequently should be thought of as a true game changer for that disease. But only about *6,000* people are diagnosed with CML annually, far less than the true killers in cancer, those of the lung, colon, breast, pancreas, and prostate, which account for just under 1 million diagnoses and 300,000 deaths per year.

How do we know this? There are two indirect but very persuasive lines of evidence. The first way involves cancer statistics over decades. The details are hidden within a database that is freely available online and is known as the Surveillance, Epidemiology, and End Results program, or SEER, as it is more commonly called. SEER is a by-product of the Nixon administration's War on Cancer; today it contains all of the information on every type cancer ever diagnosed in the United States since the early 1970s, as well as all the deaths that result from those cancer diagnoses. Because of Nixon's political calculation, we have an extremely good idea of how well our therapies stack up against the past and how well we are performing with respect to cancer treatment.[‡] It is at least as important a legacy of his time in Washington as Watergate.

When the statistics relating to the diagnosis and mortality of cancers are analyzed over this period, several of them show a remarkably similar pattern despite their underlying biological differences: the total number of diagnoses, year after year, tends to rise, while the total rate of death remains basically the same. In the *Journal of the National Cancer Institute* in 2010, H. Gilbert Welch, a professor of medicine at Dartmouth and the author of the groundbreaking book *Overdiagnosed*, performed a survey of five different cancers and saw this pattern, as seen on the following page.

Either this rise in the total number of cancer cases is due to overdiagnosis, Welch argued, or the increasing incidence is occurring simultaneous to major advances in these fields that is improving survival. But this seems implausible, as these advances aren't hailed in the medical literature. Moreover, if there really were dramatic improvements, one would expect the data to "jump" with quantum changes in relatively short periods. The death rates of these cancers, by contrast, are smooth lines across time.

Why the rise? The answer is almost certainly because we have created technologies that are ever more sensitive at detecting abnormalities that we *call* cancer, and at a cellular level they *are* cancers, but they turn out

---

‡ Irresistible political footnote: SEER, which is a tremendous achievement of public health and epidemiology, is only possible through a well-run, nonpartisan, technocratic organization funded by a centralized federal government. It would simply be impossible for this to be undertaken by a conglomeration of academic medical centers. I so tire of the canard that governments can't do anything. *Only* a government could build SEER!

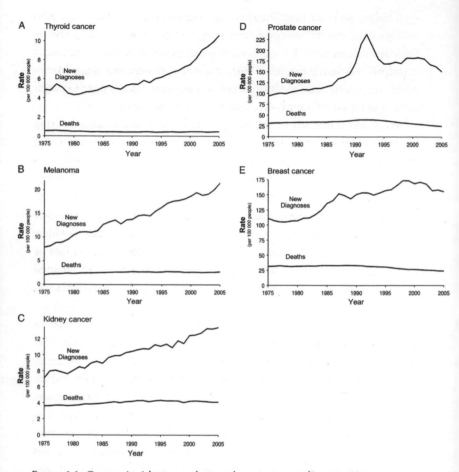

FIGURE 1.1. Cancer incidence and annual cancer mortality over time.
SOURCE: Welch, H. G., "Overdiagnosis in Cancer," *Journal of the National Cancer Institute* 2010; 102:605–613.

not to be the kind of cancers that threaten lives—in short, we find "cancer" that isn't "cancer" in the way both doctors and patients understand the term.

The single most convincing illustration of this can be found in the graphic on prostate cancer. As you can see in the figure, the rise in prostate cancer has a fairly slow but steady increase from 1975 until 1990, after which the diagnosis rate quickly spiked to more than double the number seen fifteen years earlier. The total number of cases of men diagnosed with prostate cancer has since declined—a feature not shared by any of the other diseases here with the possible exception of breast cancer—but is still well above the incidence when the statistics were first kept. Meanwhile, the death rate hardly budged during that time, hovering right around the mark of twenty-five deaths per 100,000 people.

What was it that led to this sharp increase in prostate cancer during the 1990s? Could it have been that men serving in wars were coming of age and some chemical they were exposed to during the war caused prostate cancer, such as Agent Orange? It's a plausible hypothesis, but there's a better one: by the early 1990s the prostate specific antigen test, or PSA, was becoming commonplace in the offices of urologists and primary care physicians across the country. Since there hadn't really been a widely available test that looked for prostate cancer before the PSA, the fact of its existence led to its extensive use and caused a sharp rise in the incidence of prostate cancer. The death rate proceeded as if none of this was happening at all.

The rise in rates of most of the cancers shown in the figure can be attributed to some technology becoming popular. In addition to the PSA and the mammogram, ultrasound has become the mainstay for the initial diagnosis of thyroid cancer, while the CT scan has been used for kidney cancer. Only melanoma, whose diagnosis relies initially on physical exam, can't be explained by a novel technology for screening. In that case, it is due to the rise in physician awareness through systematic medical education in medical school and residency; ironically, physician education seems to have the same effect on overdiagnosis as a CT scan has on, say, kidney cancer.

Cancer cannot be diagnosed by any of these technologies, however. What is required for a diagnosis is a piece of tissue viewed under a microscope by a trained pathologist. If this is so, one might wonder what pathologists are finding when given biopsies triggered by those ultrasounds, mammograms, and CT scans. The answer is that they are definitely finding cancer. The problem is that all the new cancers they are finding aren't likely to end up killing patients. In short, the rise in diagnoses of these cancers can be seen as the principle of medical uncertainty in action: we can see that there are unnecessary diagnoses only by looking at the numbers in aggregate, seeing the incidence rise while the death rate remains unchanged.

Earlier, I was careful to say that cancer diagnosis over the past generation has resembled insanity diagnosis in the Rosenhan experiment because we have been seeing *diseases* that aren't really there. I wrote that instead of saying that we were seeing nonexistent *cancers* because that's not actually true. In these increasing numbers of biopsies, pathologists are finding clumps of cells whose overall appearance is bizarre, with the distorted architecture that is the hallmark of cancer. Unfortunately, in many cases they appear to be of little physiologic significance. They may be "cancer" in the strict technical sense of the word: a group of cells whose reproductive machinery has gone haywire. But it's not "cancer" in the way that most patients and doctors view it, namely, something that will kill if left to its own devices.

We know this because of a series of autopsies performed on people who died from causes other than cancer and had their organs examined. This is the second line of evidence suggestive of an epidemic of cancer overdiagnosis: many, many people, especially older people, die with organs containing cancers that appear to be harmless. For instance, one study published in 2005 took prostate biopsies on Hungarian men who died with no known history of urological problems. It found that nearly 40 percent of them had evidence of prostate cancer. Among the oldest age group, the incidence was more than double that. Even more telling was a study published in 1985 that looked at the thyroids of Finnish adults who died of other causes. As with the prostate study, about 40 percent of these patients were found to have some evidence of thyroid cancer. But many of these cancers were small—so small, in fact, that they could have been missed because of the distance between each section that was taken. When this was taken into account, the researchers estimated that they could probably find some kind of cancerous cells in *every* patient if they had examined enough sections. Studies similar to these can be found for many cancers, and they all indicate that many people, especially older people, develop cancers during the course of their lives that don't amount to much in any meaningful sense of the word.

One of the central problems of cancer overdiagnosis is directly related to uncertainty: we know that some of these patients with these cancers are at risk of dying from the disease, but we only have a vague idea of which ones are most at risk. A different way to picture the problem was suggested by psychology researcher Hal Arkes of Ohio State University, when discussing the effect that the PSA has had on prostate cancer screening. In a 2012 edition of the journal *Psychological Science*, he invited readers to consider two auditoriums filled with one thousand men, all of whom are fifty or older. The men in one auditorium have annual PSA for ten consecutive years; the men in the other auditorium do not. Arkes then drew upon a number of studies in prostate cancer research to demonstrate some surprising conclusions.

At the end of those ten years, about seventy men in the unscreened auditorium will be diagnosed with prostate cancer (that is, they won't be diagnosed until they present with symptoms requiring an evaluation that leads to the diagnosis). In the screened auditorium, however, ninety will be diagnosed with prostate cancer. Nevertheless, by the end of those ten years, most studies show that about seven men in each auditorium will die of prostate cancer, meaning that for those twenty extra diagnoses, there's no impact on the actual mortality. Now these numbers are estimates and as such are fiercely contested, but it's important to provide a sense of perspective on the controversy. The debate about the value of PSA boils down to whether the number of men who die from prostate cancer in the screened auditorium is *six* rather than *seven*—or, in other words, whether one life is saved for every thousand men screened over ten years.

Harm, and the Optics of Benefit

For that saved life that may not even be there, the costs (both in terms of the literal cash expenditures of the medical system and the physical toll on the many men with elevated PSA tests) are profound. About 200 screened men will have a PSA level high enough to merit a biopsy, meaning that roughly 130 men will undergo an unnecessary invasive procedure. Nine men from this unnecessary biopsy group will require brief hospitalizations from complications such as infection or bleeding. Twenty screened men will receive a diagnosis of prostate cancer that would never have come to their attention, and most will receive some form of treatment (such as radiation) that can have major side effects; as many as a

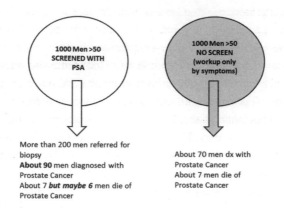

FIGURE 1.2. The effects of PSA screening. This figure estimates the difference that ten years of annual PSA screening would have on one thousand men. More than 10 percent of all men would undergo unnecessary prostate biopsies (i.e., they wouldn't have been biopsied if they hadn't been screened with PSA). Twenty men would receive a diagnosis of prostate cancer they didn't actually have and would suffer the consequences of treatment. The debate among statisticians, physicians, and other researchers is whether one life per thousand men, over ten years, is saved by this process.

quarter of them will undergo radical prostatectomy with its attendant complications, including incontinence, recurrent urinary tract infections, and impotence. These data are summarized above.

Although different professional societies have provided different recommendations about which men should be tested with PSA (or whether they should be tested at all*), not even the most vociferous advocates for PSA believe that its maximal benefit exceeds one life saved per thousand men screened over ten or more years.

But among those patients who are diagnosed with cancer following an abnormal PSA (or a mammogram, or a thyroid ultrasound, or any of the

---

* The US Preventive Services Task Force, whom we will encounter when discussing mammography, now recommends against the use of PSA for all men. As of 2013 the American Urological Association recommends that men aged fifty-five to sixty-nine should "talk with their doctors about the benefits and harms of testing" but no longer has a solid recommendation for PSA use in that age range. For all other men, they do not recommend it.

other screening methods that have become increasingly prevalent) there's a very different psychological effect. These people believe that they were saved by the screen, even if we can demonstrate in population studies that isn't the case. At best, only one man in every thousand who is screened for prostate cancer can claim to have been saved by PSA, but in reality, *ninety* men—nearly 10 percent of all men screened—feel as if this was the case because they reasonably assume that their PSA picked up an asymptomatic abnormality that would have killed them otherwise. Not only do patients feel this way, but their doctors do as well, and that explains in part the undiminished belief of some mainstream physicians in the effectiveness of PSA despite these numbers.

If you have a screening test that suggests you have cancer, and you undergo a biopsy that tells you have cancer, and you have surgery or chemotherapy or both to remove that cancer, and you are alive several years after all of this, it is completely understandable to believe that your life was saved as a consequence of that screen. But it is more often than not an optical illusion, a pseudodisease. It appears in every way to be disease, only it would have no meaningful biological effect on the course of one's life if left alone. We may live in a technologically advanced society with the tools of science within easy reach, but we—both doctors and patients—are committing the same kind of Type I, false-positive error as the mythical human ancestor who fled from a snake that was really only a stick. In that case, however, the costs of fleeing were relatively low. That same mental error, in the context of a "cancer snake" that's more akin to a cancer stick, can result in unnecessary prostatectomies, mastectomies, thyroidectomies among many other -ectomies, to say nothing of the side effects of radiation and chemotherapy. Invariably, some of these procedures will actually *become* snakes, so to speak—that is, there will be major complications from the procedures themselves—and lead directly to the deaths of some of these stick-fleeing patients.

The optical illusion of pseudodisease can be teased out only with the kind of population studies that simulate Dr. Arkes's "auditorium" thought experiment. These studies take years to perform and typically don't receive the same amount of news coverage as is seen when some famous person was diagnosed with a cancer as a result of a screen. Thus, not only do patients and their doctors become convinced of the utility of screening, but the broader public does as well.

This illusion extends to the realm of statistics. Even though the death rate of many of these cancers has remained unchanged over decades, the increasing number of cancer diagnoses has had a profound impact on a different way to measure cancer treatment: survival length. Most cancers are measured in terms of five-year survival; if you are alive and cancer-free five years from the time of your initial diagnosis and treatment, then you are considered to be cured of that cancer. If twice as many people are diagnosed with a given cancer, but the death rate from that cancer remains unchanged, then the five-year survival rate will appear to double. This makes the screen look like an even better bargain and explains to a great extent what enables overdiagnosis. It's so easy to spot the inherently bizarre behavior of psychiatrists who appear to regard everyone as insane but much more difficult to see that same behavior in one's primary care physician. Or in ourselves, for that matter.

Reification

Thus far, I have discussed overdiagnosis almost exclusively through the lens of cancer, but the psychological factors that lead to a rash of cancer-that-isn't-cancer diagnoses apply to a much broader set of diseases, in theory to every disease. In the example of our mythical ancestor assessing whether an object is a stick or a snake, nobody would doubt that there is a very real difference between those two things and that, given the proper time and the ability to judge from a safe distance, our ancestor could have figured out which was which. In medicine, we are forced to make high-stakes snap judgments only rarely. Usually, we have plenty of time to consider the implications of tests, yet there is considerable evidence that we nevertheless overdiagnose many diseases. This occurs in part because it is much more difficult to distinguish a disease from a pseudodisease than a snake from a stick.

But that still doesn't explain the mechanism by which we overdiagnose. To understand that, let's consider the diagnosis of a blood clot in the lungs—a pulmonary embolism, or PE, as it is commonly called. A pulmonary embolus is, like most cancers, a potentially life-threatening diagnosis. Also like some cancers, PEs are difficult to detect because they present with very nonspecific symptoms that can be easily confused with other conditions. Patients suffering from PEs can have fever, shortness of breath, pain when taking a deep breath, or a rapid heart rate, among other symptoms, but so can pneumonia, a heart attack, a gallbladder infection, lymphoma, and so on. Thus, it's quite valuable to have a method by which we can distinguish a PE from these other various maladies.

For the first half of the twentieth century, the PE was a well-understood and much-feared diagnosis, but there was no reliable way by which a PE could be diagnosed other than clinical suspicion. In the 1930s, EKG pioneers noticed a peculiar pattern in patients who later died from pulmonary emboli, which were found at autopsy.* One hundred years later, medical students still dutifully memorize this pattern, but it suffers from a problem we will see in example after example in this book: if patients had a PE, they had a reasonable chance of having this pattern on EKG, but it didn't follow that if patients had this EKG pattern, they were likely to have a PE. Similarly, at about the same time, a radiologist at Massachusetts General Hospital named Aubrey Hampton performed postmortem chest X-rays of patients who were found to have PEs at autopsy, and noticed that several had a hump-like opacity roughly corresponding to the site of the embolus. Unfortunately, "Hampton's hump," as it came to be known, was typically observed only in patients with the largest of clots, by which point it was often too late to make a difference. So nobody knew how to find them in time to intervene.

Then in the 1960s came a nuclear radiographic study known as the ventilation/perfusion, or VQ, scan as seen in the figure on the following page.

VQ scans look for discrepancies between two different sets of images: a ventilation scan that shows where air is flowing in the lungs, and a perfusion scan that shows where blood is flowing in the lungs. (This is done

---

* Electrocardiogram, or the graphic illustration of electrical conduction patterns in the heart. Also known as "ECGs," the "K" is still commonly used in a historical nod to the German physicians who developed the test, reflecting the Germanic spelling of "heart": *kardio.*

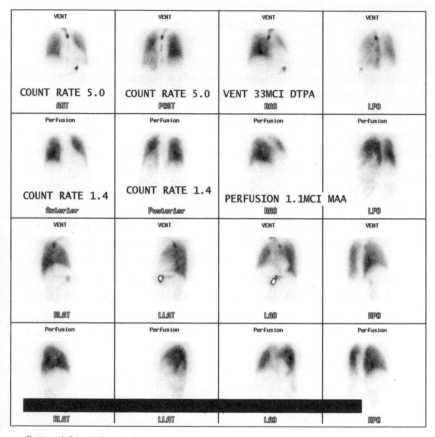

FIGURE 1.3. A VQ scan.

SOURCE: Image courtesy of Drs. Heeseop Chin, Monique Tyminski, and Robert Licho of UMass Memorial Medical Center.

by first inhaling one radioactive tracer for the ventilation scan, and then having the second radioactive tracer injected intravenously for the perfusion scan.) Any part of the scan that shows a mismatch—for instance, a dark gray splotch in one part of the lung on a ventilation scan that appears nearly white on the perfusion scan—indicates functional lung but without blood flow, and therefore suggests a clot. It was a big improvement over the crude measures of the EKG and Hampton's hump, but as you can see from Figure 1.3, the images were coarse and difficult to interpret. Ultimately, the scan had three levels of interpretation: low, intermediate, and high probability. A large number of scans, however, were read as intermediate probability.*

VQ scans were still commonplace when I was a medical student in the late 1990s, but they were displaced in only a matter of years by CAT scans. CT pulmonary angiography, as it is more formally called, provides a detailed picture of the lungs and their blood supply.† Finding a clot with these finely detailed pictures is a good deal simpler than sifting through the grainy images of the VQ scan, thus substantially reducing the number of equivocal reads. The resolution of these scans improved very quickly; the scans we perform today can generate hundreds of images with an astonishing level of precision. Comparing today's CT scans to ones from the 1990s is a bit like comparing an iPhone with Siri to a cell phone from twenty years ago. It's practically a different technology altogether, with only the most rudimentary of resemblances.

With this rapid improvement in CT resolution came an ever-greater ability to find pulmonary emboli, and the incidence of PEs from 1998 (the year in which CT pulmonary angiography made its debut) to 2006—a scant eight years—nearly *doubled*. However, the mortality from

---

* In an effort to keep the discussion as simple as possible, I've omitted another technology that came of age in the 1970s, and is now called catheter-directed pulmonary angiography. This was the gold standard for PE diagnosis until CT pulmonary angiography displaced it, but it was not as frequently used as the VQ scan because this test carried moderate risks, including kidney damage and bleeding from the catheter injection site in the groin, among other harms. There are still more tests, such as a blood test known as a D-dimer, that are also used in diagnosing PE, but an explanation of each of these tests doesn't change the underlying principle of PE overdiagnosis described here.

† Similar to the EKG/ECG phenomenon, CAT scans and CT scans are the same thing. The full name is computed axial tomography. Axial images allow viewers to look at patients as if they were looking up at them starting at the feet and going in cross-sections up the body. Over the past several years, the computerized reconstruction of images has become so much more sophisticated that scans no longer provide only axial cuts but also coronal (slicing front-to-back) and sagittal (side view) cuts, and now even three-dimensional images, so simply to call it *axial* imaging is a misnomer. They retain the informal title of CAT scan because of common usage. Also worth noting, given this discussion focuses on overdiagnosis, the CT is sometimes derisively referred to as "the donut of truth" by physicians who lament the lost art of the history and physical.

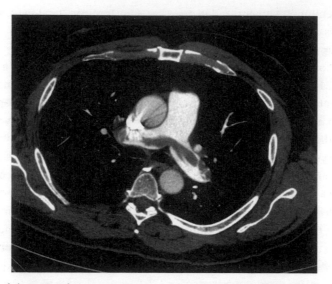

FIGURE 1.4. A CT pulmonary angiogram. It does not take a radiographer to see the superior detail of a CT when compared to a VQ scan. The dark gray areas in the midst of the white area that appears like an upside-down "T" are blood clots. This patient has large PEs that are almost certainly clinically significant, but these scans can also find much smaller clots in more distal arteries, the importance of which is unclear. Nevertheless, these smaller blood clots are also usually treated, with equally unclear benefits.

SOURCE: Image courtesy of Dr. Hao Lo of UMass Memorial Medical Center.

PE hardly budged during this time. As with the cancers discussed above, the CT enabled us to find many actual pulmonary emboli, but the PEs we have found on the whole haven't helped prevent death.

One of the important causes of the rise of overdiagnosis, especially in PEs, can be traced to the speed by which these technologies have arisen. The testing has developed at a rate that has outpaced the researchers trying to study its effectiveness, and so we cannot be certain of the true meaning of the pathology we discover when some tests turn up positive. This leads to one of the most important ways by which we rush headlong from overdiagnosis into overtreatment: we reify our diagnoses. That is, we will regard it as a *thing*—a real, unambiguous, categorically true disease that requires treatment, and in many cases fairly serious treatment, which always carries the risk of harm.

Suppose a fifty-year-old male patient comes to the emergency room with some vague chest discomfort and a rapid heart rate after a long flight. He has no history of heart disease, but both of his parents had heart attacks at young ages, so he is concerned the same could be happening to him. During his stay in the ER, the rapid heart rate goes away, as does the chest discomfort. The workup for a heart attack is negative, and the physician, rightfully concerned that the long flight could have led to a pulmonary embolism (long periods of limited movement are one of the biggest risk factors), orders a CT pulmonary angiogram. An hour later, the physician receives a report from the radiologist that the patient has a "subsegmental pulmonary embolus"—fancy medical talk meaning that there's a blood clot in one of the smaller arteries in the lungs. Not long after, the patient is admitted to the hospital and started on a blood-thinning medication, heparin.

This could be a story of a genuine PE that might have taken this man's life. Likewise, it might be a story of overdiagnosis. For the most part, we don't know what happens to people with small or medium-sized pulmonary emboli if they are left alone; there is some evidence from a small number of studies that these people do perfectly fine without treatment, but there's just not enough data to know that with great confidence. It may, in fact, be quite normal for everyone on long flights to have some level of blood clots in their bodies, whether in their arms or legs or lungs, just because they have moved so little over several hours' time. Then, over a period or hours or days, those minor blood clots resolve, never coming to medical attention. Did this man, who will soon be committed to months of blood-thinning medication, have one of those kinds of pulmonary emboli, and might he have ignored those symptoms had it not been for his family history of a different problem altogether?

The answer to this question isn't currently known, but what is clear is that he now carries an unambiguous diagnosis. The ER physician who was seeing this gentleman has the unenviable task of taking care of potentially dozens of patients simultaneously, some with trivial medical problems not even requiring an ER visit, and some with life-threatening issues. ER doctors do not have the luxury of deliberating carefully on the underlying biology of their patients' conditions; they have to make quick, real-time verdicts as to whether someone has a disease, whether treatment is required, and whether admission is necessary. So, when a radiologist's reading of a pulmonary embolism comes to that physician's attention, he or she will, quite understandably, reify it.* It's a thing—a PE—and will be approached like all other PEs that provoke a response, for it is a life-threatening condition requiring blood-thinning medications that come with real risks.

The process of reification then continues: the physician who admits the patient to the hospital will be given the diagnosis in advance by the ER physician. It is not uncommon for the handoff between the ER and another specialist to consist of a few words such as "he's a fifty-year-old with a PE." In some hospitals, this exchange may never even take place directly if the ER physician has finished his or her shift and the admitting physician hasn't started evaluating the patient. By hearing the terse summary of a busy ER doctor and reading the radiology report, an admitting physician will already be heavily influenced in favor of thinking about this as a PE, and it may never occur to that physician to think about it as a "PE"—that is, a disease that may not really be a disease, a diagnosis with quotation marks around it. Needless to say, the patient, who came to the ER in the first place because something felt wrong, will be powerfully motivated to believe in the diagnosis as well. This is how inherently fuzzy data morphs into a full-blown categorical diagnosis. We can see the effects at the population level, but it's very difficult to recognize the process, much less stop it, at the individual level.

What conclusions can we draw from this? I don't mean to suggest that patients and their families should be conversant with all manner of tests such that they should have their own independent opinions about a given diagnosis. But it is reasonable to have conversations about the confidence doctors have in their diagnoses—where on the spectrum of certainty does a given diagnosis fall? I'll talk more about conversations with doctors toward the end of the book. I also think that both doctors and patients need to carefully consider the downsides of treatments, especially in an

---

*"Reify" from the Latin *res,* meaning "thing." To use the term "thingify" would prevent a doctor from sounding, well, doctory.

age of expanding diagnoses. It's instructive to remember the bedrock principle of our profession: first, do no harm.

More Medicine. Better Medicine?

Thus far, I've described the process of overdiagnosis purely in terms of how a physician tries to solve a problem, but other factors drive overdiagnosis with equal force. Consider the CT scan used to find the might-be-PE in our hypothetical patient. Hospitals function in a competitive marketplace, where patient volume (and the insurance reimbursement that comes with them) constitutes their lifeblood. Owning the most advanced scanner in the area allows for a flashy advertisement showcasing that hospital's state-of-the-art facilities. CT scanners are very expensive, so the optimal way for that hospital to recoup its costs is by scanning as many people as possible.

Lest you think this is the beginning of a conspiracy story, when such a situation arises, nobody is forcing the ER physician to use it. Hospital CEOs don't send out memos offering bonuses for doctors who scan the most patients per month, and they don't walk around the wards trying to drum up business for radiology. But they don't have to, because there are no mechanisms to discourage their use either. When hospitals put up billboards in their communities as having state-of-the-art radiology facilities, physicians can rightly assume that they should feel free to scan away.

The structural factors driving overdiagnosis hardly end there, however. The makers of the scanners, of course, also have a financial interest in selling as much product as possible, and they advertise accordingly. The makers of pharmaceuticals used to treat these various conditions benefit from pseudodisease: more diagnoses means more patients, more patients means more medication, and more medication means more revenue. Overdiagnosis is good for business.

I don't think it requires cynicism to understand overdiagnosis, however. Pharmaceutical company executives as well as their rank and file may genuinely believe that some new medication they have developed for a serious condition carries a real benefit, even in the face of growing evidence suggesting that a given disease is overdiagnosed and overtreated. No conspiracy is required because everyone involved is already motivated to believe that more medicine equals better medicine.

What's important in understanding overdiagnosis is that although the incentives of hospitals and the biomedical industry may be different, doctors and patients are no less susceptible to motivated thinking. The manner by which it impairs clinical decision making is just as insidious, and its effects run just as deep. As health-care professionals, we want to believe that we are providing the best care for our patients by performing tests, and so we have become overconfident in what those tests tell us. As patients, we want to believe that greater technology creates greater benefits, especially because that is demonstrably true in so many other aspects of our lives, and so we tend to greet diagnoses without skepticism, even when we feel well.

By such means are sticks turned into snakes.

Overdiagnosis can be thought of as the perfect storm of our technological progress. We are hardwired by evolution to overreact to possible threats to our lives and by doing so ensure that we react appropriately to actual dangers; we develop tests that likewise find more problems than actually exist. These two factors work synergistically to expand the number of diagnoses of major disease, particularly over the past generation. Moreover, the system in which doctors and patients function is designed to create strong incentives to "make a diagnosis" (the satisfaction of a job well done for a doctor, and the relief of knowing for a patient) and create disincentives to "miss" a diagnosis (lawsuits). And, because of uncertainty, we cannot know *which* patients are being overdiagnosed—we can only see that the process is happening by looking at group data. Yet the logical consequence of a diagnosis is a treatment, and, as I'll discuss in detail later, treatments carry risks. Thus, the ultimate effect of overdiagnosis is that we consign a number of patients to needless harm.

I'll carry this subject forward as we look at screening mammograms. Screening mammograms, like screening PSA tests, are designed to detect disease in people who have no outward evidence of disease. The very absence of symptoms has a dramatic effect on the utility of such a test; in other words, the amount of uncertainty in interpreting a screening mammogram is much higher than interpreting one in which a woman presented with a lump in her breast—even though it is the exact same test. If this sounds strange, it is. How this happens is something I'll explore in detail, for it is crucial to appreciate the mathematics of overdiagnosis to grasp how much misunderstanding surrounds the practice of mammography. So, to help familiarize ourselves with how a patient's overall state of health can influence the uncertainty of a test, before diving into mammograms let's take a brief look at one patient's experience with a different screening test, the results of which led the person to assume his life would be over very soon.

2

VIGNETTE: THE PERILS
OF PREDICTIVE VALUE

Perception requires imagination because the data people
encounter in their lives are never complete and always
equivocal.

—LEONARD MLODINOW

"The data people encounter in their lives are never complete and always equivocal"—so says physicist and author Leonard Mlodinow in his book *The Drunkard's Walk,* a meditation on randomness and how people choose to incorporate it, or ignore it altogether, as they go about their daily lives. But how much imagination is required for a person to perceive the equivocal nature of a blood test that informs them they are going to die?

A lot, as it turns out.

Yet these tests are administered all the time, and only infrequently do patients or doctors account for their equivocality. We saw this in the previous chapter when we looked at the prostate specific antigen test: positive tests only very rarely uncovered disease that would have led to terrible outcomes, and yet because of the equivocal data that the PSA testing produced in groups, many men ended up enduring fairly terrible treatments that they otherwise would not have undergone.

Another way of thinking about this is to ask the following question: What happens when we approach the middle of the spectrum of certainty? In this equivocal territory, it becomes vitally important to understand the size of the risks and the magnitude of the benefits. Again, we observed this with PSA: the risks of being overdiagnosed were quite real, and fairly common, while the benefit, if one exists at all, is on the order of one life saved per one thousand men over ten years' time. When I go on to discuss screening mammograms in the following chapter, we'll need to keep this in mind.

But *how* do we overdiagnose? What are its statistical mechanics? Why can't we just develop a test that's 99 percent accurate and be done with it?

In fact, we can, and we have. Most tests aren't *that* good, but some are, and despite this we can still produce overdiagnosis. To understand this point is to understand at least part of the controversy about screening mammogram recommendations. So to more fully appreciate this phenomenon, let's see how this played out when one patient learned the news of a routine blood test.

Mlodinow's Story

On a Friday afternoon in 1989, one man in California received some very discouraging news from his doctor. The chances that he would be dead within a decade were "999 out of 1,000," according to the doctor. "I'm *really* sorry," the doc added as he relayed the news, by telephone.

The test was, of course, for HIV. It was a positive test as part of a routine insurance screen. The gentleman in question had been diagnosed with the virus that would eventually cause AIDS and lead to his demise. At that time, there was very little in the way of treatment: AZT, the first drug for HIV, had been approved two years before, but patients who took the drug got better initially only to succumb to illness as the virus became resistant to the drug's effects. So-called triple therapy, which has allowed doctors to turn HIV into a chronic and manageable disease, was still more than five years away. This test signified a death sentence, although in the world of medicine at that time it constituted yet another routine blip in the ever-growing pile of cases as the HIV epidemic spread, especially in California.

There was one aspect of this test that was unusual, however. It involved the person being tested: the very same Leonard Mlodinow whose quote opened this chapter. Because of his training, Mlodinow understood the nature of numbers and statistics. After what must have been a very harrowing few days and perhaps weeks of concentrated thought and research on the HIV test, he was able to figure out something quite remarkable: his "positive" test for HIV could actually be interpreted to mean *that it probably wasn't positive after all.* Which, in fact, was the case: Mlodinow wasn't infected with HIV, and he has kicked around ever since, producing several very readable works of popular science to an audience grateful for the misdiagnosis.

How could this be? Overall, at the time the HIV test was, in fact, quite accurate. A person with HIV was very likely to have a positive test, and an uninfected person such as Professor Mlodinow was very likely to have a negative one. And yet the counterintuitive third fact is that, despite these two statistical truths, a random positive HIV *test* was very likely to be a mistake. The insurance company and the physician both got it badly wrong.

Mlodinow's story throws a few features of modern medicine into sharp relief. The first and most obvious is the way in which highly accurate tests can nevertheless lead to deeply inaccurate interpretations. A second issue Mlodinow's story raises is the process by which we understand what it is for a physician to "know" something. Part of why the story is so jarring is how spectacularly the physician fails Stats 101: rather than having 999 in 1,000 odds of being infected with HIV, Mlodinow relates that more likely he had about *1 in 9* odds. This is a whopper of a mistake, and what makes it so troubling is that we're not inclined to think of physicians as the kind of people who make such critical errors. When coupled with his questionable judgment in relaying such news over the phone rather than scheduling a face-to-face visit in the clinic, the doc doesn't come across as particularly professional.

But again, how could this be? The answer can be found in the idea of what constitutes predictive value. Predictive value refers to whether a given test result can truly be thought of as representing the presence or absence of disease—that is, if a test is positive and has a high positive predictive value, then that person probably does have the disease. Similarly, if a test is negative and has a high *negative* predictive value, then a negative test really is cause for reassurance. For instance, in a few chapters, we'll see how the Lyme disease test has very good negative predictive value if a patient has been symptomatic for several months—if the test is negative, then whatever the problem is, isn't Lyme.

However, *accuracy* and *predictive value* aren't the same thing, and this is because predictive value is determined in part by the probability that someone has a disease. Unsurprisingly, this is referred to as the pretest probability. In other words, even when dealing with a fairly accurate test, if the pretest probability of someone having a given disease is low, then the positive predictive value will suffer. The lower the pretest probability, the lower the positive predictive value. Similarly, the lower a test's accuracy, the lower the positive predictive value.

The reason Leonard Mlodinow's positive HIV test was unlikely to be positive is because his pretest probability was low. You can't perform a blood test to define someone's pretest probability, but we can infer that it was low because Mlodinow was being tested as part of an insurance screen without any signs of illness. If, by contrast, he was experiencing unintentional weight loss, moderate fatigue, and a persistent nagging cough, especially as someone living in that place at that time, his pretest probability would have been much higher, and so the likelihood that his positive test was really positive would have been much higher.

Note however that I'm not talking about *certainties* in either direction. A positive result from a low positive predictive value test still *does* sometimes truly indicate that someone has disease, and a positive result in a high positive predictive value test is sometimes wrong. Uncertainty is ever present, but there is power in being able to quantify the uncertainty. Certainly someone receiving a diagnosis of HIV in the days before effective therapy would have been disconsolate by being told the odds the test was positive was 999 in 1,000; the same person who learned the chances of really having HIV were 1 in 9 would likely have breathed more deeply, though perhaps not altogether normally.*

In the next chapter, we'll keep this concept of positive predictive value in mind, as I give numbers to the predictive value of screening mammograms, looking at the diagnosis of breast cancer in women who learn such a diagnosis in much the same way that Leonard Mlodinow learned his test meant that he was infected with HIV. I'll quantify the levels of uncertainty surrounding screening mammograms, and in doing so illuminate one of the most impassioned topics in public health today.

---

* That was true of HIV screening in the late 1980s but has not been true for many years because of additional testing that has eliminated the false-positive problem for that disease. So, please, get your HIV screening test done!

3

SNOWBALL IN A BLIZZARD

Two enlargements required for [education] are: first, to feel
sympathy even when the sufferer is not an object of special
affection; secondly, to feel it when the suffering is merely
known to be occurring, not sensibly present. The second of
these enlargements depends mainly upon intelligence. It
may only go so far as sympathy with suffering which is portrayed vividly and touchingly, as in a good novel; it may, on
the other hand, go so far as to enable a man to be moved
emotionally by statistics. This capacity for abstract sympathy is as rare as it is important.

—BERTRAND RUSSELL, "THE AIMS OF EDUCATION," 1926

When uncertainty in medicine is ignored, one consequence can be
confusion in the public dialogue, where misunderstandings arise
because different parties are operating with different sets of assumptions
about the utility of some technology. We saw how our sometimes misplaced faith in any number of advanced diagnostic tests can lead to the
phenomenon of overdiagnosis. This occurs precisely because doctors have
failed to account for uncertainty, thinking they were at the far left of the
spectrum of uncertainty rather than somewhere near the middle.

Here, I consider a special case of overdiagnosis. Screening mammography—that is, the practice of using mammogram technology to look for
breast cancer in otherwise healthy women—has been regarded by many
as one of the cornerstones of women's health. Nevertheless, there has
been a slow and inexorable reconsideration of its value. But the public
discourse about it has been so fraught with heated accusations and

charges that it becomes difficult to sort out the data that led to this reconsideration. This chapter will try to strip away the rhetoric and see the uncertainty in the numbers.

Before I begin, I want to underline that what follows is a discussion about *screening* mammography. Part of my goal in writing this book is to encourage readers to view national health guidelines with a healthy skepticism, and to use uncertainty as a tool to know whether they really should take a medication or sign up for an annual test or stop smoking and so on. In discussing screening mammograms, I hope to show that its positive predictive value is not nearly as high as most people assume, just like Leonard Mlodinow's HIV "positive" test that we encountered in the last chapter. But I cannot emphasize enough that this does not apply *to women who feel new lumps.* The presence of a new lump in one's breast dramatically changes one's pretest probability of having breast cancer, and consequently a mammogram for such a woman is an unambiguously useful and lifesaving tool. If you are a woman reading this and discover a previously unknown lump in your breast, please see your doctor immediately for further evaluation, which may include a mammogram.

The Public Health Earthquake

In November 2009 a relatively unknown branch of the US federal government made a very big splash by compiling, in the words of one of its critics, "a pile of bland data" and making some conclusions based on what that little pile of data showed. The group, the US Preventive Services Task Force, or USPSTF, had just revised its recommendations about when and how often women should obtain screening mammograms. Based on this data, they believed that screening mammography was no longer an unambiguous lifesaver in particular populations of women. Moreover, its report indicated something even more shocking, which was that screening mammograms, when used in the wrong context, might in fact represent a significant *danger* to women.

The language was in the characteristically cautious style of medical science, with several built-in linguistic hedges about the strength of the evidence. The bottom line, however, was unmistakable: it was time to reconsider the practice of recommending annual mammograms for all women after age forty.

A political firestorm ensued. Outraged women called up congressfolk and other government officials and complained about how their lives were being devalued. The *New York Times* ran a story within twenty-four hours of the release of the new guidelines detailing the backlash. "My big fear is that coverage will be diminished and that a very valuable tool to detect something at an early stage could be taken away from me," said Karen Young-Levi of the organization breastcancer.org. In stronger wording, its founder, Dr. Marisa Weiss, said in the same article that the new recommendations were "a giant step backwards and a terrible mistake." The American College of Radiology suggested that the Obama administration had released the new recommendations in a push to save health-care dollars as part of its support for the health-care reform legislation working its way through Washington at the time. The GOP put up a post on its website describing the new guidelines as "bogus scientific analysis."

For its part, the White House ran away from the recommendations with a don't-look-at-me shrug and pointed the finger at the previous tenant. Kathleen Sibelius, the secretary for the Department of Health and Human Services, distanced the administration from the new guidelines by noting, in an interview with CNN, that the panel had been appointed under the tenure of President Bush. Either sensing an opportunity or feeling the pressure, the US Senate rushed to include an amendment to the health-care bill to cover the mammograms its own USPSTF no longer recommended.

The members of the task force seemed to be caught flat footed. The vice chairwoman of the committee, Dr. Diana Petitti, said she was taken aback by the reaction, noting that she had been relatively unaware of the intensity of the controversy that surrounded mammography screening. She was surprised that the task force's report would be met with such a visceral rejection by public health and women's health advocates. "I have been made aware of it now," she added ruefully.

The essence of the controversy lay in the task force's insinuation that screening mammograms really *didn't* save that many lives, even under best-case scenarios, or at least weren't especially likely to do so. This came as a splash of cold water to the public health community, for many practitioners had been reared to think of screening mammograms as one of the most important lifesaving technologies of modern medicine. Consider my own training: I had gone to medical school and residency and had memorized the previous iteration of the guidelines. I knew exactly what every woman should do based on her age and was pleased with myself when I displayed this knowledge to the senior physicians.

Yet, despite my rote memorization of these recommendations, like nearly everyone else I had no idea that the benefits of mammography were modest, and moreover came with some real risks. We'll look at the data to support those contentions shortly. Not many people, whether doctors or laypeople, were keenly aware of this. The controversy was caused by this disconnect; the experts knew one thing, and the general public, something else entirely.

The vehement reaction to the 2009 USPSTF guidelines raises two separate questions: First, how did this disconnect come to be? Second, why there was such fierce resistance to a change in the guidelines for a medical technology whose overall utility was somewhat good in some age groups, marginal in others, and quite likely harmful in others still?

There are many answers. *Control* was a theme flowing beneath the surface: women—entirely appropriately—wanted to be in control of their bodies and not subject to the whims and misconceptions of what until recently was a nearly exclusively male profession. After generations of women dealt with medical management largely at the hands of these men, in ways ranging from mildly patronizing to actively hostile to what can only be thought of as physical assault and battery, the screening mammogram had become one among many symbols of women taking control of their destinies. Though I am assured that it is not among the more pleasant of procedures to endure, given the positive vibe with which the mammogram had become associated, it was understandable that there was such an emotional response. It *felt* like doctors were trying to take back that control. But, as I will show, that feeling can interfere with a cool appraisal of the data; the message that got lost in the translation was that the task force members were, in fact, actively trying to avoid *repeating* the mistakes of previous generations.

Another entirely understandable narrative involved the faceless committee that issued the recommendations. If one hears of a scientific committee sitting in some conference room somewhere, it is hard not to conjure up an image of mostly middle-aged men, which reinforced the notion of male control over female bodies. The faceless committee was perceived as having no understanding of the social implications of the data and, because its members were not women (the unstated assumption), they had no notion of the impact of mammography on preserving women's lives.

This particular narrative was demonstrably untrue. In the popular press, because there was little actual investigation of the data that led to the revised guidelines, most of the coverage was devoted to the heated accusations being levied at the committee. But there was other data beyond the raw numbers and advanced statistics used to evaluate mammography that could have been publicized. Consider the following list:

Diana
Kimberly
Rosanne
Lucy
Bernadette
Virginia
Judith

This series of names is data in the true meaning of the Latin word *datum,* roughly meaning "information bit." Although it may not seem so at first blush, this list is not really different from the kind of data generated by multimillion-dollar biomedical research projects. What defines data is that it doesn't simply speak for itself: one can generate data in all manner of ways, but whether it comes in the form of a 10,000-cell Excel file or a *New York Times* headline, it must be contextualized and analyzed to be understood.

The context of these data points is that they represent the first names of the seven women who served on the US Preventive Services Task Force on mammography in 2009. In total, they comprised nearly half of the committee. Physicians, epidemiologists, and biostatisticians fill their ranks. In their professional lives they are referred to as "Doctor" because that is what they are, and highly accomplished ones at that. They have mothers, they have sisters, they have daughters, they have lovers. And they have themselves to see in the mirror on a daily basis. Surely, in addition to their professional pursuits, they know something of womanhood, and the devastating impact that a disease like breast cancer can have on a woman's sense of self.

Yet in the bewildered public reaction following the report, the fact that those exact names were intimately involved in drafting the recommendations was almost entirely overlooked. Because it didn't fit into the narrative of the faceless male committee, the inherent assumption behind the more vociferous criticisms of the panel was that this was yet another chapter in medical misogyny, a further organized attempt on the part of mostly male physicians to codify indifference to women's suffering through the power of guidelines.

But it wasn't so. In part, the recommendations were based on the kind of mathematics that can generate seeming paradoxes and counterintuitive conclusions, concepts that are far too difficult to encapsulate in a headline. So, newspeople around the US—of whom only a precious few had any acquaintance with basic statistics, even among reporters whose job it is to cover science and medicine—were faced with a simple question: *What* will be the headline? The answer seemed obvious, and every major outlet ran with a variation on the theme of "Task Force Recommends Fewer Mammograms, and None Under Fifty." It seemed like reasonable journalism because it was entirely factual. Whether such stories helped to provide a deeper understanding of what was going on is a different matter entirely.

Any woman unfamiliar with something as obscure as an advisory panel with the tongue-twisting name of the United States Preventive Services Task Force, and no knowledge of terms like "false-positive test" or even a mental framework to make sense of the term, could only read that headline with the deeper narrative of medicine's war on women in the back of her head. *Doctors want less for you,* is the easily grasped message. Had the headline been written along the lines of "Task Force Finds Mammograms Associated with Harms to Women," the entire reception might have been substantially different.

Perhaps the panel members might have been more media savvy about announcing their new recs, and perhaps they might have more shrewdly strategized how to get this information out. Ironically, that very naïveté came about as a consequence of the USPSTF's reason for existence: the group was deliberately designed to insulate scientists and physicians from the politics of screening recommendations. The original task force was created during the Reagan administration, when many of the screening methods for breast cancer, heart disease, and diabetes were just becoming widespread, and also when the costs of many of these tests weren't being covered by insurers. It was consciously constructed to have an arm's length relationship with its sponsor, the Department of Health and Human Services. Moreover, the task force was explicitly prohibited from considering the cost of tests when it issued guidelines, which made the charges that this was motivated by penny pinching as part of a desire to pass "Obamacare" seem particularly amusing.

While the task force could be chided for its lack of preparation for the resultant media tempest that its recommendations produced, the notion that the revised guidelines are part of science's ongoing war against women is not merely shortsighted, it almost certainly ends up *harming women.* Yet it's this very concept that seems to have been uncritically bandied about by people in positions of authority in both government and academia following the release of the 2009 guidelines—and hasn't much abated, though nearly seven years have passed. That several people who should have known better were yawping through the airwaves, scurrying about to champion a practice under all circumstances for all women, even when the evidence of its utility among some women was vanishingly thin, speaks to a general lack of appreciation of the subtleties involved in evaluating diagnostic technologies that form the basis of national health panel recommendations and the reason these panels recommend what they do.

A good example of the rush to judgment can be found in the online archives of *NBC News.* Immediately following the announcement of the recommendations, one commentator took to the electronic soapbox to explain the tempest as the cluelessness of a bunch of stats geeks. In making his case, the author performed a rather remarkable intellectual pirouette, choosing not to deny the scientific validity of the task force's conclusions, but arguing that they had failed to appreciate the cultural significance of mammograms. Since women *feel* that mammography is helpful, he appeared to reason, we should plow ahead, even if their value is found to be marginal:

> Screening is what responsible and health-conscious women do to take control of their bodies and prevent disease. Those are commendable and powerful virtues, and—it seems—*more compelling than a pile of bland data.*
>
> Doing the right thing and taking the time to protect yourself against breast cancer has moral weight that policy makers, as Secretary Sebelius found out, ignore at their peril.
>
> *There is no reason to doubt the accuracy of the scientists' finding that evidence does not support routine mammography for most women under 50. But there is every reason to doubt that the numbers they compiled will be sufficient to overturn a medical practice that carries so much ethical weight for women.* (my emphasis)

In sum, according to this commentator, the problem with the recommendations was that they took no account of what screening mammograms *meant* to women and offered up only cold, lifeless statistics. The argument wasn't that some smart number-cruncher got the equation wrong, but that they weren't "doing the right thing." The *right* thing was self-evident, for it was a "powerful virtue" that had "moral weight." So of course the task force missed the mark. It was only looking at the spreadsheet and not thinking about the real lives the data represented.

Never mind, for the moment, the significant number of women serving on the task force, who might have found this (male) writer's lecture about "taking control of their bodies" faintly patronizing. Condescending or not, his commentary is a perfect illustration of the intellectual thickets in which one can get caught when casually disregarding carefully assembled data as being merely "bland." Nearly one hundred years ago the philosopher Bertrand Russell, whose quote began this chapter, had understood that numbers can tell stories equally compelling—and indeed, as tragic— as those portrayed in a good novel. And the numbers reviewed by the task force *do* tell stories. They are not quite simple and straightforward stories, but neither are they so complicated that they can't be understood in broad outlines. I would also argue that the task force members were perfectly aware of the stories that the data told, in part because they had thought about the uncertainty inherent in the technology, and what that could mean for a woman.

As I've indicated, one critical reason there was such consternation in the public reaction had to do with a misunderstanding of the degree to which screening mammography is reliable. Many had assumed that mammograms deliver a black-and-white solution to a vexing national health problem. Yet a mammogram is, in a very literal sense, a *gray* technology. Teasing out its value requires sifting through numbers that do not speak unambiguously. Appreciating what's at stake in the Great Mammogram Flap of 2009, and why uncertainty plays a starring role in the saga, requires an understanding of tests and their accuracy. For mammograms, despite their popular portrayals as tools that in general uncover hidden truths—that is, cancers—are rather slightly foggy lenses that look out upon the world. The *degree* to which those lenses are foggy, and the consequences of imperfect vision, forms the core of the debate.

Before discussing exactly what the USPSTF actually said, it is important one last time to emphasize that we are talking about mammography *as a screening tool.* Mammograms, even if they use the exact same technology, can be understood in two different contexts. The first context is one that most people think of when they go to a doctor because something is awry. Either they are sick or they just don't feel right or they discover an unusual rash, and so on. When they come to the office, the doctor would offer testing—sometimes blood tests, sometimes radiology tests, and sometimes invasive tests—to help identify the problem. In the case of a mammogram, a woman would come to her doctor having felt a lump. When used in this way, a mammogram is *not* a screen; it's a diagnostic test in the context of some real physical symptom or abnormality and is being used as part of a process to evaluate that abnormality.

A screening mammogram, by contrast, is the very same mammogram, but it is performed on *healthy* women who have no evidence of disease. The notion that mammograms are lifesaving lies in the idea that they detect cancers *before* a lump is palpable. The added time between the detection of a cancer by a mammogram, and when the patient or doctor notices a lump, is what the mammogram provides. Since cancer is a disease always on the move, and one that becomes more lethal the longer it is left to fester, the rationale is that this added time leads to saved lives.

In principle, this benefit can be studied and quantified in a relatively straightforward way. You take a large cohort of women and randomly assign them to two groups. The women in the first group have annual mammograms, while the women in the second group have no mammograms and go to their doctor either on an as-needed basis or have an annual physical. Women in *both* groups, over the years, will be diagnosed with breast cancer. At the end of some defined period—usually between ten and twenty years—researchers tally the number of deaths from breast cancer in both groups, and any differences that result can arguably be attributed to the use of the mammogram. If a significantly smaller percentage of women in the mammogram arm die of breast cancer, then that extra time between mammogram and a palpable lump can be shown to have a clear mortality benefit.

The research is simple in theory. In reality, researchers have been investigating mammography for just about half a century, performing trials costing tens of millions of dollars and involving hundreds of thousands of women from countries around the world. And yet, despite this massive use of resources, critical questions about mammography as a screening tool remain unsettled. When the researchers of the US Preventive Services Task Force sat down to review the mountains of data, they used a variety of mathematical models to help them define, in as precise a manner as possible, the value of a mammogram. Their conclusions forever changed the mammography debate.

2009: Turnaround

The 2009 task force issued several recommendations that differed from previous guidelines, and each of these recommendations was based on slightly different issues related to statistics and uncertainty. By far, the most contentious recommendation was that women under the age of fifty not have annual mammograms, which represented an almost absolute about-face from what had come before. What had happened in the intervening years to cause such a change?

The answer can be found in the heaps of data that had been compiled over the previous twenty years, but it boils down to two simple numbers: the first is that about 50,000 women between the ages of forty and fifty develop invasive cancer each year in the United States; the second is that there are about 22 million women in the United States in this age range. Why is this important? Because it shows that breast cancer in this age group is still *relatively* uncommon, especially at the younger end. The annual incidence increases with each passing year (thus, of these 50,000 women, more of them are forty-eight or forty-nine than forty or forty-one). By the time a woman is sixty-five, by comparison, that incidence roughly doubles.

These baseline numbers have a dramatic effect on the accuracy of a mammogram. This is a wildly counterintuitive concept, but it is critical to understanding the task force recommendations. I foreshadowed this with the vignette about Leonard Mlodinow's HIV screening test. In the following paragraphs, I'm going to run the numbers so that you can actually see how even accurate tests have lousy predictive value when applied in the wrong population, like women under the age of fifty. Even a small error rate for a screening test like a mammogram can have a huge impact on how confident we can be that a "positive" test is really positive.

Let's assume for the moment that mammograms are 99 percent accurate—that is, they detect ninety-nine cases out of one hundred women with breast cancer, *and* they *don't* show cancer in ninety-nine of one hundred women who do not have breast cancer. By current medical standards, this would be an extremely accurate screening tool. So if a forty-three-year-old woman goes for a mammogram and, at the follow-up visit, is told by her physician that the mammogram was suggestive of breast cancer, that test is 99 percent likely to be correct, right?

In fact, it's not right at all. Indeed, almost the complete opposite is true. When you multiply the error rate (1 percent) by the actual size of the two populations (those with disease and those without), something strange happens. If you screened all 22 million women who *don't* have cancer (technically, it's 22 million minus 50,000, but that's essentially 22 million to keep the number simple), a 1 percent error rate would be approximately 220,000 false-positive tests—women who don't have cancer but are read by the radiologist as possibly having cancer. Of the 50,000 women who *do* have cancer, 49,500 are read as positive. Because this false-negative rate is negligible for the purposes of the example, I'll round the true positive number back up to 50,000 to keep the math simple.

So now you have 270,000 positive mammograms—that is, women who receive a diagnosis of potential breast cancer—but the majority of these mammograms are actually inaccurate, because as we've just seen 220,000 of the 270,000 are false positive! The bizarre truth, then, is that even if a mammogram is 99 percent accurate, the likelihood is *over 80 percent* that this forty-three-year-old woman's "positive" mammogram is actually *negative*.

A visual, not-to-scale representation might help drive the point home, as seen in Figure 3.1 on the next page. The false-negative rate of mammograms is a tiny speck on the already small square of women who actually have breast cancer. Now you can compare true positives to false positives for mammograms, and see the result. Look at the boxes representing positive tests: the false-positive box is much larger than the one representing true positives. And there's no simple way other than doing a breast biopsy to know which positive mammogram belongs in which box—and more on biopsies, and the uncertainty surrounding them, shortly.

Figure 3.1 could just as easily describe Mlodinow's HIV test. The reason his doctor had been so confident in his diagnosis was because he had considered only the *black* box—those tests that picked up people who are actually infected. In this respect the test is virtually error-free. But Mlodinow was much more likely to be in the *gray* box just by random chance, because there are so many more people in the general population who don't have disease—that big, *white* box. As a consequence, an extremely accurate test in a low-incidence population produces a relatively large number of false positives when compared to the number of people actually infected. This is the central problem in screening tests—*all* screening tests. We saw it with the PSA blood test to screen prostate cancer, we saw it in Mlodinow's HIV screen, and we'll see it again in the Appendix when I briefly discuss lung CT scans for smokers.* False positives are the bane of a screen's existence, for exactly the reason outlined in Figure 3.1.

---

* I repeat: HIV tests no longer have this problem. Please, get screened!

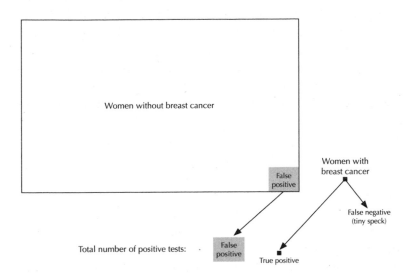

FIGURE 3.1. Positive predictive value of a mammogram among women under fifty. If the total number of women who have breast cancer is small, even a minor error rate among the women who don't have breast cancer leads to there being more false-positive mammograms than true-positive mammograms—that is, one can easily see here that of the total number of positive tests, many more are of the gray, false-positive variety than the black, true-positive kind. And there is no way for a radiologist, or anyone else, to distinguish true positive from false positive except in thought experiments like this.

This is the reason the USPSTF believed that there was no evidence for a benefit to mammography in women under fifty: there were too many false positives leading to too many unnecessary procedures. Moreover, women who fall into the gray, false-positive category receive *none* of screening mammography's benefits but also might incur substantial harm, from the unnecessary fear produced by being handed a potentially life-threatening diagnosis to undergoing unnecessary surgery.

To emphasize, even though this discussion of black, white, and gray boxes might imply otherwise, in a real-life situation there is no way to discern whether a woman's mammogram is a false positive or a true positive. All that she will know is that the radiologic evidence indicates there is something that looks very suspicious for cancer, and she will therefore be referred for a biopsy. Out of every ten women under the age of fifty who are sent for these biopsies, about *eight* will have no cancer at all—a staggering number that speaks to a large group of women who will wait around days or weeks for the biopsy to be performed, worried sick that they might die, and maybe die horribly. It is part of the toll that did not appear in the calculus of those lobbing insults at the task force, but it was very much on the minds of the members of the task force itself. For them, such data didn't seem so bland and indicated a huge amount of anxiety and, as I'll soon explain, physical risk.

The Blacks, Whites, and Grays of the Mammogram

Thus far we have looked at the problem of mammography screening for women under fifty with the mathematical assumption that it is 99 percent accurate. But it is not, and it is not by a long shot. Numbers from various studies show a wide range, but it is safe to say that mammograms have, at absolute best, a 90 percent accuracy rate, and more likely worse, making it a more unwieldy tool than even what is described above.*

To demonstrate this, it's helpful to explain the basic concept behind the X-ray, one of the most powerful tools in medicine. X-rays, as most of us learned in high school science class, are high-energy forms of radiation that can be detected by photographic film. X-rays can move along totally unimpeded by air, but they are stopped in their tracks by thick metals. So placing a piece of metal in front of X-ray film should leave a white outline; where there is nothing but air in the X-ray field, the color will be black.

---

* For the purposes of this discussion, I am using "accuracy" in a deliberately vague manner as it doesn't dramatically affect the gist of this issue. In reality, accuracy (and therefore error) is described in medical research by either *sensitivity* or *specificity.* Sensitivity describes the ability of a test to "catch" disease in a population: that is, a very sensitive test will be positive in most patients who have some disease. Specificity, by contrast, describes the level of certainty that a positive test really does mean that someone has the disease and not something else. An ideal screening test is one that is highly sensitive (it finds disease in most people who otherwise would have no idea they had a disease) and at least reasonably specific. In the above example, I've lumped these two concepts together and called it "accuracy," but what I really did was assign the exact same value of sensitivity and specificity (i.e., 99 percent) to keep matters simple. It is generally uncommon for a test's sensitivity and specificity to be exactly the same number.

The human body is composed of tissues of different densities, however, and the images produced by an X-ray of a person are seen as various shades of gray. Bone is, of course, much more dense than skin and muscle, and so appears as a lighter image because fewer X-rays pass through to the film, instead blocked by the bone itself. This is a point worth keeping in mind because those high-energy waves of radiation that *don't* pass through, and in doing so create the varying shades to make an X-ray what it is, are radiation that is *absorbed* by the body (meaning that mammograms may—and I emphasize that this is highly speculative because no well-designed trials have ever been performed to address this question— ever so slightly increase one's risk of *developing* cancer in addition to detecting it). Thus, when metal, bone, and soft tissues are superimposed, you see an image like that in Figure 3.2.

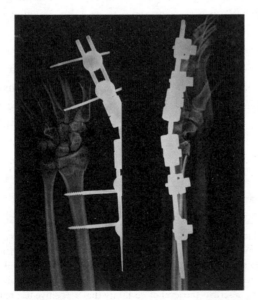

FIGURE 3.2. Bone, metal, and soft tissues form varying shades of gray in an X-ray of the arm and hand. Roughly, there are four separate shades easily seen in this film: the white of the "external fixator" here that is used to stabilize this patient's fracture, which represents metal; the somewhat more translucent white of the bones; the dark gray of the soft tissues; and finally air, which is black.

SOURCE: User Ashish j29, at https://en.wikipedia.org/wiki/External_fixation#/media /File:External_fixator_xray.jpg.

If the goal of the mammogram were as simple as the exercise of finding the metal in the picture, not only would mammography be of enormous benefit, many radiologists would be looking for other work. But, alas, locating a tumor—which is, in fact, nothing more than human tissue whose cells act in a peculiar, ultimately life-threatening manner—is a significantly greater challenge and requires years of training. Even then, radiologists are constrained by the limits of the technology. Figure 3.3, for instance, is a "blizzard" of breast tissue in one mammogram. And Figure 3.4 is a different mammogram.

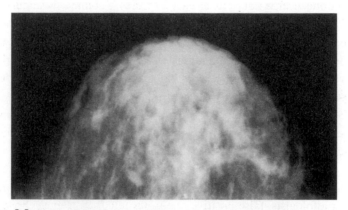

FIGURE 3.3. Mammogram 1.

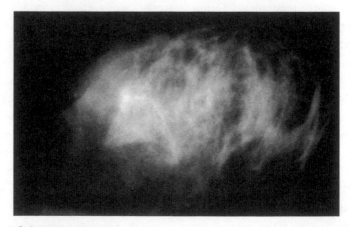

FIGURE 3.4. Mammogram 2.

Where is the "snowball" in these "blizzards"? Which one shows cancer and which does not? Or do they *both* show cancerous tissue? Or is *neither* positive? These photos, taken from publicly available electronic archives of the National Cancer Institute, are pretty good illustrations of how tricky reading a mammogram can be. As it turns out, the first image is considered to be negative (although abnormal, for which a near-term follow-up is recommended), while the second turned out to be positive for breast cancer.

As can be imagined by looking at these images, separating cancer from noncancer is not quite as easy a task as is commonly understood. And the interpretation can be highly dependent upon whose eyes are doing the reading: a study in the *Journal of the National Cancer Institute* published in 2002 looked at a radiology practice composed of two dozen doctors and found that some members of the group had up to six times more false-positive diagnoses than did their colleagues. This marked variation was true even among experienced radiologists in the group: the radiologist with the highest number of "reads" had a false-positive rate of just over 4 percent, which is laudable. Yet the radiologist who had read the second-highest number of mammograms had a false-positive rate of nearly three times that number. Other factors that might influence radiologists' false-positive rate are where they trained, how long they have been in practice, whether they have been sued, and so on. Since a mammogram isn't a number, whoever is sitting in front of the computer can have a major impact on whether a given woman will be referred for additional imaging or a biopsy. These are the ways in which uncertainty multiplies.

Unfortunately, many advocacy organizations, as well as the medical establishment, do not as a rule acknowledge these caveats when discussing the value of mammography. Further, the media, almost genetically programed to avoid discussions involving uncertainty, dodges the subject as well, which contributes to the misperceptions about the predictive value of a screening mammogram. When the task force reviewed the data in 2009 and concluded that the situation was more complicated, it was inevitable that many would react with outrage.

Harm

You might read all of this and think that, although perhaps steep, the error rate associated with mammography is a reasonable price to pay for saving a woman's life. This is essentially the boiled-down argument that our commentator made when he took to cyberspace with his dismissal of the task force's "bland" data: sure, mammograms may result in many overcalls, but when compared to doing nothing at all, it is unambiguously beneficial. Without doubt, that logic is compelling. Unfortunately, it ignores one highly important variable: the amount of harm that comes from a false-positive diagnosis.

The act of *measuring* such harm is not easy. I've already alluded to the distress that a false-positive mammogram, and possibly a follow-up mammogram, can generate. In a series of eloquent essays for the *New York Times* in late 2010 and early 2011, Dr. Ellen Feld of Drexel University noted the feelings that swirled about as she awaited the reading of the pathologist. Her words are a case study of the kind of paralyzing fear that women must deal with when faced with the possibility that they have a tumor in their breast: "For the next 48 hours, as I wait for her call, I feel suspended, hanging from a strap cinched too tightly around my chest. Waiting to hear just how bad the news is. Waiting to hear when I will move forward and to what unfamiliar places I will go."

Dr. Feld *was* subsequently diagnosed with cancer, although one can safely assume that she speaks for tens of thousands of women who had similar experiences. For those women under the age of fifty, the majority would never have experienced such emotions had they never undergone the mammogram in the first place.*

---

* Dr. Feld's breast cancer came to her attention when she noticed a lump in her breast rather than by screening mammography. It's worth emphasizing here yet again that the above discussion about mammography refers to its value as a screen—that is, its ability to find disease in people *without any indication of disease.* When women such as Dr. Feld *notice* a lump, they must be evaluated by a physician and, in most cases, referred for mammography. My single biggest fear in writing this chapter is that this message will get twisted in the public discourse in such a way that women will take to heart the message that somehow mammograms should *never* be performed, which couldn't be further from the truth.

But there are more sinister complications than mere dread, and they relate to the uncertainty inherent in the *next* layer of testing: the biopsy itself. It is difficult to know how many biopsies are read incorrectly and how many unnecessary lumpectomies or mastectomies (along with chemotherapy and radiation), and all of the attendant complications and disfigurement associated with such procedures, take place. One of the more sobering assessments came in 2004, when researchers in Norway and Sweden indicated that as many as *one-third* of cases of invasive breast cancer were overdiagnosed. It's worth letting that sink in: they estimated that one out of every three women who were told they had invasive cancer in fact had no cancer at all. Although these researchers were not focused on the question of a mammogram's accuracy in women under age fifty, their findings are potentially suggestive of the relative harm that can come of a screening tool used in the wrong population for the wrong purposes.

The balance of benefit and harm was the central issue behind the second recommendation of the US Preventive Services Task Force that caused such a furor: that women aged fifty to seventy-four should no longer receive annual mammograms, but have them every *other* year instead. The researchers used a variety of advanced statistical models to analyze the effect of how often a woman underwent a mammogram, tying these models into the known growth rate of breast cancer in most women.

Reading the reports that formed the basis of the guidelines is a difficult exercise even for those with a working knowledge of study design and statistical analysis. There are dozens of mathematical models that are simulated and analyzed, each with a Table and Figure spitting out dozens of numbers. Reading it can induce vertigo. Yet in the midst of all the if-this-then-that scenarios, one message cannot be missed: the number of women whose lives are saved by annual mammography is not appreciably different whether they have an annual or biennial (i.e., every other year) mammogram. What *is* different is the number of false-positive diagnoses: the amount of women who would end up not suffering the harm of a false positive is reduced by nearly half.

To give a sense of exactly what kind of numbers I'm talking about, let's look at one particular calculation to serve as a representative for the various models. According to this calculation, in women aged fifty to seventy-four, about ten lives were saved for every thousand women screened over twenty-five years. (That is, if one thousand women eschewed annual mammography in this age group, about ten more women would succumb to breast cancer than a similar group of women who had annual mammography over this time.) The cost, however, would be in the number of false positives: for the ten saved lives there were *110* unnecessary biopsies, which as I have discussed may in turn lead to further unnecessary interventions—maybe even more than thirty additional false-positive diagnoses of invasive breast cancer, if the Scandinavian data above is to be believed.

At any rate, if the same thousand women changed their screening strategy to every other year, the number of lives saved would indeed drop, though it would drop only to eight. But for those two "missed" lives, the number of false-positive diagnoses drops to *sixty six*. That's a dramatic reduction and represents in its distilled mathematical essence the reason for the every-other-year recommendation. Both the annual and every-other-year strategy entail uncertainty, but in the case of the every-other-year strategy, the uncertainty is associated with a significantly lower level of harm, without a huge corresponding cost in the number of lives saved.

Absolute and Relative Benefits

What I've tried to do thus far is walk you through the logic of the US Preventive Services Task Force when they issued what appeared to be revolutionary guidelines in 2009. I have not gone into detail about the Task Force's recommendation to *stop* mammography of any kind after the age of seventy-four. Suffice it to say that the principles that guided such a recommendation are part and parcel of what is written above, and that the panel was not convinced of any demonstrable benefit for mammograms in this age group, although they uncovered fairly good evidence of potential harms.

But there is one last matter that is critical to an understanding of the task force guidelines. Because of the tempest surrounding the under-fifty recommendations, to say nothing of the advice to have biennial rather than annual mammograms, this last matter was mostly an afterthought in the squawking that surrounded the report. It was couched in the very cautious language of scientists, and so its importance may have been underestimated. But it is no less important than the debates about when to start mammograms or when to stop them or how often one should have them in between.

The heart of the matter was this: the Task Force wasn't convinced there was unequivocal evidence that mammography was the remarkable lifesaving force that its proponents often proclaim it is.

To help unlock this, let's use some data from an old study—the original major mammography trial, begun in the 1960s and run by the New York Health Insurance Plan, which I'll call the HIP study for short. The HIP study is generally not included in modern analyses of mammography trials due to a variety of design flaws. Because of these flaws, most researchers believe that the HIP study overstates the value of mammography by almost double. This is precisely the reason I want to use these numbers, for even in a study that shows what nearly all statisticians today consider an outsized effect, you will see that the *absolute* benefit is very different from the *relative* benefit of mammography.

Recall from the beginning of the chapter where I said that, in principle, measuring the benefit of a mammogram was simply a matter of dividing women into a "mammography group" and a "no mammography group," and then over a long span of time counting how many women in each group are diagnosed with breast cancer, and comparing at the end of that period how many women died from breast cancer in both groups. Assuming both groups were equal, if more women died from breast cancer in the no mammography group, then mammography can be said to be beneficial, and it simply becomes a matter of describing the effect in mathematical terms.

After about ten years of the trial, the researchers from the HIP study presented their data at the Conference on Breast Cancer supported jointly by the White House, the National Cancer Institute, and the American Cancer Society in 1977. At the conference their presentation had shown something fairly dramatic: they noted a roughly 33 percent relative reduction in mortality.

This was, indeed, a number worthy of attention. But what does it mean? Here the actual data are crucial. At about the ten-year mark, the number of women in the trial who had passed away from breast cancer in each group was 91 (mammography) and 128 (no mammography), respectively. Because the total number of cases of breast cancer in each group was roughly equal, the relative difference in percentages of breast cancer mortality was about one-third.* The relative mortality measures only greater or smaller proportions of one group relative to another.

But these numbers represent only the numerators—in other words, it's telling you the number of breast cancer deaths without telling you the total size of the group studied. The real question is how many women needed to be recruited and followed to find this difference. The answer to that question is *more than 60,000* (31,000 in each group). That's a staggering number of women to follow in order to find what appears in retrospect to be a small number of lives that were saved. This is known as the *absolute* risk reduction, and it's incredibly small: about one-tenth of one percent (91/31,000 compared to 128/31,000). The small size of the absolute risk reduction seems especially underwhelming when considering the number of false positives and the potential harm that can follow from such false positives discussed above.

Depending on whether one focuses on *relative* risk reduction or *absolute* risk reduction, one can view the same data and arrive at very different conclusions regarding mammography's benefits. Through the lens of relative risk reduction, mammography is clearly beneficial; through the lens of absolute risk reduction, one may be more guarded and skeptical of its value.

This in part explains the abundant confusion of the mammography debate. If one is predisposed to the former view, mammograms sound like a great public health bargain—a 30 percent reduction in mortality. If you take the latter, mammograms don't seem to be the enormous benefit that they're billed to be, if they are a benefit at all. Most recent studies quote

---

* There were 299 cases of breast cancer in the mammography arm, and 285 in the no mammography arm, for a relative difference in the mortalities of 0.30 (91 divided by 299) and 0.45 (128 divided by 285). As a statistical side note, these numbers demonstrate that the lower the *mortality* of a given cancer, the harder it is for screening technology to provide a benefit. Breast cancer, in a relative sense, carries a good prognosis, as these numbers demonstrate. Even down to Stage IIIa cancer, five-year survival rates are well above 50 percent; more than 90 percent of women with breast cancer present at a stage that has greater than 80 percent five-year survival.

the relative risk reduction to be somewhere in the range of 15–20 percent. Yet, according to one study, the *absolute* risk reduction for women undergoing mammograms is *0.05 percent* (90.25 versus 90.30 percent after ten years). Even if one were to cite rosier estimates, it's a very small number.

Because the total number of women who were either diagnosed with or died from breast cancer is so small, even a minor, unintentional bias could artificially create a benefit where none really exists. For instance, how do we decide that someone has died from breast cancer? This may seem like a ludicrous question, but it's actually quite difficult. Consider the following problem: a sixty-four-year-old woman is diagnosed with breast cancer and undergoes lumpectomy, local radiation, and adjuvant chemotherapy. The following year she has a heart attack and dies. Should she be categorized as having died from breast cancer? What if she died of a pulmonary embolus, a common complication seen in people with various cancers? What if she died in a car accident, which might have happened because her brain bled from a metastatic tumor or might have happened because she was simply at the wrong intersection at the wrong time?

These are the kinds of questions that face researchers, and there are no simple, right-versus-wrong answers for such questions. In short, these questions cut right to the core of uncertainty in medical research. We cannot *know* that every patient who dies within one year of a breast cancer diagnosis died of breast cancer itself. We can be fairly certain in some cases but have no idea in others. If there are *large* numbers of patients, and fairly strict and agreed-upon criteria to categorize patient outcomes, then our degree of certainty can be a source of comfort. But small numbers—such as roughly 100 deaths out of 30,000 over ten years—suggest much uncertainty.

Nevertheless, one can attempt to minimize bias in such studies, and some of the bias can be minimized by having researchers who know nothing of the mammogram study decide on the cause of death for all of the deceased women in the trial because these "blinded" researchers won't have a horse in the race. That is, you don't want to have the very researchers who might have the strongest hopes for mammography's success in charge of deciding post hoc who actually died from breast cancer and who didn't; you want the most objective person possible so that no bias creeps into the results. (The categorization of deaths in the HIP study was done by its organizers, and this fact is routinely cited as one of the important reasons the data is considered unreliable.)

Particularly when the numbers are so small, where only a few borderline calls of "breast cancer deaths" are included in the control group while a similar few are excluded from the screening group, a very long, painstaking, and expensive study can end up creating a benefit where none exists or erasing one that does. (Another way of eliminating bias is simply by looking at *all* deaths regardless of cause because a true benefit should still be observable even if we include everyone who died; it's just a smaller benefit at that point. I'll take up this topic of evaluating studies by looking at "all-cause mortality" in the next chapter and beyond.)

How does a scientific body like the USPSTF boil this down into a bite-sized chunk for the interested and educated layperson? The simple answer is that they hedge. In issuing their recommendation for biennial mammograms in women age fifty to seventy-four, the task force thought there was *high* certainty that there was *at least a moderate benefit,* or conversely that there was a *moderate* certainty that there *might be a substantial benefit.* This is known as a Grade B recommendation. The Grade A recommendation is defined as showing high certainty of a substantial benefit. The task force couldn't say this with confidence, and so mammography fell to the second tier of beneficial tests.

In changing its guidelines on mammography in women under the age of fifty, the task force was equally careful in its wording. This recommendation carried a C grade, which meant that "professional judgment" and "patient preferences" could be taken into account and that mammograms might be *selectively* offered. The Grade C classification also meant that they believed there was a moderate certainty that the net benefits would be small. In short, they were stating that screening mammograms for women under fifty were in the dead center of the spectrum of certainty. But based on the data, they did not feel that it was reasonable to issue a Grade D recommendation, which would have unambiguously advised avoiding the practice. In essence, the task force tried to skirt the controversy about the cultural value of a screening mammogram, providing just enough intellectual wiggle room to sanction the test in patients with, say, strong genetic predispositions or other risk factors, even though there was no evidence one way or the other to indicate this was a lifesaving strategy.

Before I conclude this chapter, let's revisit the essay from the *NBC News* website. "How did the poor scientists of the U.S. Preventive Services Task Force go from being the 'gold standard' for deciding what works in medical screening on Monday, to a bunch of irrelevant nerds by Wednesday?" the writer asked with a verbal flourish. He then supplied his own data-minimizing answer: "that's because data and evidence have not, do not and never will be the sole determinants of health coverage."

"Data" can come in the form of a story just as much as it can as a number, and so perhaps we should consider the story of Monica Long of Cheboygan, Michigan. Long's story was reported by Stephanie Saul in the *New York Times* in July 2010, not long after the task force's recommendations were issued. It makes for grim reading. Thorough in its details, exquisite in its reportage of shock, horror, and regret, Saul documents Long's long saga with the medical system that can be understood as the living, nightmarish embodiment of a false positive. For Monica Long turned out *not* to have breast cancer, an error that was discovered only after additional review of several slides from the original biopsy. This review occurred only after part of her right breast was excised by a surgeon's knife and she was referred to a new oncologist for follow-up. "Psychologically, it's horrible," she said in the interview. "I should never have had to go through what I did."

The *Times* piece goes on to note that the field of biopsy interpretation, especially in the early stages of breast cancer, is contentious in the extreme.* "As it turns out, diagnosing the earliest stage of breast cancer can be surprisingly difficult, prone to both outright error and case-by-case disagreement over whether a cluster of cells is benign or malignant," the article states. Even in major, prestigious academic medical centers, where pathologists have significant experience reading breast biopsy slides, there

---

* Specifically, this stage is known as "ductal carcinoma in situ." Several extra paragraphs could be devoted to the special challenges involving mammogram interpretation when the subsequent biopsy reveals ductal carcinoma in situ. I have opted not to discuss it here because one can get bogged down in technicalities fairly quickly, even though the underlying themes about the precision of a mammogram, and its overall benefit, aren't dramatically affected.

are not universally agreed-upon standards as to what truly constitutes cancer and what does not. Whether you are referred for lumpectomy and radiation might be due to as random a factor as whether you live in Boston or San Francisco.

Monica Long's story is unusual in only one key respect: she learned that her original diagnosis was wrong after the fact. In essence, she became retrospectively aware of her status as a false positive, which is rare indeed. Surely the realization that her retrospective nondiagnosis meant she was unlikely to die anytime soon from breast cancer must have been cold comfort in the extreme. But she is only the tip of an iceberg. We *know* that there are thousands of other women out there, just like her. Do their stories not carry ethical weight?

"Data and evidence have not, do not, and never will be the sole determinants of health coverage"—surely this is an enlightened view of medicine. But its truth is limited here, and it is a rhetorical trick, a play to the crowd, rather than a deep consideration of the real-world consequences of scientific policy. Should we not heed that very data if it means that we don't have to put one hundred women through Monica Long's experience? Or should we be comforted that most of them will remain blissfully ignorant that they have been carved up unnecessarily?

O Canada

Nearly *seven* years after the USPSTF guidelines were issued, it is unclear whether they have had any effect. In 2013, a group of researchers looked at changes in mammography rates among nearly 30,000 women who participate in a study known as the National Health Interview Survey. While it is an annual survey, questions about mammography screening are given only every three years, the most recent years being 2005, 2008, and 2011. The final two time points allowed for a natural experiment to see whether the new guidelines had any impact on screening.

They didn't. In fact, the trend over these periods showed a slight *increase* in mammograms, although it was not a statistically significant difference and thus could still be within the natural range of variation. Nevertheless, the study highlighted the fact that the rates didn't go *down* in the immediate period after the guidelines were issued. Compare this to the dramatic decline in the number of women who took hormone replacement therapy following the early termination of the Women's Health Initiative: one study estimated that in 2000 approximately 38 percent of women used some form of hormone replacement; by 2010 it had dropped to just under 6 percent. (I'll discuss what happened with hormone replacement therapy in a later chapter.) Both events were hugely publicized, so an inability to get the message out can't account for the difference. The authors of the study noted that the ongoing recommendations of several professional and advocacy organizations probably account for at least some of the effect. Why the new screening mammography guidelines, years after their publication, have not yet caused a rethink among those organizations about the wisdom of screening mammograms in women under fifty is left unaddressed in their analysis.

In the meantime, further evidence has accumulated supporting the USPSTF's conservative approach to mammography. In February 2014, the news media reported on the completion of a massive study on the effectiveness of mammograms in Canadian women that was published in the *British Medical Journal*. The study followed women aged forty to fifty-nine over a twenty-five-year period; women in the control group received annual physical exams designed to palpate lumps, while the other group underwent these breast exams in addition to mammography. The bottom line was stark: the researchers found no benefits at all to women in this age range. Each group had roughly 45,000 women. Roughly speaking, about 3,200 women in each group developed breast cancer, of which 500 in each group died. Compared side by side, one doesn't even have to resort to statistics to see that there was no benefit to mammography.* Moreover, that held true for women in the fifty to fifty-nine age range as it did for those under fifty. No matter how one looked at the data, one couldn't find any evidence of benefits, which made the harms of false-positive diagnoses even more dramatic.

As I completed the first draft of this book in the summer of 2014, the Canadian mammography study—which by all accounts should have

---

* The screened group enrolled 44,925 women, and 3,250 were diagnosed with breast cancer, of whom 500 died. The control group included 44,910 women and had 3,133 cases of breast cancer, of whom 505 died.

caused a massive public reconsideration of the value of mammograms for all women under sixty but especially for women under fifty—had not led to any announcements about a change in policy at Komen or the American Cancer Society. Considering that the Canadian study wasn't the first of its kind and had come nearly *five years* after the USPSTF's systematic analysis, it becomes increasingly difficult to understand their rationale.

It is possible that by the time this book is published, one or both of these groups will have decided to change their recommendations. Nevertheless, the fact that those recommendations have not *yet* changed is a story unto itself, and worthy of consideration in its own right. Why was there such resistance to the 2009 guidelines, whose wisdom has now been borne out by further research? I think one does not have to stray far beyond that *NBC News* online essay I've quoted above to arrive at an answer. When health technologies are discussed in terms of righteousness, and aren't simply thought of as tools by which we *might,* or might *not,* extend our lives, it becomes difficult to evaluate the technology for what it is. For screening mammograms are not, and never were, a moral good: they are *X-rays* whose interpretations incorporate an element of uncertainty. The rhetoric surrounding the value of screening mammograms has been so overdetermined, so loaded with metaphor, that we are blind to what the data tells us, which is that the old policies made matters worse for women's bodies rather than better. And *that* is quite astonishing.

The Medical-Industrial Complex, Up Close and Personal

Just after the publication of the Canadian mammography trial, I came to the office of Dr. Judy Ockene at the University of Massachusetts with these thoughts on my mind. Judy was one of the dozen and a half experts who formed the committee that issued the 2009 USPSTF report. Her work on that committee is only the latest accomplishment in a career that has spanned five decades, and she considers it one of her proudest. I met her through some seminars that I had attended about the structure of modern scientific collaboration—a subject on which she had considerable expertise after working with colleagues from across the US and for several years on those guidelines.

As one of the senior faculty at UMass who has been centrally involved in resident and faculty development, she's a woman who always has a kind word and an encouraging smile. She's one of the types that large academic institutions are exceptionally good at producing: a scholar of the highest order who also fosters the careers of the next generation of researchers and beyond, a pillar of the academic medical community. Even though I tower over her physically, to me and many other junior faculty members who have encountered her, she's a titan. Yet you would brush past her in a supermarket without any awareness of her importance in this critical chapter in the history of American medicine.

She is, in some sense, the face of the medical-industrial complex—that nebulous entity by which certain patients and advocates, sometimes with justice and sometimes without, conceive of the modern medical system. Or at least she is one face that comprises it in part, and mine is another. In its featureless form, the medical-industrial complex is vaguely nefarious; looking at Judy, who stands not much more than five feet, if that, you see a real person who has devoted a lifetime to research on a subject that leaves her eminently qualified to be listened to with care. Talk to her about mammography, and you'll have a much harder time envisioning the USPSTF as a disembodied aggregation of cold and uncaring scientists, and, in doing so, it becomes a lot harder to ignore the substance that led to the guidelines.

"I think it was a failure of communication, a big failure of communication," Judy said as she reflected back on the aftermath of the guidelines in 2009. She noted that the actual report was submitted well in advance of the actual publication date, which could have provided an opportunity to carefully consider the publicity that would inevitably ensue, and perhaps to control the message to a much greater extent. "The failure was that we didn't ask the questions, 'How do we frame it in a way that *doesn't* get people irritated? How do we help them understand what the recommendations mean?' There's a lack of understanding by the public—and even by clinicians and researchers—what these guidelines mean, and that's understandable," she said.

"The people on the committee are scientists, and they're very busy scientists, but there are communications experts with important public relations skills and knowledge at most of the institutes involved in this work who could have been thinking about those questions. Unfortunately, communication errors were a large preventable problem."

I see her point, although I am less sure that even the best PR firm could have added enough spoonfuls of verbal sugar to help these medicine recommendations go down. The concept equating mammography and health had become so entrenched in the public mind that any departure from that, no matter how mild and carefully packaged such statements may have been, would have been a very difficult sell. Coupled with the story line that the medical establishment is capable of bureaucratic indifference—or even hostility—to women through any number of policies, the 2009 guidelines faced a steep uphill battle to be accepted by the public as being in the best interests of women.

Having a feel for uncertainty in medicine allows us to think about risks and benefits. We compare the size of a benefit with the level of risk, and then consider how sure we can be about those risks and benefits to locate a spot on the spectrum of certainty. The reason the debate about the 2009 USPSTF screening mammogram guidelines is so instructive is that the public, and a good many physicians, was saying, in effect, *Screening mammograms are way over here on the spectrum!* The Task Force's reply was, in effect, *No, actually it's over* here, *much closer to the middle.* The red-shift in perception was caused, to a very large extent, by a lack of appreciation for the uncertainty that comes with the technology.

The experts, however, who were fully aware of that uncertainty, were in consensus. In the following chapter, we'll see what happens when the uncertainty is so significant that even experts can't agree what to do. It is perhaps the most difficult and technical to read in this book, thick with studies and numbers, so it is worth considering getting a cup of coffee before proceeding (and I'll discuss coffee in a later chapter, too).

THE PRESSURES OF
MANAGING PRESSURE

Dum in dubio est animus, paulo momento huc illuc impellitur.
(When a mind is in a state of uncertainty, the smallest impulse
directs it to either side.)

—ROMAN PLAYWRIGHT TERENCE, *ANDRIA*, ACT 1, SCENE 5

We've just seen how uncertainty can have a major impact on public health guidelines and how the consequent public discussion is framed. In approaching guidelines, doctors and patients alike *might* regard them as simple yes-or-no, up-or-down recommendations. However guidelines could likewise be understood as policy statements of relative benefits versus relative risks, documents that eschew the hard-and-fast language of "do this, don't do that" and opt instead for a more nuanced view of what the scientific research can actually tell us about some topic. One of the reasons the US Preventive Services Task Force's 2009 mammogram recommendations induced so much cognitive dissonance in the public when the report was issued was that the vast majority of the public (to say nothing of the many doctors who focus on women's health) assumed the recommendations were going to look like the first kind of "marching orders" guideline, although the task force itself consciously intended to provide the second kind of recommendation, which put the uncertainty surrounding screening mammography's benefits front and center.

Yet it is important to note that although many physicians strongly disagreed with those guidelines (and, indeed, nearly seven years after the report's publication, many still do), the committee itself was unanimous. The experts assembled, sixteen in all, reviewed a mountain of data and presented a picture of screening mammography as a technology that occupied more than one spot on the spectrum of certainty, depending on a woman's demographics. The value of screening mammograms for healthy women above the age of fifty but under the age of seventy-four was regarded as being to the left of center. They believed there was either a big suggestion of a small benefit or possibly a small hint of a big benefit. In other words, there was moderate uncertainty of its benefits, but the benefits seemed persuasive (although these recommendations came out before the results of the large and well-designed Canadian mammography trial that showed no benefits at all, which may have influenced the 2009 report). But the evidence in the benefits of screening mammograms in women under fifty was regarded as far less persuasive, and so screening mammograms in that group was placed either in the absolute center, or possibly a little to the *right* of center on the spectrum of certainty, where it suggested net harms.

The bottom line was that these sixteen experts, who had laboriously reviewed the evidence for months, and who must have had marathon discussion sessions about how to convey the subtleties of these findings, were completely unified in standing behind these guidelines. While there was a "controversy" in the public debate, there was nowhere near the same level of contentiousness within the task force itself.

The following story, however, is about a guideline task force in which the experts *did* split, and as such this chapter represents the relatively rare moment when true biomedical controversy exists on a large scale. While there are many disputes in medicine about the optimal treatment for a condition, or the best strategy to manage a given disease, or the most accurate method to arrive at a diagnosis, most of these arguments deal with fairly fine points, and there is much consensus on the general approaches to various maladies. But here we'll see an example of a situation where even highly trained doctors looked to the experts and saw nothing but discord.

It may seem ever so slightly sadistic to include a chapter dealing with this degree of uncertainty in a book for a general audience. If the experts can't even agree, then how on earth should a layperson be able to sort it out? I include this story not because I wish to induce a sense of throw-your-hands-up hopelessness, but rather because understanding the role that uncertainty plays in genuinely controversial policies allows all of us to establish what we do know and do not know about a medical topic. And as I hope to underline further at the conclusion of the book, having the ability to sort out what is known from what is not can be genuinely liberating for patients. Moreover, I include it to underline that treatments always carry the risk of harms, and any time we pop a pill, we should regard that action as the culmination of a risk-versus-benefit equation that should land squarely on the side of benefit. As patients, we should always be cognizant of that equation.

So there is *good* news in this chapter, although at first glance it may seem daunting and frustrating. But bear with me. Go slow as you read this, for the data can seem confusing—not surprising, because it caused the expert consensus to crack! But even for nonmedical laypeople it's not impossible to understand the parameters of the debate. If you start to get bogged down in the studies, just remember that the question that divided the specialists was this: For people with high blood pressure, what is the optimal level to which we should attempt to lower it?

Time to dive in.

JNC8, or Breaking Up Is Hard to Do, Expert Edition

In February 2014, the members of a group in the United States called the Joint National Committee (a panel of more than a dozen experts assembled by the National Heart, Lung, and Blood Institute, which is a key division of the National Institutes of Health) issued its long-awaited recommendations for the diagnosis and management of high blood pressure. Because high blood pressure has been one of the central and most lethal problems facing Americans for several generations, the JNC has been periodically updating its guidelines since its first report in 1977. This most recent report was the seventh revision of the original, and thus has been shorthanded in the medical community as the JNC8.

It is safe to say that there will not be a JNC9 anytime in the near future, for the process of producing JNC8 was so fraught with contentiousness that the entire method by which US national guidelines are generated is unlikely to continue. Seven months before the publication of JNC8, the leadership of the National Heart, Lung, and Blood Institute issued a long statement discussing the process of the guideline formation, and although the text of the announcement is somewhat cryptic—they state, for instance, that they would publish "five integrated cardiovascular guideline products . . . as evidentiary reviews," whatever that means—it seemed clear that they were getting out of the guideline business.

The source of the dispute could be found in matters both practical and theoretical to the function of the JNC8 committee. The practical issues centered on blood pressure targets for one particular group of patients, while the theoretical issues related to how one included or excluded evidence in forming the guidelines. By the time the JNC8 guidelines were issued, a minority group had published its own separate report in a different journal.* Not only would patients find such conflicting recommendations difficult to absorb, workaday docs would be equally hard put to the task of knowing which set of recommendations to follow unless they immersed themselves in the data to arrive at their own conclusions. In the case of the JNC8 guidelines, immersion can quickly lead to drowning.

JNC8 represented a departure from JNC7 in a manner similar to the revised mammography recommendations by the USPSTF in 2009 in that they proposed scaling *back* treatment goals. The table on the next page summarizes the differences between the two sets of guidelines:

In patients over the age of eighty, there were no changes: the goal blood pressure was 150/90 or lower. There were new, *higher* goal blood pressures for patients with either concomitant diabetes or chronic kidney disease, with the previous target being 130/80 and the new target 140/90. This may seem counterintuitive for people who have long heard that a "normal" and healthy blood pressure is 120/80, but when the committee reviewed the data, they believed that there was no evidence to suggest that the lower blood pressure prevented the complications of these diseases.

---

* Five of the members of the JNC8 committee peeled away from the remaining twelve to issue their report in 2014. Again, contrast this with the 2009 USPSTF recommendations on screening mammograms, in which all sixteen authors supported the report. Controversy has its gradations, and, as we'll see in the next chapter, on Lyme, sometimes patients think there is a raging debate with much uncertainty, when in fact there's virtually no debate at all and a pretty high degree of certainty about the major points of diagnosis and treatment.

Table 4.1

Patient Group	Old JNC7 Target BP	New JNC8 Target BP
Anyone with diabetes	130/80	140/90 (not controversial)
Anyone with kidney disease	130/80	140/90 (not controversial)
Age 60–79 without diabetes or kidney disease	*140/90*	*150/90 (controversial)*
Age 80 and up	150/90	no change

Although these were higher goals, the full JNC8 concurred on the new targets for these patients.

Yet the real dispute came in patients between the ages of sixty and eighty who did not have kidney disease or diabetes. The JNC7 goal was a pressure below 140/90, whereas in JNC8, the committee basically said that they should be thought of as the same way we think of patients over eighty, with a revised target blood pressure below 150/90. At its core, the dissenters were saying, *we believe that we should get our patients below 140!* while the majority opinion offered the following reply: *we can't confidently say that dropping below 140 confers unambiguous benefits.*

Currently, an estimated population of nearly 42 million people are above the target pressure by JNC7 criteria; with the revised JNC8 guidelines, that number drops to about 14 million.[†] The minority essentially rejected this reclassification scheme, but, as I noted, they didn't reject all of it. The sticking point revolved around whether it was legitimate to raise the goal pressure of patients between ages sixty and eighty if they did not have the complications of diabetes and kidney disease. Should the goal be a systolic blood pressure less than 140 or 150? That was the crux of the

---

† With the reclassification, a little under 10 percent of patients would no longer be regarded as in need of therapy—about 6 million out of the 70 million people whom the JNC7 guidelines considered treatment eligible. Therefore the bulk of the controversy lay in how aggressively to approach the approximately 30 million people who are already on treatment but are above the previous (JNC7) guideline's goals.

matter: one group insisted the lower target was the ideal, while the other group (the majority) was skeptical of the benefits of this lower target.

How could such experts be so divided? In large part, it's because of a legitimate dispute about what we can reasonably infer about *three points of systolic pressure.*

One particular contested trial highlights this conundrum: the Systolic Hypertension in Elderly Patients, or SHEP, trial. SHEP included nearly 5,000 patients older than sixty, most of whom had not been treated for hypertension before enrolling in the trial. Researchers gave them a combination of antihypertensive medications or placebos, and followed them for more than four years on average.* The trial was a resounding success: the total number of strokes was nearly cut in half, the amount of heart failure cases decreased by *more* than half, and there were more modest reductions in heart attacks, heart bypass surgeries, and transient ischemic attacks (so-called ministrokes, which can be harder to diagnose than full-blown stroke events). SHEP showed, without any doubt, that lowering blood pressure results in big gains.

But how to translate SHEP to a set of guidelines by a committee that has been tasked to weigh in on the bright line of 140/90 versus a higher target? Herein lies the problem. The average starting systolic blood pressure of the SHEP participants, that is, both the placebo and treatment groups, was 170. The placebo group dropped its average pressure to 155 over the course of the trial, while the treatment group dropped its average pressure to . . . one hundred forty *three.* Therefore, the majority of the JNC8 panel concluded this study provided strong evidence that lowering systolic blood pressure below one hundred *fifty* carried benefits. However, because the final blood pressure of the treatment group was just *above* that 140 cutoff, SHEP was not deemed to support the lower target that the previous guidelines had advocated.

Before I continue to analyze the dispute, it's worth considering how the placebo group dropped its pressure if the researchers were not giving them pharmacologically active medications. This is a beautiful illustration of what is known as the "placebo effect," where symptomatic or other changes take place in patients who are not given pharmacologically active

---

* A placebo is a "do nothing" pill, which I'll discuss in Chapter 6.

drugs but believe they are. In the eyes of many believers in "alternative medicine," the placebo effect is evidence of the magical and secretive powers of the human mind to heal the body, and much claptrap is devoted to the topic.

More on alternative medicine and pseudoscience in the next chapter, but in this case I think there's a pretty good explanation for why the placebo group in SHEP dropped its average systolic pressure by fifteen points. Simply put, by *becoming aware* that they had sky-high blood pressures—which they had been told could lead to very scary outcomes as part of the consent process for enrolling in the trial—they suddenly became focused on their mortality and made, consciously or otherwise, healthy lifestyle changes, probably by increasing their physical activity and eating either less or better, or less *and* better. In this respect, SHEP (and all trials of this ilk) probably underestimates the magnitude of benefit of lowering blood pressure, because a comparison of properly treated patients with a group of people who maintained a systolic blood pressure of 170 would almost certainly show an even greater reduction in cardiovascular events and overall mortality when compared to the difference between the treated and the placebo group (with its lowered average pressure of 155, which was still higher than the treatment group). Such a trial is no longer considered ethical, however.

Keep in mind that SHEP was but one among many tiles in the mosaic of studies that the JNC8 experts were forced to sift through on their way to issuing blood pressure guidelines. Thus, one can pretty easily comprehend why a minority group could have split away and cried foul at the decision to change the recommendations—keeping in mind that the previous guidelines had taken nearly a decade to inculcate into the brains of primary care physicians, in the estimates of one group that wrote a mildly skeptical editorial in the same issue in which the JNC8 report was published.

The question the dissenters were asking was this: Was the JNC8 willing to scrap the "140/90 is the target" message, which had become the equivalent of a public service announcement, especially to the community of primary care docs who may not have the time to delve into arguments about the nuances of study design, because the average blood pressure of this universally acknowledged well-designed trial was *three* points higher

than the previous guideline? No matter where one falls on the specific issue of what the optimal blood pressure of this patient group should be, it
isn't especially difficult to see why they were so troubled by the change.

Moreover, SHEP wasn't the only prickly piece of evidence that caused
headaches and led to the minority group's decision to break with JNC8.
One can get the feeling of entering Wonderland when reading about the
controversy, but here is a glimpse into the debate. In expressing its skepticism of the benefits of lowering pressures below 140, the JNC8 cited two
other studies that went by the acronyms JATOS and VALISH. These
studies *did* get the average systolic blood pressures below the magic 140
mark, but neither study showed a benefit. So the majority of the committee believed that represented evidence that 140 should no longer be the
goal, but 150 instead.

Unfortunately, both JATOS and VALISH were considered to be of
inferior trial design largely because they didn't enroll enough patients to
demonstrate positive effects if such effects were present (I'll talk more in
the later chapters, and in the Appendix, about the size of trials). Nobody,
as far as I can tell, disputed the value of the SHEP study. The majority of
the JNC8 felt the JATOS and VALISH studies provided indirect evidence
against the lower target, but the minority said these studies shouldn't be
considered at all and were biasing the group. The dissenters further noted
that JATOS and VALISH were Japanese studies and thought that it was
potentially inappropriate to generalize studies from Japan anyway, given
the significantly different diet and lifestyle of those patients.

The dissenters were also upset about the *exclusion* of a trial that went
by the acronym FEVER, which *did* show benefits for the lower target
blood pressures, even though FEVER was a Chinese study, enrolling patients with what one would assume are equally different dietary and lifestyle differences compared to Americans (even if these differences aren't
the *same* differences as those of the Japanese study subjects). All I can
conclude with confidence after poring over these papers is that the lead
scientists need to work on developing better acronyms for their trials.

As we saw in the data on screening mammography, another issue that
at least indirectly drove the debate about the optimal target blood pressure involved the difference between the *relative* and *absolute* benefits of
aggressive blood pressure control. Recall that when we looked at

mammography, we found data showing that even big reductions in relative risk might translate to only modest absolute benefits. A look at the SHEP trial highlights a similar phenomenon with respect to blood pressure control.

At the end of the trial, 149 out of the 2,371 patients in the placebo group of the trial had a stroke (in this trial, stroke was considered to be the primary outcome); in the treatment group, there were 96 strokes out of 2,365 patients. So although the *relative* risk reduction in strokes is 0.63—that is, treatment cuts the rate of strokes almost by half—the *absolute* risk reduction is about 2 percent, or about fifty strokes saved per nearly 2,400 patients over five years' time.* What that probably means is that there's a *big* benefit to dropping your blood pressure if you start out at 170, but those benefits get smaller once you're down in the low 140s and you and your physician are contemplating adding a drug to get you to the low 130s.

Stop for a moment, and reread that last sentence, for it is absolutely critical to contextualizing the JNC8 dispute. If one can grasp the essential principle, one can apply the lesson to much more than just blood pressure management. The biggest benefits of blood pressure management come for those already at the higher end and diminish as we move closer to the "normal" value of 120/80. That's true for many other diseases as well: for instance, diabetes may be diabetes, but very poorly controlled diabetes is much, much more dangerous than even moderately controlled diabetes. So patients need not feel like failures if they aren't "at goal" with some disease—*any* kind of improvement tends to reap huge benefits. Even *a little* exercise is likely to provide real protection against heart attacks, heart failure, and strokes. Do patients who walk for half an hour twice a week derive the same level of protection from heart disease as those who transform themselves from couch potatoes to marathoners? No, but instead of becoming dispirited for not hitting that goal and losing their motivation to keep walking, such patients should feel accomplished that

---

* Because of dropout rates over the course of the trial, the study authors used some more sophisticated statistical tests and concluded that the medications reduced thirty strokes per one thousand patients, a slightly higher benefit than my raw calculation implies.

they've made a big difference in their lives. And their doctors should be encouraging this way of looking at the world instead of obsessing about hitting a given target.*

This is how understanding uncertainty can aid you as a patient when you talk with your physician, for with uncertainty comes a framework for knowing when it's a really, really good idea to get treatment for some condition, or it's perfectly fine to hold off. We'll see the same kind of effect when we look at how high cholesterol is treated later in the book.

Harm

It might cross your mind to ask *why* we would want to stop lowering blood pressure, even if the benefits diminish as the numbers decline. Isn't any benefit, even a little one, worth it, if it prevents something as devastating as a stroke? Again, the SHEP data can help explain in part why we shy away from being overly aggressive. While the reduction in cardiovascular events from SHEP is quite striking, hovering around 40 percent, the reduction in "all-cause mortality" (that is, just adding up all the people who died in each group regardless of cause) is a much more modest 10 percent, sufficiently small that the lower number of deaths in the treatment group *might* simply have been a matter of chance.

Why is there such a discrepancy between these two measurements? Why doesn't the reduction in mortality match that of strokes and cardiac events seen in the trial? The authors of SHEP don't speculate, but all internists routinely encounter medical problems in the elderly that are often direct consequences of a blood pressure being *too* low. Keep in mind that blood pressures, like body temperatures or heart rates, fluctuate throughout the course of a day, and in older patients the swings can be more dramatic as the elasticity of blood vessels decrease. Thus, even simple

---

* The increasing emphasis on adherence to national guidelines, coupled with the computerization of patient health information, has had the unintended effect of forcing doctors, in particular primary care physicians, on achieving bright-line goals for their patients. That is, if some patient lowers their blood pressure from a systolic of 180 to 152—which confers a *huge* protective benefit—the physician may face lower "performance scores" because he or she is not at the goal of less than 150, and such performance scores can affect reimbursement.

maneuvers like rising from a seated position can cause major drops in pressure, and if the starting point is lowered through medications, such precipitous shifts can cause people to faint.

Among the most common problems caused by fainting is a broken hip. Far worse than a broken bone almost anywhere else in the body, broken hips cause patients to be bedbound for long stretches, which increases their risk for blood clots, pneumonias, and other complications associated with surgery. Estimates vary, but the one-year mortality following a broken hip is probably somewhere between 10 and 40 percent—at least as bad as or worse than many cancers. At first glance, hip fractures may not seem like the kind of event that a blood pressure study should evaluate (and few have done so), but that hidden variable probably accounts for a chunk of the reduction in lifesaving benefit seen in SHEP. *That* is why being overly aggressive in lowering blood pressure in patients over the age of sixty might be dangerous.

The question, then, is where this happy medium can be found, and the current evidence suggests that the benefits clearly outweigh the risks for these patients when their pressures are lowered to somewhere in the range of the low to mid-140s on average. Whether there is *additional* benefit to lowering one's pressure even further than that is very much a matter of debate.

The key to understanding how one can use uncertainty as a helpful tool lies in realizing that *nobody* truly knows the optimal low point. Indeed, it's very clear that there is no *single* optimal low point for all patients, because factors like genetics, other disease, and smoking will all contribute to one's risk of stroke, and some will require lower sustained pressures over time than others. But appreciating the value of uncertainty involves knowing oneself.

Nobody expects patients to solve the problem of knowing their optimal blood pressure. But what goals do they wish to achieve, and are they willing to tolerate side effects, and even more serious problems, in pursuit of a particular goal? It may be that a given patient, having watched a loved one suffer a major stroke, wants to do as much as possible to minimize that risk, even if he or she understands that means complications like a broken hip—which has the potential to be lethal—may arise. Other patients may have very wide pulse pressures—high systolic blood pressures coupled with normal or even low diastolic pressures—for which aggressive approaches may carry significantly more danger. Others still may hate taking medications and find themselves after one drug in the mid-140s, but are looking at having to start a new class of medications to drop them further. *These* are the kinds of factors that patients can think about and should discuss with their doctors. Similarly, they should expect honest and informed replies about relative risks and relative benefits (to say nothing of *absolute* risks and benefits). I'll say more about how to have that conversation in the Conclusion.

The JNC8 brouhaha highlights as much about our emotional responses toward data as it does about the underlying disease process and the science we use to analyze it. Glenn Kershaw, a nephrologist (kidney and blood pressure doctor) with whom I work, summed up the controversy this way: "The old school view is that guidelines express certainty. The new school view is that guidelines emphasize the limits of evidence, and the unique role of the practitioner and patient." To my mind, it is not that one approach is right and the other wrong; they're doing *different things,* and, when we are at the limits of our understanding, struggling in the world of known unknowns, finding ourselves in the middle of the spectrum of certainty, conversations about medical guidelines must take this into account.

In the previous chapter, we encountered a body of experts who presented a set of guidelines that incorporated uncertainty to its core. Although they were unified, the guidelines led to public controversy. In reviewing the JNC8 report, we observed how uncertainty and our attitudes about uncertainty can lead to controversy even *among* the experts. The next chapter will look at what happens when the experts are unified but a small and highly motivated activist group creates the impression that there is very little consensus, even though there is a very high level of it, not just among the experts, but among tens of thousands of physicians.

LYME'S FALSE PROPHETS:
CHRONIC FATIGUE, TICK-BORNE ILLNESS,
AND THE OVERSELLING OF CERTAINTY

> We are all capable of believing things which we *know* to be
> untrue, and then, when we are finally proved wrong, impu-
> dently twisting the facts so as to show that we were right.
> Intellectually, it is possible to carry on this process for an in-
> definite time: the only check on it is that sooner or later a
> false belief bumps up against solid reality, usually on a
> battlefield.
>
> —GEORGE ORWELL

In the two previous chapters, we have moved along the spectrum of certainty into ever murkier territory. In the case of mammograms, I tried to show how the divide between the experts and the public occurred because most experts were always less certain of mammography's benefits than was popularly understood. Moreover, there was a general consensus among experts that the *magnitude* of the benefit wasn't as profound as laypeople thought. The latest blood pressure guidelines in the JNC8 investigated a question that involved so much uncertainty that even the experts were split—indeed, they were so split that one group simply broke off and issued a competing set of guidelines. The JNC8 controversy also highlights the issue of what the ultimate purpose guidelines should serve: Are they simply bright-line goals, about which the less asked the better, or should they reflect the limits of our knowledge and go no further? These are, by no means, easily answered questions.

In this chapter, however, we emerge onto the other side of the spectrum of certainty—one in which we can be fairly certain that treatments carry *harm* without any evidence of a corresponding benefit. For about a generation, a small group of patient advocates, along with a coterie of physicians, have theorized that chronic fatigue syndrome is caused mainly by Lyme disease. Because Lyme is a treatable disease, and because chronic fatigue is of course chronic, these patients and this small group of physicians have advocated for, in some cases, essentially indefinite courses of antibiotics. When the experts sat down to review the data in the early 2000s, there was a solid consensus that prolonged antibiotics were not only *not* helpful but pretty clearly harmful, and so a professional society advocated for *less* medicine in its Lyme disease treatment guidelines. What almost nobody could have anticipated after the publication of their fairly dry and technical paper was that they would find themselves in court, with the real possibility of financial insolvency simply by having to defend the scientific accuracy of those very guidelines.

What follows is that story, which begins in my clinic as I evaluate David Marsh. It is worth repeating that David is not "real" in the sense that he is not a single person by that name. However, he is *quite* real in that he is an amalgam of several patients whom I have seen, and whose stories are similar in broad outline. It is safe to say that every general infectious disease doctor, to say nothing of a good number of internists and family physicians, will be familiar with David's story—certainly in New England, but also quite possibly across the United States.

David was twenty-four years old and had grown up in a small town in central Massachusetts. He came to my office seeking an answer to the question of why his life had gone completely awry. He was an exemplary student at his high school: he regularly made the honor roll, ran for the cross-country team, and took part in a variety of student activities. After graduation he attended a liberal arts college in the South, and four years later he came back to Massachusetts to start graduate school, about two years before our first visit.

It was midway through his first semester that something began to happen.

I say "something" because after meditating on his case for more than a year, I don't really know what that "thing" is. What I do know is that he began to experience symptoms that most doctors would, at first glance, assume was some kind of a viral illness. He spent the better part of a week during the first semester of graduate school in bed feeling lousy, suffering from muscle pains, sweating episodes that came and went, and a bit of tenderness in his knee and ankle joints. He never sought medical help during this period so there wasn't any specific testing done. At any rate, after that week the aches and joint pains went away, and he tried to resume his life and get back to his academic work.

But instead of picking back up, as nearly all of us have done after some brief, nonspecific bout of illness, David's body went into a long idle that continues to this day. He never finished that first semester and couldn't find a job. He stopped exercising, he didn't go out and spend time with friends, he didn't travel to try to jump-start his life again. At the time we first met, it was as if his life had just been put on a very prolonged pause.

What he *did* do was sleep. During college, David felt like he could function perfectly fine if he got between six and seven hours of sleep each night. Since that fateful illness, he began to sleep more and more, and by the time we met he was sleeping about twelve hours at night yet still required one to two prolonged naps during the day. He was exhausted constantly. His life had become confined largely to his father's couch, where he would sit and watch TV after getting out of bed and spend the day dozing before returning to his room and starting the cycle all over again. I am neither Catholic nor religious, but "purgatory" seemed the most apt word for what his life had become.

He began seeking medical opinions several months later. First he made a visit to the pediatrician who cared for him as a child, who reluctantly agreed to see him as he had never established a relationship with an internist. No diagnosis was offered. Next came his father's primary care physician, and, after a few visits, referrals to an endocrinologist, a hematologist, and a neurologist. Throughout these visits, a series of tests were ordered: routine blood work, serum chemistries, liver function studies, an HIV test, and labs for thyroid function were but a few of dozens of tests ordered to look for disease running the gamut from common to exceedingly rare. He had a CT scan done on his lungs, abdomen, and pelvis to look for some hidden cancer or infection that might be the source; the neurologist ordered a brain MRI to evaluate for any possible structural brain problems that might explain his symptoms. Every last test was normal. My office received a stack of consultation notes, lab results, and radiology reports nearly two inches thick. Not one of the doctors involved could explain what was wrong with David, and after an hour-long appointment and twice that time reviewing his records, neither could I.

Yet our visits were not, strictly speaking, aimed at finding some diagnosis for his chronic fatigue, for by the time David came to me, he had his own fairly strong ideas as to the cause. David believed he was suffering from Lyme disease. He actually had more than one Lyme test performed over the course of his prolonged evaluation, and each time it was negative. (Despite this, he had nonetheless undergone two courses of treatment with doxycycline, the gold-standard treatment for Lyme.) But David had an answer for this: the test, he said, was being interpreted incorrectly. He produced literature that backed up his claim. He noted a medical organization composed of various board-certified doctors whose website supported this interpretation of his testing. Based upon all of this, he believed that antibiotics—*months* of antibiotics, possibly years of antibiotics—were his best chance at turning his life around. Although we spoke in part about other causes of his illness, most of our discussion revolved around whether I felt comfortable giving him a three-month prescription for tetracycline for what he believed was his Lyme disease, which had not responded to treatment.

How David and I came to that point, with that specific question on the table, is a story that probably could not have happened were it not for the quirky biology of the Lyme bacteria, which produces illness ranging from something that looks like the flu to chronic arthritis to a state where the heart muscle becomes inflamed to any number of neurological problems and, of course, to chronic fatigue. It could not have happened if it were not for the difficulty in diagnosing Lyme, which at the time of this writing relies on a testing algorithm that is not without its problems. Finally, it could not have happened without the Internet, which has spread both an abundant amount of medical knowledge to laypeople as well as an equal amount of misinformation.

Thus far, this book has discussed uncertainty by emphasizing the underestimated imperfection of results. My goal has been to show that these results, whether those of an individual blood test or those of a 10,000-person study five years in the making, need to be approached with varying levels of caution. I've tried to highlight some areas in which doctors or patients or both have gotten themselves into trouble by neglecting uncertainty when they interpret results, not realizing that a positive test may sometimes be negative in reality.

In the case of chronic fatigue syndrome, however, this has been turned on its head so that *negative* tests have been interpreted by some to be *positive.* An entire medical subculture—one might, in fact, call it an alternate medical universe—has evolved, and it has exploited the complicated dynamics of Lyme disease testing, convincing thousands of patients who *don't* suffer from Lyme that they *do,* and that they will benefit from everlonger courses of antibiotics when no study has ever shown this to be true. Indeed, the lack of benefit of prolonged antibiotics is often taken as evidence by particular practitioners that *more* antibiotics are required, with the very failure of patient improvement serving to reinforce their belief that they haven't stamped out the infection that so-called mainstream physicians can't find in the first place.*

If all of this sounds confusing, it is, and yet it is the state of affairs in doctors' offices across the US. Lyme tends to be concentrated in three parts of the country: New England, the upper Midwest, and the Pacific West. Nevertheless, this has not stopped a small industry of physicians convinced of the ubiquitous menace of Lyme from cropping up across the country, all running clinics focused on patients with chronic fatigue.

---

* What's in a name? The sharply divergent views of different communities involved in the treatment of Lyme disease lead to two competing sets of nomenclature, which can be dizzying in its confusion, especially for outsiders trying to make sense of the controversy. Thus, for the sake of simplicity I refer to each of these groups by commonly used names—"alternative" and "mainstream," mainly—and won't spend much time analyzing why people have chosen that vocabulary or complain that they are misleading. What's important is that they really do refer to two distinct groups with very different assumptions about Lyme disease.

They also believe chronic fatigue is caused by other exotic infections as babesiosis, anaplasmosis, and bartonellosis. Their common denominator is that they are tick-borne illnesses, but Lyme takes center stage for these doctors, and their patients reflect these concerns. The notion that Lyme plays the starring role in the world of chronic fatigue is reflected in the name of the principal advocacy group known by the acronym ILADS, or the International Lyme and Associated Diseases Society.

There is nothing especially controversial about having specialized clinics that cater to certain patient populations; a typical infectious disease practice routinely cares for patients with such infections. But these particular chronic fatigue Lyme clinics—let's call them the ILADS group—have a very different approach than that of mainstream physicians. They interpret Lyme testing differently, often avoiding the labs and tests used by such mainstream physicians. They utilize treatment protocols that their mainstream colleagues shun. They have their own professional organization in ILADS, and ILADS engages in very little dialogue with the broader medical world. They are, in every meaningful sense of the phrase, *alternative medicine:* they have alternative theories about the causes of chronic fatigue, they have alternative laboratories who perform alternative tests not approved by government agencies, and they have alternative treatments.

For their part, mainstream physicians often react to the ILADS practitioners with a mixture of bewilderment, exasperation, and contempt. Most believe that the entire approach of ILADS relies on shoddy science and that these doctors do more harm than good in at least two ways. First, they prescribe treatments that carry genuine risk without any evidence of a corresponding benefit in symptoms. (I'll discuss some of these risks later in the chapter.) Second, they offer false certainty about the cause of chronic fatigue, and thus false hope, to their patients.

Normally these two mostly distinct worlds would just function in parallel, with one set of doctors choosing to go their own way, and the other set doing otherwise, each largely rejecting the baseline assumptions of the other group. This is the case with many of the philosophies that undergird the movement of alternative medicine, whether it be Qi Gong, reflexology, acupuncture, or the like.* But, in the case of Lyme disease, a series of guidelines issued by a mainstream physicians' organization brought the two groups into direct conflict, leading not merely to the usual heated accusations of unprofessionalism, but a full-fledged legal attack on the largest organization of infectious disease physicians in the world.

The story of Lyme disease and patients suffering from chronic fatigue syndrome reveals much about the limits of what doctors can know through testing. It highlights the problems associated with modern medicine when a patient has obvious illness but a diagnosis for it remains elusive. It illustrates the influence that the business of medicine can have on patients' perception of doctors. And it displays the impact of the Internet on doctor-patient interactions—or at least one aspect of it. To say that the Internet alone is responsible for the false prophets who trumpet "chronic Lyme" as the source of so many ills not only goes too far, it ignores the significant benefits that the Internet has had on the doctor-patient encounter. But, with respect to Lyme, the Internet has allowed a certain kind of anti-intellectual and antiscientific set of ideas to spread much more efficiently, and for like-minded advocates to join forces and spread confusion in the process. Indeed, the Internet appears to have facilitated the spread of the diagnosis internationally, with a protest outside Downing Street in the UK held in 2013.

Although there were descriptions in the medical literature throughout the twentieth century of the disease we now call Lyme, we typically date its discovery to 1975, when physicians working for the Centers for Disease Control and Prevention (CDC) in Atlanta came to Lyme, Connecticut, to investigate a cluster of cases of what appeared to be the fairly uncommon condition of juvenile rheumatoid arthritis. Several of these patients, and

---

* There is much more to be said about so-called alternative medicine that is beyond the scope of this book. What distinguishes ILADS from many other alternative movements is that it seems to accept certain baseline assumptions of "Western medicine." It appears to accept the evidence of germ theory, the molecular biology that forms the basis of Lyme testing, and the usefulness of antibiotic therapy, for instance. However it does differ, and differs mightily, with mainstream medicine on the ground rules concerning scientific evidence in how to assign causes to symptoms and how to know whether a given therapy is working and should be stopped.

subsequent others like them, were also found to have a distinctive bull's eye rash that had been described in European medical journals as early as 1909 and was called erythema migrans.

What was known about erythema migrans rashes is that they were associated with tick bites, and that became a critical clue in unwrapping the Lyme mystery. Over the next several years a variety of clinical and laboratory studies were carried out, and a researcher named Willy Burgdorfer isolated from deer ticks a type of corkscrew-shaped bacteria known as a spirochete that eventually was understood as the causative agent of Lyme, and the organism was named *Borrelia burgdorferi* in his honor.

It would become clear over the course of the 1980s that *Borrelia burgdorferi* was an odd organism. It was incredibly difficult to grow in culture, which was and remains the mainstay laboratory technique for the diagnosis of bacterial disease. Moreover, the clinical symptoms that *B. burgdorferi* produced were protean—that is, they could frequently change form, first appearing as the painless rash, then progressing to fevers and muscle pains, then to headaches or neurologic abnormalities or arthritis or a combination of these symptoms. The arthritis notwithstanding, most of the complaints were nonspecific and could be associated with dozens of diseases. Because there was no direct method for testing for Lyme infection, and because Lyme could mimic so many other conditions, it was difficult from the start to know whether Lyme was, or was not, the cause of someone's illness.

During the 1980s and 1990s, as suburbanization was bringing more and more people into direct contact with traditional deer habitat, and thus the ticks that spread Lyme, scientists began developing other tools besides culture for detecting *Borrelia burgdorferi*. The two most important types of tests that were developed for Lyme, which are still used today, were the ELISA and the Western blot. Both of these tests diagnose Lyme not by finding direct evidence of the presence of *Borrelia* in the patient (as a culture would) but by *indirectly* noting the presence of the patient's immune response to *Borrelia*. It's a bit like stumbling upon a crime scene. If you see a body lying there with a knife in the chest, then you can be pretty confident a murder took place. That's the equivalent of culturing *Borrelia* from the patient. But in the case of Lyme, the body typically is nowhere to be found. Instead, you can infer that a patient had Lyme (i.e., that there was a murder) by seeing a pool of blood and a nearby knife—the metaphor for the ELISA and Western blot.

Of course, occasionally you find blood and a knife in a room and there really wasn't a murder, but rather there was some innocent explanation for the mess: someone cut themselves shaving, it was an animal who bled rather than a person, or it wasn't even blood in the first place and merely looked like it. The combination testing of ELISA and Western blot, of which I'll discuss the biological details in a moment, is designed to minimize these overinterpretations. But the believers in chronic Lyme argue that it's the mainstream physicians who are ignoring the evidence and that they are in collusion with one another to deprive patients of care. At the heart of the dispute is how to interpret Lyme tests and what degree of uncertainty is acceptable in diagnosing a disease that often has very nonspecific symptoms.

The origins of the ELISA test date to the mid-1960s, but it became available for commercial use more than two decades later. The ELISA can be used in a variety of ways, but to keep things simple I'll discuss it mostly in relation to Lyme. The Lyme ELISA is based on the idea that the body responds to *Borrelia* infection by developing antibodies that "catch" the organism and direct it to specialized immune cells that devour and destroy the bacteria. Antibodies are made by a different set of immune cells, and what makes the ELISA work is that these cells make antibodies that are organism specific. That is, after being infected by Lyme, the body will mount an immune response by making antibodies that target unique surface molecules (mostly proteins) of *Borrelia burgdorferi*. This is true for nearly all infectious agents: infections with bacteria, or viruses, or fungi all produce antibody responses specific to that organism.

The Lyme ELISA, then, is designed to capture that specific antibody response to *Borrelia burgdorferi*. Since Lyme-infected patients have ready-made anti-*Borrelia* antibodies in their blood, they can be captured if a patient's serum is dropped into a well coated with Lyme proteins. After the patient's serum is mixed in this well allowing for the binding, the rest of the serum—with all its other antibodies that aren't specific for Lyme—can be washed away. After that, special antibodies that bind only to *human antibodies* are added. *These* antibodies are attached to fluorochromes, which are effectively tiny light beacons that can be activated, detected, and quantified by lasers. From there it's a simple matter of a second wash, adding the proper reagents to activate the beacons and placing the well in a specialized laser system designed to read ELISAs.

Keep in mind that if a person *doesn't* have Lyme, when the serum is added to the well, there won't be any binding of that person's antibodies to the Lyme antigens that coat the surface of the well. The antibodies meant for organisms other than *Borrelia* will just bounce around in the fluid, and so when the serum is washed away, *all* the patient's antibodies will be washed away, too. Thus, when the next step of the ELISA takes place, and the antihuman antibodies with the molecular beacons are added, they will have nothing to bind to themselves and will also be washed away. The resultant well will be read by the laser in the ELISA reader as negative—that is, the quantity of light emitted by those molecular beacons will approach zero.

That's the ELISA in principle, although the reality is a little more complicated, and those complications limit the effectiveness of the ELISA as the sole test for Lyme. The first is that, because the ELISA test measures the *quantity of light* emitted by the fluorochromes attached to the antibodies that bind in turn to the patient's antibodies, it is an indirect test twice removed, and its result isn't yes or no but is instead a number. Needless to say, because of the complex, multistep nature of the procedure, the numbers do not fall into nice, neat binary categories of zero and some high number that would indicate infection, but rather fall along a continuum. If we return to our body/murder crime scene analogy, the ELISA provides an answer as to *how much* blood is in the room. As a consequence, based on the characteristics of the test, some arbitrary number is chosen as the cutoff for "positive" and "negative." Anything below that number is considered reliably negative, and above that positive.

Unfortunately, the Lyme ELISA test has a false-positive problem. We've encountered this before elsewhere: the physicist Leonard Mlodinow's "positive HIV test" that wasn't really positive was an ELISA. The reason for this is that some antibodies the body produces can bind to Lyme antigens (or HIV antigens or whatever is being tested) even though they weren't produced in response to an infection. Some diseases, like lupus, are caused by the body producing an abundance of antibodies: the high level of antibodies in the serum of these patients can often cross-react with antigens in ELISA tests, producing false positives. Even among healthy people, some just happen to have these cross-reactive antibodies. The Lyme ELISA turns out to have somewhere around a 5 percent false-positive rate: that is, for every hundred people with a positive test, five were never infected.

This is where the Western blot comes into play, and it is used in precisely the same way HIV testing requires a Western blot to confirm infection (this test either wasn't commercially available or wasn't used when Leonard Mlodinow was "diagnosed" with HIV). The Lyme Western blot relies on measuring antibody responses for specific proteins found on the surface of every *Borrelia burgdorferi* bacteria. The test looks at thirteen proteins in all: ten can be bound by one type of antibody known as IgG, which are typically produced several weeks after infection, while the remaining three are bound by IgM antibodies, which are generated during the acute phase of infection and eventually dissipate. If the antibodies bind to the proteins, they are "labeled" in a manner similar to the antibodies in the ELISA and show up as little black lines, or bands, on photographic paper. Unlike the ELISA test, which in its crude form is a number, the Western blot bands either are present or not, and thus are either positive or negative.

If we return to our body/murder analogy, the ELISA provides us with a general sense of how *much* blood is in the room, while the Western Blot provides an even more specific quantification of the amount *and* confirms that the blood is from the murder victim. Over the past two decades, the Western blot has served as the definitive test for Lyme disease, becoming the final stop on a two-test system that utilizes the less expensive and less cumbersome ELISA as a primary screen, eliminating the false positives from the first test because of its greater accuracy. There are yet other legitimate Lyme tests that are beginning to gain acceptance, but the two-step testing remains the mainstay of Lyme diagnosis at the time of this writing. However, the alternative community has devised other Lyme tests that aren't nearly as reliable.

As with the ELISA (whose value is some number but gets interpreted as positive or negative), the Western blot similarly has a cutoff number: two out of three IgM bands indicates acute infection, while five of ten IgG bands make the diagnosis of past infection. Researchers developed these criteria for the same reasons that they chose the cutoff value in the ELISA: above the threshold, one can be reasonably confident that there's a real infection, but below that number the test isn't reliable. We know this by performing the Lyme Western blot on perfectly healthy people who don't live in Lyme-endemic areas. Consider going to a mountain community in the Himalayas of Nepal, where Lyme definitely does not exist and collecting blood specimens to test for Lyme. These hypothetical Nepalese test subjects who have so graciously provided their blood aren't even sick, yet even here the Christmas tree can light up to a limited extent, as some subjects will have a few IgG or IgM bands.

To be sure, it is an imperfect test. Thus, the current criteria for Lyme diagnosis, both in terms of the ELISA and the Western blot, are constructed so as to minimize the false positives.

Although I have described the Western blot in terms of clear positive or negative bands, even here the story is more complicated: sometimes the bands are *faintly* positive. Does this mean there are true anti-Lyme antibodies present in the patient's serum, or is this just a fluke related to the imperfect characteristics of the test? One Lyme researcher named Gary Wormser looked at this question in relation to IgM antibodies. Since IgM antibodies can be produced only during the early, acute phase of the infection (usually the first four weeks), we know that if IgM testing is positive in the cold and snowy New England winter, when ticks are much less likely to feed and people are far less likely to be exposed to these ticks, it is highly probable to be a false positive. Dr. Wormser reviewed the records of approximately 250 patients using criteria such as these to evaluate interpretation of Lyme Western blots. Of the 250, nearly one hundred had positive IgM Western blots, and of these, about *half* were deemed to be false positive based on commonsense criteria.

The entire Lyme diagnosis apparatus, then, is somewhat clunky, and it is sufficiently complicated that even mainstream physicians can misinterpret the tests and their cutoff points. Plus the two-step testing, in its effort to eliminate false positives, creates in turn the possibility of false *negatives*. What do you do with a person who has symptoms of textbook Lyme, lives in Connecticut, and whose Western blot has only *four* positive IgG bands and one positive IgM band? What happens when a newly sick patient has a negative ELISA, but the testing is done early enough that one cannot be completely confident of a negative result because the immune response isn't immediate? Given the ease by which Lyme can be treated—three weeks of doxycycline typically does the trick—many doctors accept that they will overtreat a percentage of their patients, either by treating patients who don't have Lyme or ones that do but don't have definitive evidence of it at the time they come to the clinic.

That said, the uncertainty of Lyme diagnosis has limits and only applies to a relatively small number of patients suffering from classic Lyme symptoms in areas where deer ticks live. For these patients, suspicion of negative tests is sometimes warranted. But the believers in chronic Lyme disease have seized upon the uncertainty inherent in Lyme testing, convincing patients that the mainstream approach is far too restrictive and thus not to be trusted under virtually any circumstance, particularly in patients with persistent, low-grade symptoms such as chronic fatigue, muscle pain, and difficulty concentrating. The alternative practitioners fashion themselves as "Lyme-literate physicians," thus implying that the mainstream doctors are Lyme *illiterate*—with the goal of maximizing doubt about the reliability of ELISAs and Western blots, unless, of course, the testing aligns with their preconceived notions about why a given patient is ill. The distrust of the standard two-test approach to Lyme, which magnifies the issue of the uncertainty inherent in the testing, is the starting point for going down the rabbit hole. Without it, the rest of the theory doesn't make much sense.

To aid those efforts, the alternate Lyme community has a panel of yet more tests for Lyme diagnosis, most of which are not approved by standard scientific labs. Among others, they include "urine antigen capture assays," which look for proteins produced by *Borrelia* in a urine sample; CD57 assays, which look for the presence of mature immune cells known as "natural killer" cells that once looked promising in diagnosing Lyme but turned out to be elevated in all kinds of conditions; and the Lyme lymphocyte transformation test, about which the less said the better. The CDC has included a page in its Lyme disease section referencing all of these tests, noting with bureaucratic dryness that "some laboratories offer [these tests] using assays whose accuracy and clinical usefulness have not been adequately established."

The website for the alternative chronic Lyme advocacy group ILADS provides a fair illustration of its suspicion of mainstream test interpretation. In a section titled "Basic Information about Lyme Disease," it argues that the CDC intended the two-step testing process to be used for only "disease surveillance," not diagnosis; that the CDC Western blot criteria are defined too narrowly and that "the Western blot should be performed by a laboratory that reads and reports all of the bands related to *Borrelia burgdorferi*"; and, moreover, that the ELISA is the wrong test to use in the first place because, according to ILADS, the ELISA misses about a third of Lyme cases to begin with.

Taken together, these objections to Lyme testing sets the stage for a two-pronged assault on the validity of the mainstream community's Lyme diagnosis strategy. The first prong asserts that alternative laboratories, which use a variety of tests that either are not approved by the Food and Drug Administration (FDA) or are not interpreted according to the CDC guidelines, are the only ones that can be trusted in diagnosing patients. The second prong asserts that Lyme is a "clinical diagnosis"—that is, labs aren't really relevant anyway. "Familiarity with [Lyme's] varied presentations is key to recognizing disseminated disease," the website says, implying that a mainstream physician's reliance on a negative Lyme test is not only misplaced faith in technology but speaks of that physician's ineptitude in clinical diagnosis.

In short, it's a heads-I-win-tails-you-lose response to mainstream medicine: first they use a different set of tests with a different set of standards, ensuring that there are far more positive than negative tests; second, in the unlikely event that a test from one of their approved labs is negative, these practitioners will often argue that the Lyme bacteria is still present and has evaded laboratory detection, or that a patient's disease is due to a different tick-borne illness such as babesiosis.*

This entire elaborate alternate hypothetical structure is founded to a large extent upon the moderate degree of uncertainty inherent in Lyme

---

* I have seen many patients referred to me with tests from these alternative companies endorsed by chronic Lyme advocacy groups. Personal experience can be trusted only so far, but with that caveat in mind, I have never once seen a patient who has had completely negative testing from them.

diagnosis, especially in the first few weeks of the infection when even mainstream doctors can disagree about cases. The mainstream approach during that window is, by and large, to overtreat some patients: give appropriate antibiotics to a plurality, or even a majority, of patients who present with these vague symptoms during the warm-weather months in Lyme-endemic areas, knowing that some people will actually have some nonspecific viral or other illness. Given the limitations of the testing, it is a balancing act between the clear benefits for those infected with Lyme and risk for those with other problems. Here, overtreatment in the right population (those with classic Lyme symptoms in the early period of disease) carries real benefits at the cost of small risks (as I'll explain shortly, the harms of antibiotics in patients who don't have Lyme but whose presentation mimics it).

Contrast this with the downsides of overdiagnosis and overtreatment of breast cancer through the false-positive problems of screening mammography, which introduces the possibility of the horrifying spectacle of unnecessary surgery. Again, we are in a different place on the spectrum of certainty: the harms of overtreating Lyme in the face of legitimate uncertainty are smaller, and the benefits real.

However, as people's symptoms become more prolonged, the likelihood that a negative Western blot or a negative ELISA really *does* mean that a patient isn't suffering from Lyme becomes more and more reliable. But ILADS and its supporters, who have overestimated the uncertainty involved in Lyme diagnosis to the point that they don't trust standard testing at all, can't be convinced of this. To me, they appear to refuse to be convinced, despite an avalanche of scientific evidence that has accumulated since the research on *Borrelia* began in earnest.

If this description of an advocacy group resisting mainstream medical opinion by evaluating evidence in a highly selective manner sounds familiar, it should: this is more or less the intellectual approach used by anti-vaccine advocates. (I will talk about the HPV vaccine briefly in the chapter on media.) But it is noteworthy that the strategies of these two movements bear a striking resemblance to one another. To a great extent, they could be described as flipping mainstream uncertainty into alternative-medicine capital-C Certainty. *This child with autism? It must have been due to vaccinations because he was vaccinated and now he has autism.* (One cannot, after all, prove the negative.) *The Lyme ELISA eliminates negative tests from consideration for the disease, and this patient with six months of fatigue has a negative ELISA? No, it's the wrong test, he needs a Western blot, and we know this because he has Lyme. The Western blot has only two positive bands? You're interpreting the test wrong, and we know this. Why do we know? Because he has Lyme!*[*]

The schism between mainstream doctors and their alternative counterparts was years in the making, with much of the contentiousness focused on what did or did not constitute unimpeachable evidence that someone didn't have Lyme. In general, among mainstream doctors evaluating patients with several months of symptoms, a negative Lyme test meant that Lyme was not to blame. The alternative practitioners, meanwhile, frequently attributed these symptoms to Lyme. Over the years, companies were founded that allowed the alternative practitioners to have their diagnosis and eat it, too, so to speak, using the testing that I've described above (and which led to real-world profits for those companies that fed this diagnostic hunger). Thus a good deal of the disagreement was based on diagnosis.

Throughout the 1980s and 1990s, there was, however, one area in which these two very distinct groups shared a somewhat similar approach: the use of long-term antibiotics in patients with lingering symptoms after Lyme infection. What was clear was that a small minority of patients who were clearly suffering from Lyme disease were failing to improve, even after completing several weeks of antibiotics. David, the patient whose story began this chapter, would have been an apt example but for the fact that his Lyme screens were never positive. Many others who did have Lyme disease had stories matching David's, however.

Unsure of what to do and without clear-cut scientific evidence to guide them, some mainstream physicians gave ever-longer courses of antibiotics under the assumption that there was some hidden reservoir where *Borrelia burgdorferi* was riding out the antibiotic storm, only to crop up after the medication was stopped. Given that Lyme had a predilection for joints, and that antibiotic penetration into joints is fairly low compared

---

[*] This also is the same type of circular reasoning used by the psychiatrist who concluded his patient lacked "affective stability" in the Rosenhan experiment.

to that of other parts of the body, the reasoning was that Lyme managed to survive there and could recur if subjected to only a few weeks of antibiotics. Thus, some physicians opted for courses as long as three or six months, and a smaller number treated patients even longer.

To give a sense of context, most bacterial infections are treated with antibiotic courses lasting from days to weeks. Osteomyelitis—infections in the bone—are often treated for up to three months. Tuberculosis is the leader in terms of length of treatment for a bacterial infection: depending on where the tuberculosis is found, courses can range from as short as four months to as long as twelve. But, barring very unusual circumstances, bacterial infections are almost never treated for more than a year; such prolonged treatments are rare, reserved for uncommon organisms in addition to TB.[†]

Of pathogens that cause infectious disease in humans, the closest bacteria that resembles Lyme in terms of its structure and clinical behavior is, surprisingly, syphilis, and the longest course of syphilis treatment is two weeks. It's also worth noting that Lyme is also like syphilis in that it is exquisitely sensitive to drugs. In a test tube, *Borrelia burgdorferi* is easily killed by antibiotics, making the idea of "antibiotic resistant Lyme" mostly implausible. By contrast, there are bacteria that are genuinely difficult to treat and for which resistance is a major issue: *Staphylococcus aureus,* more commonly known as "staph" to laypeople, is the most notorious of these. Despite all of this indirect evidence suggesting that months of antibiotics for Lyme was based on somewhat shaky reasoning, and not knowing what else to do for their patients, many mainstream doctors opted in favor of long treatments.

The alternative Lyme group embraced the concept of prolonged antibiotics to an even further extent, endorsing treatment courses lasting up to several *years.* While most mainstream doctors never went that far, the question of how long to treat patients with Lyme remained unsettled. When the mainstream medical community finally did arrive at an answer

---

[†] Patients with implanted devices (like artificial hips) that become infected but cannot be removed because the procedure is too risky for the patient, are typical candidates for "antibiotics for life." There are also a couple of unusual bacteria that require more than a year of treatment. But, again, these are exceptional situations.

and issued formal recommendations based on that answer, it found itself on the defensive in ways that essentially nobody could have anticipated.

The evidence about the value of prolonged antibiotics—or more to the point, the lack thereof—had been accumulating with a series of studies in the early 2000s. A typical example can be found in a paper published in the *New England Journal of Medicine* in 2001. In the study, researchers looked at more than one hundred patients who had persistent symptoms after having been diagnosed with Lyme disease. They gave half of these patients a month of an intravenous antibiotic known as ceftriaxone followed by two additional months of doxycycline; the other half got placebos. Over the course of several months they followed the patients, monitoring their symptoms for signs of effectiveness. In the group receiving actual antibiotics, about a third of patients felt like they improved, about a third felt the same, and the final third actually felt worse. These proportions, however, were the same as those in the placebo group, indicating there was no real value to the antibiotics.

Not only was there no evidence of benefit from prolonged treatment, such regimens were clearly associated with risks. All antibiotics destroy gut bacteria, which can lead to gastrointestinal problems, as well as the overgrowth of a toxin-producing bacteria called *Clostridium difficile* that causes intense diarrhea and, in several cases, severe illness, even including death. Antibiotics can lead to interactions with other drugs that patients take, most notoriously coumadin, a blood thinner taken typically by older patients for various cardiovascular problems (in killing gut bacteria, which synthesize the essential clotting protein vitamin K, antibiotics can significantly augment the effect of coumadin and make the blood too thin; David Marsh would be unlikely to take coumadin, but many older patients who have been referred to chronic Lyme clinics do). Oral antibiotics increase the chance of allergic responses as well as damage to the liver and kidneys, while long-term intravenous access for IV antibiotics, which had become favored by the alternative group as "stronger" therapy, could cause bleeding, blood clots, or lead to potentially life-threatening IV line infections—all in addition to the same risks associated with the oral medications.

The key here is that the risks of antibiotics accumulate over time. A few weeks of antibiotics tend to have a sufficiently small risk such that mainstream doctors are content to overtreat a certain percentage of patients for suspected Lyme disease, as I noted earlier. But months, and indeed years, of antibiotics, present much more significant hazards. By the early 2000s the evidence had filtered in, and the mainstream medical community shifted its position on the spectrum of certainty. Lacking any clear evidence of benefit, and with good evidence that long treatments for Lyme brought real possibility of harm, the stage was set for a direct confrontation between these two opposing approaches to Lyme disease.

The organizational acronyms in the story can be confusing. The mainstream professional organization of physicians that specialize in the treatment of infectious diseases such as Lyme is IDSA—the Infectious Diseases Society of America. In the case of Lyme, as I've noted above, the alternative group goes by the very similar acronym, ILADS, the International Lyme and Associated Diseases Society.* ILADS was founded in 1999 as an organized response to IDSA. Although alternative physicians had been promoting a theory of Lyme disease sharply at odds with the mainstream viewpoint for years before this, ILADS centralized these physicians under one banner. They also became a prime example of how the Internet could be used to further a particular agenda, particularly one opposed to a group like IDSA: they fashioned a website that has all the trappings of a society of academics and clinicians, albeit one with a different approach than the scientific establishment.

It is not much of a surprise, then, that the very existence of an alternative organization like ILADS strikes many as the professional equivalent of the mainstream IDSA, and that there must be a legitimate scientific controversy about even the most basic topics in Lyme disease treatment. Take, for instance, an article by that most establishment of periodicals, the *New York Times,* in which highly respected health columnist Jane Brody wrote the following in a piece on Lyme in 2008: "The treatments recommended by the [mainstream IDSA] . . . are controversial. They have been challenged by a nonprofit medical group [ILADS], which says they are inadequate to combat the infection in a significant number of

---

* I don't think it's merely a coincidence that the name ILADS is a close approximation of the mainstream IDSA, allowing confusion to be sown even in the acronym orthography.

patients." Yet the *Times* does not give the same platform of plausibility to other groups hostile to mainstream science. For instance, within a year of Brody's column, a piece entitled "Paleontology and Creationism Meet but Don't Mesh" described the horror of mainstream paleontologists upon learning how evolution was portrayed in a creationist museum in Kentucky. Throughout the article the writer never formally weighed in on the merits of the debate because, we can safely assume, he didn't really think there was a valid debate to begin with, siding entirely with the paleontologists. Likewise, antivaxxers have generally been treated by the *Times* with the skepticism they very much deserve. But Lyme was treated differently.

Despite the airtime the alternative view is given in the mainstream media, even a cursory examination of the alternative ILADS website indicates that there is a thin patina of scholarliness beneath which there's very little there. For example, of the ten people listed as officers and directors of the ILADS organization in early 2014, none had board certification in infectious diseases, and after excluding the two on the list who were not physicians, the remaining eight were board certified in either general internal medicine or family medicine. Moreover, few of these officers and directors had any history of NIH-funded research of any kind, much less on the science or clinical presentation or treatment of Lyme—an assemblage of doctors that stood in marked contrast to mainstream IDSA Lyme working groups.

It would seem absurd to have an alternative cardiology group overseen by psychiatrists and obstetricians—almost none with any experience in research—who claimed to be "heart literate," yet this is roughly analogous to the ILADS leadership who claim to be "Lyme literate."

As a final emblem of its complete break with the scientific establishment, ILADS had in the mid-2000s elected Dr. Raphael Stricker as its president, who at the time of this writing serves as one of the organization's directors. Dr. Stricker's career began in HIV research in the early 1990s at the prestigious University of California at San Francisco, where as a junior faculty member he authored an article published in the *New England Journal of Medicine*. It is hard to be off to a better start in the scientific mainstream than that. Unfortunately, the paper was ultimately withdrawn because he withheld data from his colleagues that would have invalidated his scientific claims. Following these revelations, he was cited by the National Institutes of Health for scientific misconduct, and UCSF fired him as a consequence.[*]

So when in 2006 the mainstream IDSA issued an updated set of guidelines, in which prolonged antibiotics were explicitly rejected as a valid approach, the physicians allied with ILADS rightly worried that a part of their livelihoods faced an existential threat. To understand this, it's important to realize that licensed physicians are given a pretty wide latitude in their clinical practice. It is extremely unusual for individual physicians to be subject to sanctions by fellow professionals for opting to treat their patients even in unconventional ways. As a rule, most doctors run afoul of the system by engaging in unprofessional conduct (such as sexual harassment, insurance fraud, or narcotics abuse) rather than for showing questionable medical judgment. However, if a state medical board could be persuaded that the alternative Lyme physicians repeatedly flouted accepted medical practice, mainstream physicians could conceivably use this strategy to eliminate the alternative approach. Indeed, a small number of chronic Lyme doctors had already been disciplined by these groups. The guidelines could accelerate the process, the reasoning went.

For this fight, not only did the alternative camp have a reasonably sympathetic ear in the media, but it had enlisted one of the most powerful allies one could hope for in such a dispute: government itself, which came in the form of Richard Blumenthal, the attorney general of the state of Connecticut, who had long been allied with the advocates of chronic Lyme disease. The 2006 mainstream IDSA guidelines gave alternative groups like ILADS and their supporters, through the use of the power of Blumenthal's office, reason to go on offense. The attorney general opened up an investigation of the IDSA within months of the publication of the guidelines on the theory that the IDSA violated antitrust law and that the guidelines were going to interfere with "legitimate diagnosis and

---

[*] The very fact of Dr. Stricker's fall from grace is sometimes cited by chronic Lyme advocates as evidence of his intellectual integrity, because it proves that the mainstream was so bent on suppressing his views that they concocted allegations of misconduct to have him fired. "I wonder just who [*sic*] he pissed off enough to make them trump up some charges against him," wrote cave76 to a largely like-minded audience on the website LymeNet Europe when the topic was broached on a discussion thread (which can be found in the bibliography).

treatment options for patients." Blumenthal's goal, it appeared, was to have IDSA reverse or negate its recommendations, thus giving the chronic Lyme approach, at least indirectly, the imprimatur of scientific respectability by stifling IDSA's criticism. It would also make any state medical board think very carefully before undertaking any disciplinary action against a chronic Lyme physician, lest they find themselves in court as well.

Blumenthal's allegations required a clever, unconventional premise. The problem he had, in arguing that IDSA had set up the guidelines as part of a medical monopoly to squelch competition, was to identify the smoking financial gun in a scenario where doctors were very clearly advocating for *less* treatment. The common complaint of patient and consumer advocacy groups is that physicians have far too comfortable a relationship with the pharmaceutical industry, which results in an all-drugs-all-the-time approach to medicine. Based on this reasoning, it would appear that the IDSA's stance of limiting antibiotics was laudable. Thus, in order to allege financial conflict of interest among the IDSA panel members, Blumenthal required a different group to play the role of villain.

Ironically, that group would be one of the largest industries in Blumenthal's home state of Connecticut: insurers. The logic was that IDSA had colluded with the insurance lobby to limit access to prolonged treatments. By denying antibiotics to chronically ill patients, the IDSA recommendations enabled insurance companies to line their pockets. The investigation, his office announced, was designed in part to discover whether or not there was a quid pro quo for the Lyme panel members.

As with many assertions made by chronic Lyme advocates, the charges had a surface plausibility. Big medicine is big business, after all, and the idea that a panel of physicians might be biased based on lucrative arrangements with companies who have good reasons to influence the final recommendations makes a great deal of sense. But, as with other claims of the chronic Lyme lobby, of which Richard Blumenthal had now become much more than a mere figurehead, they make less sense on closer investigation.

Why, for instance, would the mainstream IDSA suddenly opt to play footsie with the insurance industry by *limiting* the total amount of antibiotics given to their patients when so many other fields of medicine have benefited financially from a cozy relationship with Big Pharma? From a purely monetary standpoint, issuing such guidelines makes no sense. Drug companies have a well-deserved reputation for enticing physicians, through all manner of trinkets both trivial and luxurious, to prescribe expensive drugs even if they have little clinical benefit; the new recommendations would leave any company driven by profits with very little desire to try to persuade doctors to prescribe this or that for Lyme because the standard treatment advised by the IDSA for most cases of Lyme is ten to twenty-one days of doxycycline, a generic drug that usually costs a few bucks. Moreover, rigid adherence to the new guidelines would mean fewer office visits for generalists and infectious disease specialists alike, so ultimately following the new recommendations would produce *less* income for such doctors.

Contrast this with the economic incentives of the physicians affiliated with ILADS. The medical management offered by these providers involves frequent office visits, sometimes for years on end. The more serious treatments, such as prolonged intravenous antibiotics, are major money-makers for a practice, because they can be billed to the insurance companies under special procedure codes. The insertion of an IV line typically is a reimbursable expense paid to the physician's office, and whole clinics are devoted to servicing scores of patients who come in several times a week for infusions. That's an impressive number of office charges, especially when compared to the single visit that is typically required for managing an episode of Lyme disease in the mainstream medical world.

Which of these two groups of providers has benefited more in financial terms from the IDSA guidelines—the one that ignored them, or the one that followed them?

At any rate, if there were such seriously inappropriate quid pro quo arrangements between the IDSA and the insurance industry, they became of secondary importance, and by 2008 the IDSA and Blumenthal came to an agreement.* In exchange for ending the investigation, and the crippling legal expenses that had arisen from defending themselves against it, the IDSA agreed to have an independent panel review the guidelines. The

---

* None has ever been discovered.

idea was to convene a group of scientists affiliated with the finest medical and scientific institutions in the United States, who had no ties to Lyme research or Lyme treatment or Lyme anything. Their expertise would come in their collective ability to judge the quality of evidence surrounding theories of chronic Lyme, comprising essentially a very specialized and disinterested set of fresh eyes on this contentious matter. The chronic Lyme advocates would be welcome to present their viewpoints side by side with the mainstream physicians, including some of the IDSA panel members. Both Blumenthal and the IDSA were gambling that a neutral group would side with them.

The panel would be overseen by an ombudsman that IDSA and Blumenthal's office had mutually agreed upon: Dr. Howard Brody of the Institute for the Medical Humanities at the University of Texas Medical Branch in Galveston. The panel convened a one-day hearing in 2009, allowing two patients and more than a dozen researchers and clinicians to present evidence. Not long after, Blumenthal's office claimed victory: "the investigation . . . uncovered serious flaws in the process for writing its 2006 Lyme disease guidelines," a triumphant press release noted. "The [IDSA] guideline panel improperly ignored or minimized consideration of alternative medical opinion and evidence regarding chronic Lyme disease, potentially raising serious questions about whether the recommendations reflected all relevant science."

That press release was issued long before the review panel had completed its work. That wouldn't come until the middle of 2010, and its report could only be described as a stinging rebuke of the attorney general's most cherished notions about chronic Lyme or the value of prolonged antibiotics.

The panel was composed of eight members whose scientific integrity and objectivity was deemed unimpeachable by both parties. They reviewed every single recommendation from the 2006 Lyme guidelines from the mainstream IDSA and voted up or down as to whether they found each recommendation to be based on solid science and clinical reasoning. Think of it as something akin to a scientific Supreme Court assembled solely to adjudicate the question of Lyme diagnosis and treatment.

In total, the panel reviewed forty-eight separate recommendations specifically devoted to Lyme in the 2006 guidelines (the remainder dealt with other tick-borne diseases). Of these, forty-*seven* of the recommendations were upheld in 8–0 votes. The forty-eighth recommendation was this: "to date, there is no convincing biologic evidence for the existence of symptomatic *Borrelia burgdorferi* infection among patients after receipt of recommended treatment regimens for Lyme disease." Instead of the unanimous endorsement that all of the other recommendations received, this was upheld by a 7–1 vote. (That's 383 votes supporting the IDSA to *1* against. Contrast this almost complete unanimity with the *actually* contentious JNC8 blood pressure guidelines, where about a quarter of experts, whose credentials nobody questioned, had split away from the majority.)

The final section of the Lyme guideline review, though, made in the characteristically dry prose of a governmental report, contains an unmistakable message. By "unmistakable," I don't mean to imply that they used exceptionally lucid language, but rather that it was literally unmistakable: they changed the font to boldface, as I do here. They noted that the "**trials for extended antibiotic treatment of Lyme disease have demonstrated considerable risk of harm, including potentially life-threatening adverse events** . . . [but likewise] **have demonstrated little benefit.** . . . [T]he risk/ benefit ratio from prolonged antibiotic therapy strongly discourages prolonged antibiotic courses for Lyme disease.**" These sentences all but scream at the chronic Lyme advocates to cut it out.

Cut it out, they have not. The alternative ILADS continues to spread its message about the pervasiveness of chronic Lyme and the benefits of prolonged therapy as if it were 2007 and nothing has transpired since. When I completed the first draft of this chapter in the summer of 2014, their website, as well as other chronic Lyme discussion groups on the Internet, included a great deal of information about the attorney general investigation of IDSA. Yet there was effectively no mention of the review panel's vindication of IDSA.

Attorney General Blumenthal has since become US senator Blumenthal. He was so chastened by the report of the review panel that almost as soon as he joined the Senate in 2011, he introduced legislation calling for the establishment of a "Tick-Borne Advisory Committee" that would "ensure a broad spectrum of scientific viewpoints" in formulating Lyme policy. There can be no doubt that what Blumenthal means by "broad spectrum" is that it should include the very chronic Lyme viewpoint the review panel had so forcefully rejected. Indeed, at the press conference announcing the bill, he prominently showcased members of the chronic Lyme advocacy groups, as clear a message as any that his thinking had not really changed. In short, he is trying to achieve through the government bureaucracy what he could not with an independent panel of scientists—a strategy that the alternative Lyme groups have pursued successfully at the state level for several years.

David Marsh, the young man who has come to my office, is aware of this controversy, although his interpretation of it would differ from my account. In the months preceding our visits he had increasingly read up on chronic Lyme via the large number of websites devoted to the subject. He is planning on attending an ILADS conference. Because of the almost complete repudiation of the chronic Lyme viewpoint among mainstream physicians—and it should be clear by now that I am, at least in this respect, very much a mainstream physician—most patients who strongly support the chronic Lyme theories do not visit university-based infectious disease consultants. To a great extent, these patients inhabit a hermetically sealed world and have very few discussions with people like me. Our visits represented a rare moment where those two worlds interfaced rather than collided. In part, this was due to the fact that David stood on the threshold of that separate world and wanted to talk to me before deciding to enter it wholly.

What followed between us were conversations, ultimately, about the limits of certainty, and what action one should take in the face of uncertainty. I could not, for instance, say that he *never* had Lyme. He lived in a place where his risk of Lyme infection was high, and his outdoor activities increased his risk further. I could not even say that his symptoms weren't *due* to some prior encounter with Lyme: although there is almost total consensus that Lyme cannot survive the course of antibiotics recommended in the guidelines, there is an equal recognition that a very small percentage of patients who have Lyme develop the kind of chronic fatigue from which David suffers, and is referred to as "post-Lyme syndrome," though really that's just a label saying we know something is going wrong but have little idea what that something is. So perhaps this is all the consequence of a fully treated infection, and that infection triggered his immune system to go haywire. I just don't know.

Nor do I know what diagnosis, infectious or otherwise, to provide him in place of Lyme. A considerable amount of intellectual firepower and scientific resources have been brought to bear on the subject of chronic fatigue syndrome. Decades ago, some researchers working on the Epstein Barr virus (a common cause of mononucleosis) considered it to be a leading candidate as the cause of chronic fatigue. Subsequent population studies, however, made it clear that nearly *everyone* gets infected by EBV, so if it is indeed the cause, nobody has yet shown how it causes symptoms in only a small group of people.* For a brief period at just about the time the Lyme review panel was announcing its conclusions, scientists reported that a newly discovered pathogen with the nightmarish name of xenotropic murine leukemia virus-related virus looked like it was the cause, but no other labs were able to validate their findings, and the paper was partially retracted, as it appears that the virus may have been an accidental laboratory contaminant. Many other candidates have been nominated, most of them viruses, bacteria, or industrial chemicals, but nothing has thus far panned out. On the subject of the cause of chronic fatigue, doctors remain in the dark.

That's a lot of uncertainty to swallow, especially for someone who understandably is desperate for an answer and some help, but that isn't the end of the story with respect to Lyme. As I wrote at the beginning of the chapter, we occupy a spot on the spectrum of certainty that moves *away* from the uncertainties of benefits and *toward* the increasing certainties of harm. For although we don't know why some patients develop chronic fatigue, we *do* know that months and months of antibiotics don't

---

* Worth emphasizing here that the discovery that EBV was widespread wasn't necessarily evidence that EBV didn't cause chronic fatigue. The vast majority of people infected with tuberculosis live their entire lives without becoming sick from it— doctors refer to this as "latent tuberculosis infection." The discovery of latent TB, however, doesn't mean that *Mycobacterium tuberculosis* isn't the cause of the TB that kills so many, as there has been more than a century of accumulated evidence supporting that theory. So EBV is *potentially* the cause of the chronic fatigue syndrome, but there has been no convincing evidence to support that thus far.

help. We know that because multiple studies were done, and *all* of them failed to show any meaningful benefit. By "know," I don't mean know with absolute, unimpeachable certainty, but rather I mean know within the limits of what can reasonably be expected at this point in time. It's the kind of knowing that doctors require to do their diagnosing and treating every day of their careers. It's the kind of knowing that people require to do their living and functioning every day of their lives.

Moreover, I know a few other things. I know that his negative Lyme Western blot is pretty strong evidence that, whatever happened in the past, he isn't infected now. Furthermore, the Western blot was done despite a negative ELISA, and a negative ELISA likewise provides a strong degree of certainty he isn't currently infected. The test's parameters were designed specifically to exclude people who aren't infected; its shortcoming, like the ELISA test for HIV, lies in its inability to exclude uninfected patients in the *positive* range. So a negative test, with a negative Western blot, should at least provide the comfort—though granted, it isn't much—that Lyme is not the source of his troubles. The greater value in this information is that it can protect him from useless treatments that won't help him and could very possibly make his life worse. On these points, I am much more confident, and I tell him so.

But that is where we part ways, as he is bound for the ILADS conference where he will undoubtedly find a physician who will be more receptive to his request for the tetracycline, or perhaps encourage him to try a more toxic regimen. Part of what makes these visits painful is that I sense a degree of mutual respect. He is eloquent and thoughtful, reflective about his troubles. He is coping with his illness with tremendous grace. I think that he appreciates my candor as I emphasize what we do and don't know about chronic fatigue. I hope he sees that I am, despite our different views about Lyme, trying to listen to him and validate him in what ways I can. Ultimately, however, he is disappointed in me.

I am disappointed that I don't have answers for him.

THE ORIGINS OF KNOWLEDGE AND THE SEEDS OF UNCERTAINTY

There is nothing men will not do, there is nothing they have not done, to recover their health. They have submitted to be half-drowned in water, and half-choked with gases, to be buried up to their chins in earth, to be seared with hot irons like galley-slaves, to be crimped with knives, like codfish, to have needles thrust into their flesh, and bonfires kindled on their skin, to swallow all sorts of abominations, and to pay for all of this, as if to be singed and scalded were costly privilege, as if blisters were a blessing and leeches were a luxury.

—OLIVER WENDELL HOLMES

In the previous chapters, we looked at various forms of medical uncertainty and the impact that such uncertainty has on patients, whether they are submitting blood for an insurance screen, or calling the local hospital to schedule a screening test, or considering starting medications to aim for a goal blood pressure, or relieving unrelenting fatigue. But before we look further at uncertainty it is best to consider how our modern medical knowledge differs from that of the past—that is, to look at the origins of our modern "certainty," even while we keep our eyes fixed on the ever-present problem of uncertainty.

In this chapter, I will focus on how making the proper comparisons allows us to know the true value of medications. Shortly I will discuss some of the biggest, most successful drugs of our time and how their success is built on this very modern line of reasoning. As I briefly noted in the introduction, our modern medicines really *do* work in a way that medicines from two hundred years ago mostly didn't. We have much more specific indications, coupled with a considerably deeper appreciation for physiology than premodern healers could have dreamed of. From a pharmacologic standpoint, it is a remarkable time to be alive—especially when stacked against the kind of "drugs" that were considered standard fare a few hundred years ago, when establishment physicians, Western or otherwise, routinely offered treatments that would now leave us in speechless recoil.

Yet if you peer beneath the surface of this notion that nearly all drugs before the twentieth century were worthless, you will find some odd and irreducible curiosities. Take a look today at any hospital formulary or drugstore shelf stock, and you will encounter several medications absolutely central to our basic armamentarium of healing. You might be surprised to find that their properties were not only understood before 1900, they were understood long before that year arrived.

Patients who suffer from heart failure, especially in the setting of a condition known as atrial fibrillation, are still sometimes prescribed digoxin, the precursor of which (digitalis) was the dominant cardiac drug for much of the twentieth century; it is derived from extracts of the foxglove plant, whose pharmacologic properties were first described in 1785. Senna, a treatment for constipation, is still used commonly today and sold over the counter; it was introduced by Arab physicians of the ninth century. Our most important painkillers remain the narcotic family of drugs known as opiates; the first modern drug in this class, morphine, was developed in 1804, but a working knowledge of the anesthetic properties of opium dates back thousands of years. And perhaps the single most important drug in the history of humanity, salicylic acid, or aspirin—a drug with a variety of uses and demonstrably lifesaving qualities despite a reasonably low side-effect profile—was synthesized in its modern, pure form in 1899, but descriptions of the medicinal properties of willow and other plants containing salicylic acid can be found in Egyptian texts from the second millennium BCE. If these primitive healers didn't know anything about anything, how did they know these plant extracts worked? And because they *did* appear to know at least something about something, what makes our way of knowing different from theirs, or have we deluded ourselves into thinking we know stuff when we're no better than they were?

To consider this question let's pretend there's a very bad disease. First the symptoms start out in a nonspecific way: people feel fatigued and their muscles ache. But it gets worse. After a time, their skin becomes rough, and they can bruise easily. Their bones start to hurt. Wounds don't heal. Their mouth and eyes become dry, their gums swell, and their teeth fall out. Eventually their livers fail and they slip into a coma to die a few hours or days later. The cause of this disease is completely unclear. Patients are dropping like flies.

Now let's forget we know anything about modern medicine for a moment and imagine that someone proposes a series of treatments for this strange disease using some common, minimally toxic substances that we incorporate into our daily diet. They suggest that we take twelve people suffering from this malady, split them into six groups of two, and give these substances to see what will happen. Two people will be given a quart of cider to drink each day; two will add a small amount of acid to their drink; two will have a few tablespoons of vinegar added to their food; two will be given oranges to eat and lemons to suck on; two will eat food flavored liberally with nutmeg; and the final pair will drink a few glasses of saltwater each day.

Sounds like nonsense, right? Perhaps such a study might send a frisson of excitement through the homeopathic crowd, but most people would look at this "drug trial" and assume that it is distinctly unscientific in its underlying philosophy as well as its execution. After all, why on earth would one choose these items to begin with, or was it just some random hodgepodge? This "trial," insofar as it is a trial at all by modern standards, appears doomed. It's a classic nonscientific muddle consisting of taking some arbitrary substances, giving them to some very sick people, and hoping for the best. One doesn't have to be a research scientist to sense that this isn't what modern scientific research is about.

But what happens when just one pair—say, the two who had oranges and lemons—starts to recover? In fact, with their oranges and lemons, they are back to their normal selves within days. None of the other pairs have recovered in the meantime.

It turns out that although this example may seem outlandish, it isn't made up. What I've just described really did happen, and it is often regarded by historians as one of the key moments when contemporary,

Western medicine took shape. Sometimes referred to as the first modern drug trial, this is the experiment that the Scotsman James Lind performed on patients suffering from scurvy.

The research subjects, divided into pairs like I describe above, were British sailors; the two that got oranges and lemons—Lind may have been inspired by the English nursery rhyme, which dates back at least a century before his experiment—were fit for duty inside a week.* Lind performed his experiment in 1747 and published his *Treatise on Scurvy* describing this Lazarus-like effect six years after that, but it would be nearly forty more years before the juice of citrus fruits was routinely added to the grog of sailors and scurvy virtually disappeared from the British navy, in part because Lind himself appears not to have fully understood the importance of his own finding. He continued to work with the navy for the next two decades, experimenting with all kinds of dietary supplements, but never became the champion of oranges and lemons that we would assume he would have been based on the trial results.

What can we gain from this anecdote? That big, big changes to the scientific method sometimes start small—so small, in fact, that it isn't obvious to the scientists in the moment what profound discovery they've stumbled upon.

The Organized Search for Dissimilarities

So why *does* James Lind get such credit for being a pioneer of science? It hardly seems like an auspicious achievement in retrospect. His theories as to the cause of scurvy was a typical eighteenth-century morass, consisting of concerns about putrefaction of poorly digested food and living in the damp environment of sea ships. Like all physicians of that time, he didn't even possess the intellectual scaffolding to place an idea such as vitamin

---

* Lind isn't the source of the phrase "oranges and lemons," but he *is* given the lion's share of credit for the origin of the term "limeys" because once the scurvy-preventing properties of citrus fruit were finally understood, limes became the main additive to the British navy's diet. They were more abundant, apparently: in Roy Porter's comprehensive history of medicine, limes are referred to as "less effective" than lemons, but from what I can find on Doctor Internet, they both appear to have more than the necessary daily amount of vitamin C.

deficiency in his thinking. Scurvy is caused by a lack of vitamin C, and the initial discoveries of the chemical compounds we now call vitamins took place in the 1890s, one full century after Lind's death. He was lucky rather than smart, having randomly picked an effective treatment for scurvy, finding a fruit rich in a chemical he knew nothing about—indeed, to say that he knew anything of chemicals *themselves* in the way we think of that term is going too far. So why do we solemnly invoke his name at medical school convocations and the like?

The simplest answer is, he compared things. He administered such-and-such to this group, a different thing to another group, and so on and monitored the effects. That may seem like a pedestrian innovation, but it's the basis for *everything* we know in clinical medicine. All clinical research, or at least *good* clinical research, is a variation on the theme of seeing what happens when X is administered to one group, and X is *not* administered to another. We call the second group a control group, and the research controlled trials. Lind didn't actually have a control group because all his pairs of sailors were given different treatments. He ended up having controls by default—most of the other treatments had no vitamin C—but of course he didn't know that. Not all controlled trials today have only one intervention, although it's unusual today to see more than two or three interventions in a single trial.

Doing this kind of research is not especially glamorous work: it requires intellectual rigor without intellectual creativity. But without that basic tool of comparing X to not-X, we'd have no greater insights than the Quacks of Old London about what drugs are helpful and what are a waste of money and resources—and what may well make us sicker rather than healthier. Modern clinical medicine really *did* start at the moment Lind doled out those odd treatments, even though he hadn't really a clue what he was doing or how important that approach would later be.

There is another aspect of Lind's work worth noting, equally rudimentary and also equally important to our modern structure of clinical research: he compared only *one* variable—just dietary supplements—when evaluating treatments for scurvy. As noted above, Lind had complex theories of scurvy's causes, theories that were shared by his colleagues. They were all wrong, we now know, but it didn't seem so to them, and not all of their thinking was inept. The idea that damp played a critical role in scurvy no doubt came about from making comparisons about the empirical differences between a sailor's life and a landlubber's because sailors were much more liable to develop scurvy. It's easy to see the appeal of that hypothesis, especially at a time when nobody knew anything about vitamins. As we'll see in the next chapter, a similar type of hypothesis generation took place at the advent of the AIDS crisis and is a common feature of gumshoe epidemiologic work. Regardless, Lind didn't worry about the *whole* theory of scurvy when he performed his trial. He just focused on *one* variable, and in doing so he was able to make stronger conclusions about the effects of those interventions. The power of that approach went unappreciated not only by Lind himself but by pretty much the entire profession of medicine, and it did so for a lot longer than it took doctors to solve the problem of scurvy.

Now that we've seen what's vaguely modern in Lind's scurvy trial, let's focus again on what makes it seem so premodern. First, everyone in the scurvy trial was treated with *something*. Like advanced cancer today, scurvy tends to have an inexorable path toward death. But the majority of diseases *aren't* like that: people often naturally recover from a given malady. Think of allergies, depression, and reflux, or even a much more serious life-threatening condition like bacterial pneumonia: do nothing at all, and a certain percentage of people will get better anyway. In experimental conditions, we have artificially introduced that "do nothing" element, and we call it a placebo, and our comparisons are "placebo controlled."

Of course, to make that comparison, everyone needs to believe that they are in the trial as equal participants, and so modern trials also engage in a process known as blinding. In his scurvy trial, Lind knew all the details: he knew which sailors were given each treatment, and for that matter he knew which sailors *weren't* given any treatment at all. That may seem trivial for his research because the apparent effects of oranges and lemons was so dramatic, but if he had a particular theory as to which of his interventions was most likely to succeed, he might have been unconsciously biased to interpret his results either favorably or unfavorably depending on the treatment. It turned out by accident that none of the other treatments in the scurvy trial contained any appreciable amounts of vitamin C. Had these treatments contained varying levels such that some of his sailors made a partial recovery, the data may have been much less obvious, and his interpretation of them could have been affected by internal biases.

Researchers can often be motivated to believe in a theory so powerfully that they neglect evidence that would seem obvious to a disinterested observer. In Chapter 1 we observed a similar phenomenon in overdiagnosis; individual doctors can become powerfully attached to their diagnoses in like manner. Nobody really understood this in Lind's time, but now we have a deeper appreciation of the role that psychological factors can play in creating bias in clinical trials. In today's drug studies that bear a surface resemblance to the scurvy trial, we've learned to avoid introducing this bias at all costs. And we don't merely blind the scientists performing the experiment: patients likewise do not know whether they are receiving active drugs or placebos.

Finally, part of the process of blinding involves deciding which patients are selected for the treatment arm, and which for the placebo arm. Again, subtle biases may lead a researcher, for instance, to unconsciously place healthier subjects in the treatment group and sicker ones in the placebo group. That would then create the appearance of benefit where none actually exists. So we pick who goes where blindly as well—that is, we randomize patients. Nowadays, we usually randomize through a computer program. Someone enrolls for a study, the research staff enters the data into a computer, and the computer spits out some identifier that will be used later to analyze the data because, at a meaningful level, only the computer now knows which arm of the study that patient is in. The pharmacists giving the experimental drug, as well as the doctors and nurses and other staff following the patient, to say nothing of the patients themselves, have no idea whether they're getting the actual drug or a sugar pill.

Thus, the modern standard for a drug trial is that it be randomized, double-blind, and placebo-controlled. The first of this kind of trial actually didn't occur until almost exactly two centuries after Lind's groundbreaking work, when a group of British researchers performed a series of studies on male patients using an experimental drug known as streptomycin. The first of these papers was published in 1948, and even then, although the trial was randomized in much the same way that they are today (though without computers), it was a single-blind trial: the physicians knew which patients were getting the streptomycin. Moreover, it wasn't placebo controlled, as the controls were simply given the standard treatment of the day for severe tuberculosis, which was simply bed rest. In fact, the controls didn't even realize that they were involved in a trial at all. (This would not be considered ethical by today's research standards, or at least it would have serious problems if the design were brought before an ethical review board, the type of group involved in the oversight of all legitimate modern medical research.) But the streptomycin trials laid the groundwork for genuinely modern medicine, and they mark the first time scientists truly understood the purest way that we can know whether some treatment actually works.

The Mechanics of Certainty and Uncertainty

This is the *how* of modern medicine. It is simple in outline. In practice, however, it is cumbersome and expensive. The process of blinding and random allocation, the creation of placebos (it costs money to make fake pills that look exactly like real pills, and to put them in packaging that can't be distinguished by even the most skilled pharmacist), the generation of heaps of documentation, as well as the efforts of countless administrators, scientists, and other support staff required to oversee the work is phenomenally costly and time-consuming. When people speak of the medical industrial complex, *this* is the creature to which they are referring. This book is a consideration of some of the dilemmas that result from the products of this massive machine. But it *does* work on the whole, and it works largely because of this simple principle used in making comparisons between two relatively equal groups, with much modern science and physiology undergirding the work.

The process of comparison making in biomedical research on humans applies not only to drug trials but also to investigations on the causes of disease, the utility of blood tests, the natural history of a condition like, say, schizophrenia, and all manner of scientific inquiries besides. In this chapter, however, I will focus specifically on how we use comparisons to decide which drugs make the cut and which do not, and we'll consider the implications of these findings.

One important quality of James Lind's scurvy research that appears on the surface to have very little in common with modern trials is the size of his cohort, as his work involved a scant twelve sailors. That doesn't seem to square with the contemporary trials we read about in the news, where thousands, or tens of thousands, of volunteers are followed, sometimes for years. But why do we recruit so many today, and why was his trial a success with so few back then? The answer lies in part in the nature of scurvy, and again Lind was remarkably lucky in choosing the disease he did to perform his investigations. Because scurvy's effects are so profound, and because complete recovery from scurvy happens in a miraculously short time, Lind was able to witness a radical transformation in his patients almost instantaneously when administering his vitamin C–supercharged oranges and lemons.

Most modern diseases, however, don't work like that. Symptoms are more subtle, and healing through medications can take longer. What, for instance, would have become of Lind's treatise if the natural history of scurvy required a *month* rather than a *week* of treatment for recovery to commence, and Lind had abandoned his work after a fortnight? What would he have done if scurvy wasn't so lethal, where *some* people succumbed to disease but most did not, similar to how influenza affects us today? If only one in twenty sailors died of scurvy, and most just puttered on in a weakened state, Lind would have had a strong chance of not noticing the effect by monitoring only twelve subjects in his trial. Moreover, although he might have stopped scurvy in the two sailors who did get oranges and lemons, surviving in a weakened state would likely have been par for the course above the crowded, fetid below-decks atmosphere in which low-ranking sailors lived, so he could easily have overlooked their recovery and misinterpreted his results. Solving problems like this is a daily task in the field of work we call biostatistics. You don't have to become a biostatistician to appreciate the basic principles of how it works, however: the more dramatic the impact a treatment has on a disease, the fewer people are required to demonstrate that effect; treatments with a less dramatic impact require many more such people.

But what does *any* of this have to do with *un*certainty? Haven't I just argued that, whatever happened in the past, we've now solved the problem of how to know things through the practice of randomization, blinding, and controlling with placebos?

The answer depends in part on the meaning of the word "know." Knowledge in medicine is virtually never absolute, and it cannot in general be thought of in the same way we think of *facts*—that is, unimpeachable bits of information. Knowing the benefits of a medicine, for instance, much more often than not means knowing the *relative* likelihood that the medicine will make things better. Take *this* drug for *this* condition, and there's a *very* good chance you'll get better; take *that* drug for *that* problem, by contrast, and it *may* be helpful, but because the effect is smaller, we can be less certain it will be helpful in any individual case.

This lack of certainty relates directly to the question of sample sizes when investigating the benefits of a medication. Suppose you have a disease with a 100 percent mortality rate—not unlike untreated scurvy, in fact. Now recruit twenty people for a trial to administer some experimental drug in the modern randomized, double-blinded, and placebo-controlled method. At the end of the study, ten of the patients have made a full recovery, and ten are dead. The blinding is lifted, and lo and behold, all ten patients who recovered were given the experimental drug, and all ten who received the placebo succumbed to the disease. That would seem to be extremely strong evidence that the drug worked, right? If someone argued that we needed to repeat the experiment with twenty *thousand* people instead of just twenty, you would almost certainly argue that's a waste of time and resources, and likely unethical, especially if the disease was spreading.

Now let's complicate matters a bit, and suppose there's a disease with a 50 percent mortality rate. For this study, with another drug, we decide to recruit a larger number of people—say, two hundred, with one hundred participants in each arm. At the end of this trial, fifty of the subjects in the placebo arm have passed away, entirely consistent with the predicted mortality rate of 50 percent. Meanwhile, in the treatment arm, only *forty eight* have died. That is, of those who received the experimental drug, two additional people are alive compared to the placebo group. So is this drug effective? What if the number of people who died in the treatment arm is only forty-*six* compared to fifty in the placebo arm? What if it was forty-*four*? Or thirty-eight? At what point do you cross over the line and have the same level of confidence in this drug that you had in the much smaller hypothetical trial done in the previous paragraph?

The value of these examples lies in their demonstration that the ability to compare a treatment group with a placebo group, in a precise, randomized, blinded manner, doesn't in and of itself provide you with clear answers; it provides you with *numbers*. And the numbers have to be interpreted. Moreover, because the numbers can potentially fall along a continuum, there is no single moment where one can look at the results of a drug trial and exclaim, "Eureka!" knowing that a drug has shifted from the status of totally useless to totally effective. If the two groups of subjects look *exactly* the same at the end of a trial, the drug probably has no effect, but as the two groups differ in terms of the proportions of who improves, one only becomes *gradually* more certain that the observed difference is due to the drug.

In other words, there's a constant recognition that all the changes observed could be due just to chance alone, and the question is, How likely are the observed changes just due to chance? Because the oranges and lemons made such a huge difference to Lind's sailors, he didn't need to perform a trial with hundreds of people. But when we deal with drugs that have smaller effects, our ability to know their value is much more appropriately expressed in terms of levels of confidence. In modern medicine, we have introduced statistical cutoffs by which we allow people to claim that a result is "significant," but *significance* is different from *truth*. Significance simply allows us to say that the observed differences between two groups is so large that it is highly unlikely those differences could be due to chance alone.

The drugs of antiquity that have endured into the age of modern medicine—the salicylates, the sennas, the opiates of the world—had such obvious and profound benefits that this kind of technical study was not required to know their value. But knowing that a plant extract can ease pain immediately is much easier to observe than whether a synthetic compound can produce a 30 percent reduction in the risk of a heart attack three years hence or, for that matter, whether saw palmetto "supports healthy prostate function," as the herbal supplement company General Nutrition Center claims on its website. Modern drug trials have largely been able to quantify with a fair degree of precision the value of new treatments for the maladies that afflict us, and they are responsible for the big industrial machinery of medicine required to generate those benefits.

But these treatments aren't perfect, and viewing them through the lens of uncertainty can help reveal their limitations. Let's consider some of the most important medications of our time, looking at them in part through James Lind's eyes, and see what they can tell us about medicine today.

A Tale of Two Drugs

In the annals of pharmacology, 1987 will be remembered as an auspicious year. Two new medications were approved by the FDA that year to treat diseases that had come to be among the dominant illnesses of the industrial age: coronary artery disease and depression, literally drugs to treat the ailing heart and soul. It wasn't that there weren't already medications for these maladies, but these two drugs represented wholly new molecular approaches to their respective diseases, and as such constituted a quantum leap in treatment. Their approval represented a moment when the advanced biochemistry that would have been unimaginable to a physician from early twentieth century finally produced highly effective treatments with relatively minimal side effects, and as such could make a reasonable claim to the title "miracle drugs." Although the specific drugs that were approved have since been eclipsed in sales by others within their respective classes, the classes of drugs themselves have remained central to medicine to this day.

The first, whose generic name is lovastatin and trade name is Mevacor, is perhaps not well recognized by most. However, the trade names of others within this class of drugs, commonly known as statins, are omnipresent: Zocor (simvastatin), Pravachol (pravastatin), Crestor (rosuvastatin), and the biggest selling drug ever, with total sales at more than $125 billion, Lipitor (atorvastatin). Critically important drugs for treating heart and other vascular diseases, they are all household names, as much cultural phenomena as pills dispensed by specialists: indeed, one can hardly sit through a televised football game without seeing an advertisement for one of these medications, typically showing some middle-aged male performing a faux end-zone dance in front of bemused family members, all for the joys of having gotten a new prescription for his beloved drug. (Such commercials often come on the heels of ads for nationwide fast food chains such as Buffalo Wild Wings or Dave & Buster's, establishments that, if attended regularly and with gusto, will contribute quite directly to the metabolic problems leading to the prescription in the first place.) Make no mistake, as measured in raw dollars, collectively they have been a gigantic success. Somewhere, in the cellars of many a pharmaceutical executive, are a substantial number of bottles of fine cabernet sauvignon, all acquired as a result of the healing properties of this new class of cardiac medication.

Although Mevacor itself never attained great popularity, the depression drug approved that same year of 1987 needs little introduction. Having attained the status of cultural icon, Prozac (fluoxetine) has become as tied to notions of mental health as the anxiety medication Valium was for the previous generation. Prozac was famous not only for its mood-altering effects but as the symbol of the medicalization of everyday life and the particular societal ills of the past generation, perhaps because of the depersonalization that the medication was said to be capable of inducing. The psychiatrist Peter Kramer observed this strange new drug in his clinical practice and wrote of it in the classic medical reflection *Listening to Prozac* in 1993; the following year a young woman named Elizabeth Wurtzel wrote a memoir of her bouts with depression, and the role the drug played in treating it, with the all-encompassing title *Prozac Nation*. Both were international best sellers; *Prozac Nation* was adapted into a movie in 2001.

Like Mevacor, Prozac was just the first drug of a group that worked in the same manner, a mechanism known as selective serotonin reuptake inhibition, and the drugs are thus known as SSRIs. Other SSRIs would follow, such as Paxil (paroxetine), Zoloft (sertraline), Luvox (fluvoxamine), Celexa (citalopram), and Lexapro (escitalopram). Along with other classes that work in relatively similar ways, these new medications account for the bulk of drugs used for depression in the world today, having replaced the then-dominant class of drugs used for depression known as tricyclic antidepressants, or TCAs (such as amitriptyline, nortriptyline, and imipramine among several others, which have become second-line agents because of their higher side-effect profile).

Statins and SSRIs are arguably the key examples of modern medicine's success. They stop heart disease in its tracks and lift our spirits skyward. As we consume them, we consume health itself.

But is that portrayal accurate? Let's return to the question first posed at the beginning of this book: *How* do we know that medicines work? What evidence allows us to regard these medications as the blockbusters they have become? Where do we encounter such drugs on the spectrum of certainty—toward the far left end, where we can be very confident of net benefits at the cost of very low risks, or is it more toward the middle, where they work only a little and carry the possibility of some harm?

Heart

In the case of statin drugs like Mevacor, finding the answer relied on an approach that James Lind would have been able to grasp in general outline, although the structure of the research was considerably more sophisticated than what he had used in investigating treatments for scurvy. Statins were developed as treatments for coronary artery disease—the gradual occlusion of the arteries that supply blood to the heart itself to keep it healthy and pumping. Because many people die from heart disease, evaluating these drugs for effectiveness involved splitting patients into a treatment (statin) versus no-treatment (i.e., placebo) arm, following them over time, and counting the number of events caused by heart disease.

By "events," I'm being deliberately vague here. You can measure events in a number of ways, and dozens of trials of statin drugs done over the past twenty years have measured them in these different ways: You can measure events by looking at heart attacks, or you can look at events that aren't classically thought of as heart attacks but indicate a heart attack may be imminent (for instance, tabulating the number of admissions to the hospital for chest pain). You could, in fact, just look at the *total* number of hospital admissions and compare them, hypothesizing that the benefits of statins extend even into "events" that in theory have nothing to do with cardiac chest pain. More on that in a moment. At any rate, the strategy is take two groups, give placebos to one and active drugs to another, define some event worth measuring, and wait. And count.

These methods introduce uncertainty into their numbers, however, because sometimes events can be missed by the researchers tabulating the data. Some heart attacks are so obvious even medical students can correctly diagnose them with the proper testing, but others are subject to interpretation, where even seasoned cardiologists have differences of opinion. What happens if an eighty-year-old with underlying heart disease develops pneumonia, causing the heart to beat quickly from the physiologic stress of the infection, which in turn leads to a small amount of heart muscle not being able to receive adequate oxygen through the blood? We call this process "demand ischemia"; sometimes it actually leads to a full-fledged heart attack, but often it doesn't. The specific blood tests used to diagnose heart attacks are frequently positive in these situations, and thus the criteria used to distinguish coronary events from noncoronary events can be somewhat arbitrary. Therefore, some of these measurements are capable of introducing bias into the process of categorization, and the fuzzier the definition of some event, the greater the uncertainty that the results have any real meaning.

There is one category of measurement that ostensibly is immune to this kind of misinterpretation, however: mortality. If the process involves, to put it somewhat indelicately, counting the bodies from the treatment group at the end of some defined period, and comparing that figure to the number of bodies in the placebo group, you can observe differences and apply statistical models to see how likely any observed differences are due to mere chance, or might be legitimately attributable to the effects of the drug.

Even here, however, investigators have had some false starts: Do you count mortality from heart attacks *alone,* or do you simply look at *everyone* who has died in both groups? If you opt for the former strategy, you run the same risk of miscategorization as you do by tallying "cardiac events." For instance, if statins really are tremendously beneficial at reducing risk of heart disease, then in theory they should *also* be beneficial even when patients develop noncardiac problems, because patients taking statins have healthier hearts and can cope with other stresses, such as pneumonia or a gastrointestinal bleed or any number of other conditions where a weaker heart can be the difference between life and death. This is generally why opting for the latter strategy, or looking at what is called "all-cause mortality," has become the standard in studies on "lifesaving" drugs. (Compare this to the trials looking at the relationship between blood pressure and deaths due to stroke—often the reduction in all-cause mortality was lower or in some cases wasn't even evaluated, and the lack of concordance is probably due, at least in part, to the fact that lowering blood pressure too far led people to be saved from strokes but to die of something else like a broken hip and its complications.)

The first of these "count 'em up" statin trials, which looked at the same kinds of endpoints as James Lind did in his scurvy research, didn't actually get published until seven years *after* Mevacor was approved. Somewhat surprisingly, the FDA had approved Mevacor *not* because it directly proved it could save lives. There was good evidence based on other trials with *other* drugs that lowering cholesterol saved lives (particularly the so-called bad cholesterol known as LDL), so the makers of Mevacor argued that they didn't have to demonstrate that it saved lives, but simply that it could reduce cholesterol levels. This Mevacor did, and did so fairly dramatically, with fewer side effects than the standard drug being used at the time, cholestyramine. James Lind, though, would have found this approach baffling; it would have been like measuring the heart rate of his sailors instead of counting who lived and who died. The FDA approvals of Mevacor and other statins were all based on indirect reasoning. In the next chapter, I'll highlight a case where that kind of indirect reasoning seemed ironclad but ultimately didn't work out very well.

Happily, the early statin trials of the mid-1990s that looked at patient outcomes rather than cholesterol levels were indeed successful. Moreover, those first papers were the beginning of an impressive streak: essentially every large-scale trial that has been performed since, more than two dozen in all, has shown that there were fewer events among people taking statins compared to those taking placebos. Initially, "events" was defined narrowly—usually a heart attack—but subsequent studies expanded the measurement to include the "all-cause mortality" parameter mentioned above. It didn't really matter what way the investigators measured the effects of statins. They were lifesavers. They *are* lifesavers. The data at this point is overwhelming.

But how *big* a lifesaver is a statin? Compared to vitamin C in the setting of scurvy, the answer is, not much. But vitamin C is, of course, *essential* to survival. Essential as in you cannot live without it. You need to enroll only *one* patient, deprive them of vitamin C, produce scurvy, and then give the patient orange juice and watch the healing to make your point. Statins, by contrast, are nowhere near that successful, although that shouldn't be much of a surprise, so some recalibration is in order.

One of the earliest outcome trials of statins, known as the 4S Study, was published in the British journal the *Lancet* in 1994. Looking at patients who were already known to have coronary artery disease, they enrolled 4,444 subjects—proving that doctors can occasionally, if only accidentally, demonstrate a flair for the dramatic—and followed them over a span of five years. At the end of the trial, about 250 patients of the 2,200 in the placebo arm had died, compared to only about 180 patients in the statin arm. Thus, based on this trial, statins could reasonably be estimated to save, or at least significantly prolong, the lives of about 70 people out of every 2,200 in a five-year span. That's pretty impressive, for few other medications can match that, especially those used to treat chronic conditions like coronary artery disease.

One might be tempted to just wrap up the statin story on this feel-good note, but there is more to the story, and this part of the story is where uncertainty takes center stage. For it is worth keeping in mind that although that number is big, there are a lot of people in this trial who did fine anyway *regardless* of whether they got the medication or not (and, of course, a lot of people still died as well). Therefore, a different way to measure the lifesaving impact of the drug is to consider how many people need to be taking it in order to save a life. In this trial, a rough estimate is that *thirty* people need to be on a statin in order for *one* person to be saved. This "number needed to treat" statistic can be thought of as a direct measurement of the certainty of benefit, for if one needs to treat, say, two hundred people in order to save one life, patients and their doctors might rightly assume that there's a great deal of uncertainty in terms of the benefit a given drug may have for them alone.

Earlier, I noted that the justification for statins was based on the indirect reasoning that high cholesterol was associated with an increased risk of death, especially death from heart disease, so lowering cholesterol should bring about better outcomes. In the 1980s, there were many studies that demonstrated this effect, an effect seen in the figure on the following page.

What you can see is that there isn't a completely linear relationship between cholesterol levels and death: the death rate of someone with a total cholesterol of 240 is roughly double that of someone with 200, but those with 200 have only a modestly higher risk of death than someone whose cholesterol is 160.

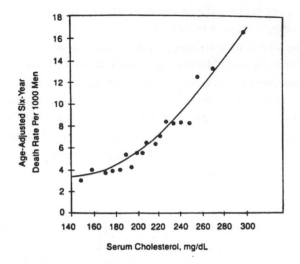

FIGURE 6.1. From the *Report of the National Cholesterol Education Program Expert Panel on Detection, Evaluation, and Treatment of High Blood Cholesterol in Adults*, 1988. Referenced in Witzum, J. L., "Current Approaches to Drug Therapy for the Hypercholesterolemic Patient," *Circulation* 1989; 80:1101–1114.

So if the "cholesterol theory" is correct—and there are decades of research suggesting that this is, at the very least, partially true—and lowering cholesterol through medications does prolong lives, then the biggest bang for the buck should be seen in people with either very high cholesterol levels or existing heart disease or both. The 4S trial, and many others like it, owe their great success in part to the fact that the right *kind* of person who was most likely to benefit from statins was enrolled in the studies.* But as time has gone on and statins have enjoyed ever-greater success, both in the commercial and scientific sense of the word, there has been a steady expansion of the "statin market"—that is, the kind of people for whom statins are recommended. With this expansion, the dramatic beneficial effects of statins become smaller, the number of patients that need to be treated for a

---

* The average total cholesterol for the 4S cohort was about 260, with an average LDL of just under 190. These are extremely high numbers. Additionally, to be eligible for the 4S trial, one had to have a history of heart disease, so these subjects were, in some sense, cherry-picked to be the most likely to benefit from statins.

life to be saved rises steadily, and one can be less certain that taking such drugs will be of unquestionable benefit.

Late in 2013, the American Heart Association and the American College of Cardiology issued a new set of guidelines for treating cholesterol with statins. The revised guidelines rely on a complicated algorithm that is difficult even for physicians to grasp; a calculator is required to assess one's lifetime risk of having heart disease for which a statin should provide protection. Complex or not, the guidelines appear to have dramatically increased the total number of people for whom statins are now recommended, and moreover they appear to depart significantly from using "bad" LDL cholesterol levels as one of the principal points of entry for assessing statin eligibility. An analysis of the new guidelines that appeared in the *New England Journal of Medicine* suggested that as many as 13 *million* new people are now theoretically in the statin pool, representing a 30 percent increase from the previous guidelines.

Whether the vast majority of these newly statin-eligible patients will *benefit* from treatment, however, is much less clear, and we lurch toward the middle of the spectrum of certainty. A major segment of this new group includes people who have a variety of increased risks for heart disease *regardless* of their LDL cholesterol level (such as smoking and high blood pressure). But there have been precious few trials that have evaluated whether using a cholesterol-lowering medication in people whose cholesterol is *already* relatively low will make much of a difference.

"As compared with the [previous] guidelines, the new guidelines would recommend statin therapy for more adults who would be expected to have future cardiovascular events . . . *but would also include many adults who would not have future cardiovascular events,*" the authors of the *New England Journal* article wrote (my emphasis). Therein lies the rub. As the number of patients considered appropriate for statin therapy grows, the number of people needed to be treated by statins grows as well. Would it make sense to take a drug when one has a 1 in 200 chance of preventing one's heart attack, especially if it means that one could have an *equal* risk of suffering a moderate or serious side effect from that medication, such as liver toxicity or diabetes, which are small but well-known complications of treatment? Statins are generally safe drugs, but as their benefits become ever smaller, those risks loom ever larger.

Soul

Compared to statin manufacturers, the makers of SSRIs have faced a much more difficult challenge to prove their drugs are worthy of widespread use: How do you measure outcomes?

How, indeed, do you measure depression? Fancy medical degree or no, many people can recognize a depressed person when they see one, but how does one quantify this in order to know that an antidepressant makes one less depressed? James Lind needed only to see whether his patients lived or died, and statin makers ultimately did so as well. Moreover, statin makers had a surrogate metric (cholesterol levels) that allowed them to measure the potential benefits of their drug, albeit indirectly. The same cannot be said for researchers evaluating the possible benefits of SSRIs like Prozac.*

The solution to this problem lay in a variety of "depression scales," more than a dozen in all, that attempt to quantify the severity of mood disturbance. One of the most commonly used scales is known as the Hamilton Depression Rating Scale, which was first devised by the eponymous psychiatrist in 1960 but has been revised multiple times. The Hamilton Scale consists of approximately twenty questions scored by the evaluator, in which responses suggestive of depression are given points. The worse the symptoms, the more points. The number is tallied and, based on that score (which ranges from zero to fifty-two), one is categorized as having either no depression, or depression rated as mild, moderate, or severe.

A close look at the scale, though, makes the subjective, fuzzy nature of the test apparent. One of the questions evaluates psychological anxiety: "no difficulty" is given zero points, with increasing points provided for "subjective tension and irritability," "worrying about minor matters,"

---

* One could, of course, theorize that SSRI-treated patients are less likely to commit suicide, but unlike heart disease, which is incredibly common in the developed world, suicide remains a relatively rare event, and the number of patients needed to test that theory would number in the tens of thousands and would require years, perhaps decades, of follow-up. In short, it's a study that can be performed only as a thought experiment, although researchers have looked *retrospectively* at suicidal risk factors. A discussion of the challenges of retrospective analysis can be found in the following chapter.

"apprehensive attitude apparent in face or speech," and finally, "fears expressed without questioning." Worrying about minor matters could just as easily be defined as *being an adult,* which means that a large number of people reading this are now two points closer to a diagnosis of depression than they were at the beginning of this paragraph. Similarly, a "work and activities" question would provide points to anyone who exhibits any reaction to the usual stresses and anxieties associated with the workplace. Three questions in total deal with insomnia, potentially inflating the size of that problem. And *most* of the questions don't quite work their way around the problem that *everyone* has a bad day at least once in a while. How many days have to be blue before one is labeled depressed? The Hamilton Scale doesn't directly answer that question.[†]

Looking over the Hamilton Scale, it becomes apparent that one *can* separate those who are *not* depressed from those who are moderately or severely depressed with great confidence. Unfortunately, it's much harder to distinguish mild from moderate, and moderate from severe depression—a few answers that are different here or there and you suddenly find yourself in a different category, all of which may be due to the subjective impressions of the person who is evaluating you. And *that* fact becomes very important when we consider the value of SSRIs, for much the same reason that we can be confident about the value of statins for patients with very high cholesterol, but less so for those who have only mildly elevated cholesterol.

As with statins for heart disease, there have been dozens of trials performed on SSRIs for depression, and, like the statin trials, the vast majority of SSRI trials have shown a clinical benefit. However, unlike the statin trials, whose primary aims were generally to evaluate how many lived or died, SSRI trials for effectiveness have to look for improvement in depression scale scores. Taken as a group, these studies have generally shown the benefits of SSRIs to be in the range of about two to four points—a benefit, to be sure, and one that is often

---

[†] Several professionals consider the overemphasis on insomnia a major flaw of the Hamilton Scale. Worth emphasizing that there are more than a dozen of these depression scales in all, each subtly different from the other, but all face the same problem of applying precision to a medical and psychiatric problem that cannot easily be quantified in a precise, or even reproducible, way.

reproduced, but a mild one (though if you read only one footnote in this book, read this one).* Moreover, those with higher scores (i.e., those more depressed) tend to reap the biggest benefits, an effect similar to that in patients who benefit from statins.

The fact that the value of an SSRI is probably most pronounced in the most depressed patients hasn't stopped SSRIs from being marketed as something of a panacea: according to CDC data, about one in every ten Americans now takes an antidepressant, the majority of which are SSRIs. According to official NHS data, the picture is similar in the UK where approximately one in fifteen are on an antidepressant. These aren't prescriptions being written by psychiatrists doing careful assessments with Hamilton Depression Scales, however. A recent study in the *Journal of Clinical Psychiatry* estimated that nearly three-quarters of all antidepressant prescriptions are given by primary care physicians, a group much less likely to be adept with depression scales and with little time to read the literature on outcome studies.†

Primary care physicians must manage an astonishing number of medical problems of their patients, of which depression is only one in a list that can be extensive, particularly if the patient is elderly. It also means that the assessment of depression can often be given short shrift, with the

---

* In writing this, I am ignoring an entire area of controversy, that of the selective publication bias. A 2008 study in the *New England Journal of Medicine* looked at antidepressant drug trials that had to be registered with the Food and Drug Administration, and found that out of thirty-six trials that did not show benefit, only *three* were published, while eleven were published but "spun" to appear more positive than was merited, and the remaining twenty-two weren't published at all. That contrasted with thirty-eight antidepressant trials that did show benefits, of which all but one were published. The large majority of these trials involved SSRIs. "Selective reporting of clinical trial results may have adverse consequences for researchers, study participants, health care professionals, and patients," they write in conclusion, in what was almost certainly the *New England Journal*'s award winner for understatement of 2008.

† Even among psychiatrists, the utilization of depression scales is hardly widespread. A survey of British psychiatrists published in 2002 indicated that nearly 60 percent of them never used a depression scale to monitor response to treatment. Presumably, however, shrinks are able to assess the severity of depression with greater accuracy than primary care physicians even without formal scales, due in part to their clinical expertise, as well as the fact that PCPs must manage the entirety of their patients' medical issues, while psychiatrists concern themselves exclusively with the soul.

"diagnosis" made following a rapid-fire question-and-answer session that can range from eating habits, exercise regimens, and discussions about "bad habits" like cigarettes and alcohol, to say nothing of a physical exam and a review of any pertinent laboratory tests. The diagnosis of depression can be made at an even greater remove in the case of elderly, who are frequently accompanied by family members who serve as surrogate "historians," quickly summarizing details for hurried and harried doctors whose minds can be just as focused on documenting all the findings as considering their implications.

And once patients *start* an antidepressant, they tend to *stay* on it, especially because the very doctors who might have made a hasty diagnosis in the first place do not often consider what the endpoint should be, and do not have a strategy to evaluate whether the patient has improved. By such means a condition that used to be considered a largely transitory state becomes morphed into a permanent feature of a patient's medical profile, as unchanging as DNA. Whether there are any discernible benefits for these patients—and whether there may be risks, either due to side effects or interactions with other drugs—is much less clear. The use of long-term antidepressants is very much in the middle of the spectrum of certainty. There is a paucity of information about the risks versus benefits in people who stay on treatment for years, even though millions may take such drugs for that long.

The Escalation of Medicalization

What I have tried to describe above is something approaching the catch-22 situation of modern drugs. We have built a formidable formulary of medications that would have been the envy of healers of yore. Statins really are quite remarkable as well as lifesaving, and SSRIs are at least reasonably safe drugs that may be genuinely beneficial for certain patients. But the trend over the past decade or more has been to gradually expand the indications for various drugs.

My point here is that, as the indications for these medications continue to reach into populations previously considered "normal," our confidence that we are helping our patients becomes ever more shaky, and what benefits that can be accurately measured are ever smaller still. As I have tried to show, when this happens, our uncertainty increases, and the harms become more worrisome. When that middle point is reached on the spectrum of certainty, the Latin phrase floats to the front of consciousness: *primum non nocere.* First, do no harm.

This holds true for medications well beyond drugs for cardiac disease and depression: it can be seen in guidelines for hypertension that I discussed earlier, or the gradual lowering of the blood sugar levels that define diabetes, to name but two critical categories. No sane physician denies that hypertension and diabetes are conditions that must be treated, and moreover that our modern treatments are unquestioned scientific triumphs. However, the lifesaving value of lowering one's systolic blood pressure from 180 to 150 is much, much greater than lowering it from 150 to 120—a point I will return to at the end of the book. Similarly, reducing someone's hemoglobin A1C (which measures the severity of diabetes) by two points is tremendously beneficial if one drops it from 10 to 8; it's not nearly as lifesaving when it drops from 8 to 6.

What I've also hinted at thus far is that there are other drivers of medication prescription and medication use besides pure scientific knowledge of a drug's precise benefit. It is unclear whether pharmaceutical companies *consciously* sought to have primary care physicians become the main dispensaries of antidepressants, but it would certainly make perfect business sense to encourage this group to feel comfortable writing SSRI prescriptions. It bears emphasis that PCPs are *busy,* and the Hamilton Scale clearly cannot be performed accurately without a lengthy evaluation. But these PCPs, who are almost certainly struggling to stay on top of the revised statin guidelines or the mammography guidelines or the blood pressure management guidelines, among many other medical matters, almost never have the luxury of time to make a careful assessment about the risks and benefits of SSRIs. Because they are generally well tolerated (like statins), many PCPs must assume that it is easier to just prescribe (and maintain) an SSRI than it is to have a prolonged discussion about whether a given patient will experience a true benefit. The avoidance of such topics in a primary care office must benefit the financial bottom line of drug companies, whether that was by design or was simply a happy accident.

Drugs are neither miracles nor curses—they are, alas, *both*. Their value can be properly assessed when the size of their benefit is weighed against the risks of their use. Doctors must weigh these two variables every day when faced with their patients' needs. In some cases, the task is easy: the smoking septuagenarian fresh from a recent hospital stay for a heart attack really *does* need to start taking a statin barring some compelling reason not to.* Yet does an otherwise healthy fifty-year-old whose father smoked require a statin with the same level of urgency? It's the same drug, but when we consider that drug in relation to the second patient we suddenly find ourselves somewhere else on the spectrum of certainty. Understanding these shifts—both as physicians and as patients—is critical to understanding the *true* value of a drug, and whether we're willing to tolerate the harm that it may do us for the benefits that it may offer.

As we move to the next chapter, we'll look more directly at how uncertainty and the corporate world's need for profits can prove a combustible combination and change the lives of millions of people in practically the blink of an eye—or at least a few minutes after a health report is broadcast by the media and circulated on the Internet. Just as in this chapter, the final arbiter of a medication's value will be found in a double-blind, placebo-controlled trial.

However, unlike the statins and SSRIs I discussed in this chapter, there was *already* an established practice of giving a medication *before* critical trials were performed. How did that come about? And what was the scientific evidence that supported its use? The answer is that a different type of study was used. We still commonly use this type of study today, and although it can be an effective tool to understand medicine, it introduces new elements of uncertainty. Exploring the parameters of that uncertainty is where I will begin, by looking at a small group of young women who developed a strange and devastating disease just over fifty years ago.

---

* In medical parlance, the "compelling reason not to take it" is referred to as a *contraindication*.

THE CORRELATION/CAUSATION PROBLEM, OR WHY DARK CHOCOLATE MAY *NOT* LOWER YOUR RISK OF HEART FAILURE

The science was accurate but it was extrapolated beyond imagination.

—CYNTHIA PEARSON, EXECUTIVE DIRECTOR OF THE NATIONAL WOMEN'S HEALTH NETWORK, ON HORMONE REPLACEMENT THERAPY RESEARCH, 2002

Uncertainty in medicine takes a variety of forms. When we looked at the drug trials in the previous chapter, we witnessed a variety of questions, each dealing in whole or in part with uncertainty, that affect our perception of the value of a drug. First, what will be the yardstick by which we will measure a drug's value? Will it be something indisputable (like dying) or something subject to interpretation, and thus more difficult to quantify and measure (like feelings)? Second, how big will any potential observed benefit need to be before we consider it a success? Third, what are the potential harms of the treatment? Every type of treatment we offer our patients, from drugs to surgery to electroshock therapy, involves consideration of each of these factors. Because the answers to these questions differ for each treatment, and the fact that the answers tend to fall onto a continuum rather than cozy themselves into a tidy binary yes or no category, both doctors and patients alike need to carefully consider the data before "knowing" that a drug is right for them.

Nevertheless, the power of the double-blind, randomized, placebo-controlled trial lies in its ability to ask these questions in an organized and systematic way. We can say *this* drug saves *this* many lives (great!) but comes at the cost of *these* side effects, of which *these* particular effects are truly dangerous (not great). They do not settle questions; they give us a framework by which we can ponder uncertainty and allow us to decide where we can place a drug's value on the spectrum.

In this chapter, we add a new form of uncertainty to the mix. Drug trials like the kind I have just discussed look *forward* in time. But not all clinical research is performed this way, and sometimes we look *backward* to see whether some remote event led to a disease that we're seeing now. We can compare people who are suffering from a disease to those who are not and look for meaningful differences between the two, whether they be lifestyles, education levels, general emotional outlook, or medications, among many other factors. But we're not waiting around to see which of them will develop disease and testing whether something prevents it; we're looking at the disease *right now* and wondering whether something in the *past* brought them to their current state.

For instance, we could design a study where we took one thousand people with lung cancer, compare them to one thousand people who don't have lung cancer, and see whether there's a difference in the proportion of people who smoked cigarettes.* Similarly, we can look directly at those factors and then see whether the factors are associated with more or less disease. In this case, we would compare those who have smoked, that is, the cases, to those who have not, that is, the controls. At least part of that language should seem familiar because the controls in this research comprise the same kind of "do nothing" control category that we saw in drug trials. From there, we can calculate the percentage of lung cancer in the case group, do the same for the control group, and evaluate the relative proportions to see whether there is a statistically significant difference between the two. At the end, we have generated a case-control study. This type of research is known as retrospective, and its calling card is that it looks for meaningful associations in the past. We call those meaningful associations *correlations*.

The additional layer of uncertainty involves whether a correlation can be considered equivalent to causation. Can one *know* that smoking causes lung cancer from a study like these? This seems a naïve question because

---

* Discussed in the Appendix.

everyone knows almost by instinct that of course smoking causes lung cancer. Yet one of the greatest biostatisticians of the mid-twentieth century remained skeptical of the link when looking at the early smoking–lung cancer retrospective studies, in part because of his insistence that correlation does not equal causation. (That he was a chain smoker might have influenced his interpretation of the data; you can meet him—and his fibrotic lungs—later in the Appendix.)

"Correlation does not equal causation"—graduate students in public health or biostatistics memorize this phrase when learning about retrospective studies. If I take my umbrella to work, and it rains as I walk, it didn't rain *because* I did so. Here the chain of causation is totally reversed. Again, this is the easy example, as we can immediately grasp the chain of relationship between rain and umbrella use. Just because two things are related by time and one thing happened to happen before the other, it hardly means that the first thing *caused* the second thing to occur. So why bother with this kind of research at all if it is so hopelessly mired in an Escher-like unsolvable loop?

For starters, to dismiss retrospective studies as useless is to turn our collective scientific back on an enormous volume of high-quality research that really *can* teach us things about our bodies, what makes them work and what makes them fail. Consequently, having a nuanced understanding of the scientific ambiguity produced by the correlation/causation problem is a valuable next stop on the tour of uncertainty. Moreover, studies don't have to be retrospective to have correlation/causation problems, as we'll also look at some prospective studies that are plagued by the same issue.

In this chapter, we'll encounter correlations that really *did* turn out to be causations. But we'll also see some pretty dramatic failures. Only by looking at both can we start to appreciate the value of research that utilizes correlation, which is commonly retrospective in nature.

Tragedy, Illustrated Through Statistics

In 1965, a young doctor named Arthur Herbst joined the faculty of the Boston Lying-In Hospital, a venerated institution in Boston circles, which had been established more than a century before as one of America's first

health-care facilities devoted exclusively to obstetrics.* Herbst had gradu-
ated from Harvard Medical School not long before, and after finishing his
residency took up his clinical work with aspirations of becoming an academic physician, pushing the boundaries of what was known about the
practice of obstetrics and gynecology.

It would not take long for him to get his wish, and, as is so often the
manner of physicians who become known to posterity, his academic acco-
lades came about through the dutiful and perfunctory documentation of
the sufferings of patients. Just as Herbst joined the faculty, a small number
of young women were sent to the Lying-In for vaginal bleeding. In and of
itself, this was, then as now, a fairly common problem. But these particular
women would leave the hospital with the most unlikely of diagnoses, not
to mention having their sense of womanhood utterly shattered. For the
women, who numbered about a half dozen, underwent biopsies to discover
they had a cancer known as clear cell adenocarcinoma, and, following the
biopsies, underwent hysterectomies to save their lives.

Clear cell adenocarcinoma under any circumstances is unusual, but in
young women it was essentially unheard of, as this was widely known at
the time to be a cancer of postmenopausal women. This made no sense.
Herbst must have treated hundreds, perhaps thousands, of women during
this time, yet six or seven unusual cancers in a span of a few years made
an impression. There was no description of this phenomenon before. So
Herbst, along with a senior colleague named Robert Scully, wrote a paper
about these cases in what is known as a case series.

The case series is, in some sense, about the lowest form of medical
investigation, meant only to communicate some novel finding. *Look here,*
a case series says, *something odd is happening.* It is a flare sent up through
the technical language of journals, asking aloud, in effect, whether anyone else has seen similar stuff. Herbst and Scully's paper was published in
the journal *Cancer* in April 1970.

The acceptance of such a paper in a prestigious journal like *Cancer*
bodes well for the career of a young clinical researcher, but if the paper

---

* The Lying-In Hospital would merge in 1966 with the Free Hospital for Women—
  itself nearly one hundred years old—and after a series of successive mergers would
  become what is now called the Brigham and Women's Faulkner Hospital.

had ended there, it would not merit particular attention more than forty years later. The medical literature is studded with reports such as this, some of which are meticulous in their collection of details and learned in their explanation of the importance of their findings. But there are many reports of strange illnesses that befall people, or groups of people, that have been reported for centuries. A case series in and of itself simply isn't particularly profound. Herbst made no effort to describe the mechanism by which these rather remarkable cases came to pass but merely noted that they simply *were*. Indeed, the paper did not even venture a guess as to why this strange cancer would suddenly be so prevalent, and the absence of a guess is startling.[†]

It's what happened *after* the *Cancer* paper that completely changed Dr. Herbst's professional life, to say nothing of the lives of millions of women. Still, outside the world of medicine—indeed, even largely *within* the world of medicine—Arthur Herbst is barely known. The names of early 1970s celebrities such as second-tier baseball players and mediocre actors from sitcoms like *The Partridge Family* (which debuted about the time of the *Cancer* paper) are much more likely to be recognized. In fact, it isn't even close. And yet, due in large part to Herbst's research, people think about pregnancy in a completely, utterly different way than they had before.

What happened was this: Dr. Herbst was approached by the mother of one of the women included in the case series. The *Cancer* paper had received some media publicity, and this mother had followed the coverage. She contacted Herbst and asked him a question. *You know, I was*

[†] Compare the absence of a discussion about a proposed mechanism for the clear cell cases to another famous case series, the 1981 CDC *Morbidity and Mortality Weekly Report* in which the first cases of what is now called AIDS were reported. Although the CDC staff must have been no less mystified than was Herbst by what they were seeing in previously healthy young gay men dying of a strange pneumonia known as *Pneumocystis carinii,* they make a foray into considering the cause. The easy part was that they all had the same sexual practices—almost anybody would have noted that this wasn't coincidental—but they go further and get the essential drift of how HIV works the very first time out: "All the above observations suggest the possibility of a cellular-immune dysfunction related to a common exposure that predisposes individuals to opportunistic infections," they wrote. That's a pretty accurate description of HIV, and they provided this depiction two years before the virus itself was discovered.

wondering, she said. *When I was pregnant, I took a medication to stop bleeding. Could it be connected to my daughter's cancer?*

Intrigued, Herbst ended up asking the other mothers of the young women from the case series, and was surprised to find that essentially all of them had taken a drug called diethyl stilbestrol, or DES, during their pregnancies. DES was a synthetic estrogen, initially approved by the FDA in 1941 mainly for symptoms associated with menopause. Not long after it came to market, the drug's maker, Bristol-Meyers Squibb, sought approval for its use in aiding the pregnancies of women with a history of miscarriage, which it was granted in 1947. Within a few years, however, there was evidence that DES might not be especially useful in helping these women carry their babies to term: a group of obstetricians from the University of Chicago performed a double-blind, placebo-controlled trial to evaluate its effectiveness and found that it made no difference in pregnancy outcomes. That didn't stop DES from being widely prescribed to another generation of pregnant women, even though multiple obstetric textbooks noted that it wasn't effective treatment. Its heyday, though, was in the early 1950s, just about the time these young women were born.

Herbst reviewed the data on the women with the clear cell cancer with several colleagues, and they collectively decided to perform something akin to a retrospective survey to learn whether DES might be associated with this rare cancer. In other words, they set up a case-control study like that discussed above. The seven women from the case series, along with an eighth who had come to their attention from a private-practice physician, were grouped into one cohort and then "matched" with a larger group of young women of the same age who *didn't* have cancer. They asked questions about their medical, and especially gynecological, histories: Was there some factor that separated the young women with cancer from the control group? The women reported whether they smoked, whether they had pets, what cosmetics they used, how old they were when they began having periods—anything to try to tease out what might be linked to this unusual disease. They didn't find any differences.

Then they looked at the *mothers* of the girls and asked questions about their pregnancies, and based on what they found the practice of obstetrics was never the same. On the following page is the Table from the article, published in the *New England Journal of Medicine* in 1971, showing the relevant data.*

They found three factors that were significantly more common among the case mothers compared to the control mothers: bleeding during pregnancy, a history of previous miscarriage, and the use of DES. The statistical analysis of significance is discussed in the Appendix, but the table is a mathematical description of the likelihood that such factors could be different by chance. For instance, three of the eight case mothers, or 37.5 percent, had bleeding during their pregnancy, while only one of the thirty-two control mothers—a measly 3 percent—had the same problem. The likelihood that this was just due to random chance was calculated to be less than one in twenty.

This was an intriguing finding, but what practically leaped off the page was the DES use: seven of eight of the case mothers used DES during the first trimester of their pregnancies; *none* of the thirty-two control mothers had done so. The difference in those proportions is much more dramatic; the likelihood that nearly all of the mothers would use DES and none of the control mothers would just due to random chance was calculated to be less than 1 in 100,000.

There were two consequences of that one column in that one table. The first was that, later that year, the FDA withdrew approval for DES to be marketed for the prevention of miscarriage. (It was pulled entirely from circulation four years later.) The second was that nobody, whether inside or outside medicine, ever thought about pregnancy in quite the same way.

It is hard now, in an age when many women won't so much as *look* at a tuna steak during pregnancy for fear of being contaminated by trace amounts of heavy metals, to imagine a time when doctors provided drugs to pregnant women without much thought about how it might affect the

---

* Table 1 of the article briefly summarizes the clinical aspects of the cases: how old they were when symptoms began, year of birth, year of treatment, and the therapy. The final column provides their clinical status as of the article's publication in 1971: one had died the year of her procedure, while the others were described as "living and well." Living? Sure. *Well?* Well, one supposes that Dr. Herbst and his colleagues were talking in the narrow, clinical sense of "well," rather than their overall spiritual state at the time, because all of the women had just undergone total hysterectomies and would never bear children.

Table 2. Summary of Data Comparing Patients with Matched Controls.

CASE NO.	MATERNAL AGE (YR) CASE	MEAN OF 4 CONTROLS	MATERNAL SMOKING CASE	CONTROL	BLEEDING IN THIS PREGNANCY CASE	CONTROL	ANY PRIOR PREGNANCY LOSS CASE	CONTROL	ESTROGEN GIVEN IN THIS PREGNANCY CASE	CONTROL	BREAST FEEDING CASE	CONTROL	INTRA-UTERINE X-RAY EXPOSURE CASE	CONTROL
1	25	32	Yes	2/4	No	0/4	Yes	1/4	Yes	0/4	No	0/4	No	1/4
2	30	30	Yes	3/4	No	0/4	Yes	1/4	Yes	0/4	No	1/4	No	0/4
3	22	31	Yes	1/4	Yes	0/4	No	1/4	Yes	0/4	Yes	0/4	No	0/4
4	33	30	Yes	3/4	Yes	0/4	No	0/4	No	0/4	Yes	2/4	No	0/4
5	22	27	Yes	3/4	No	1/4	Yes	1/4	Yes	0/4	No	0/4	No	0/4
6	21	29	Yes	3/4	Yes	0/4	Yes	0/4	Yes	0/4	Yes	0/4	No	0/4
7	30	27	No	3/4	No	0/4	Yes	1/4	Yes	0/4	No	0/4	No	1/4
8	26	28	Yes	3/4	No	0/4	Yes	0/4	Yes	0/4	No	0/4	Yes	1/4
Total			7/8	21/32	3/8	1/32	6/8	5/32	7/8	0/32	3/8	3/32	1/8	4/32
Mean	26.1	29.3												
Chi square (1 df)*			0.53		4.52		7.16		23.22		2.35		0	
p value	(N.S.)†		0.50 (N.S.)		<0.05		<0.01		<0.00001		0.20 (N.S.)		(N.S.)	

* Matched control chi-square test used as described by Pike & Morrow.[9]   † Standard error of difference 1.7 yr (paired t-test); N.S. = not statistically significant.

FIGURE 7.1. The single column that changed the practice of obstetrics. Of eight young women who had been diagnosed with the rare vaginal cancer known as clear cell adenocarcinoma, all but one of their mothers had used the drug diethylstilbestrol during pregnancy. By contrast, *none* of the thirty-two mothers of otherwise healthy "matched controls" had used the drug.

SOURCE: Herbst, A., "Adenocarcinoma of the Vagina: Association of Maternal Stilbestrol Therapy with Tumor Appearance in Young Women," *New England Journal of Medicine* 1971; 284(16):878–881.

baby. But until the 1950s and 1960s many, if not most, physicians believed that drugs could not cross the placenta, and thus rigorous safety studies were never performed on pregnant women.

The drug that would initially lead to a reconsideration of this bit of received wisdom is infamous: thalidomide. Thalidomide was initially developed as a sedative by a German pharmaceutical firm in the late 1950s but was quickly appreciated for its antinausea properties and subsequently marketed for morning sickness. Nearly fifty countries in all approved thalidomide. In the United States, however, one woman working in the Food and Drug Administration named Dr. Frances Oldham Kelsey found the safety studies on thalidomide wanting, and she insisted on further studies proving its safety in order for it to be approved. The studies never came because around the time of Dr. Kelsey's act of bureaucratic stubbornness, thousands of thalidomide-using mothers in Europe (where the drug had been approved and was commonly prescribed) bore children with malformed limbs, a condition known as phocomelia. Many of the children did not survive. Thalidomide was withdrawn within a few years, having never been stocked on pharmacy shelves in the United States. Dr. Kelsey saved tens of thousands of lives, and in doing so became one of medicine's greatest heroes.* She retired from the FDA, Nestor-like in her knowledge of the institution, at the age of ninety in 2005, and she is still living in British Columbia as I complete this book in mid-2015.

Thalidomide began the paradigm shift with respect to environmental effects on fetal development, and the DES paper a decade later largely completed it. By the end of the 1970s, the Food and Drug Administration introduced a set of drug classifications based on fetal risk. Category A drugs were found to be safe based on quality studies; Category B drugs did not *appear* to show risk, but there was not the high-quality evidence seen in the Category A drugs; Category C drugs—a fairly confusing category for clinicians—had animal but not human studies showing adverse

---

* Although she is a bit more well known than Arthur Herbst, she is significantly more obscure than physicians such as Deepak Chopra and Andrew Weil, whose contributions to the profession, even if viewed only through the lens of public education and outreach, can be described as harmless but mostly useless, at absolute best.

fetal effects, so they may be considered helpful "despite risks"; Category D drugs were likely harmful but might be warranted because of their use (i.e., to save the mother's life); and Category X drugs were unambiguously harmful and had no legitimate uses in pregnant women. (Thalidomide, which is still used today for such varied diseases as leprosy and multiple myeloma, was, of course, Category X.) Today, this classification scheme remains in effect, and doctors carefully scrutinize drugs for their pregnancy category before prescribing them to their pregnant patients, all a consequence of the one-two punch formed by the research on thalidomide and DES.

If this category scheme has a familiar feel to it, it should: the FDA fetal risk classification is essentially its own spectrum of certainty, specifically in relation to the harms that a given drug carries for the baby.

The DES data was at once striking and slightly quizzical, for although the association between the drug and the disease seemed to be beyond doubt, clear cell adenocarcinoma of young women remained a very rare disease despite the fact that millions of women had used DES during their pregnancies. If you *had* the cancer, the odds were overwhelming that your mother had taken DES (in technical language, this is known as the odds ratio). Yet that wasn't true in the reverse: if a mother took DES, the chance her daughter would develop cancer—statistically, the absolute risk—was estimated to be about one in one thousand, based on later studies.

But the most important aspect of the DES study is perhaps one of the least understood, and as I said at the outset of the chapter, it directly relates to this new layer of uncertainty introduced by the backward-looking aspect of this research. The paper didn't demonstrate that DES *caused* clear cell adenocarcinoma; it merely noted that the two things seemed to be *linked.* In an interview commemorating the fortieth anniversary of its publication, Dr. Herbst made this point perfectly clear. "Actually, at the time, [we wanted to write the paper] in clear language that didn't result in claiming more than an association," he said, underscoring that they weren't suggesting causation at that juncture. The only way that causation could be proved was by performing laboratory studies—first in a test tube, then in animals—that showed the mechanism by which the DES led to cancer. Those studies would be done over the next generation, and as a result much more is understood about the behavior of DES in utero, as well as the passage of all sorts of drugs across the placenta and what kinds of effects they might have on a developing fetus. In essence, it paved the way for an entire subspecialty in obstetrics as well as pharmacology.

Correlations—the careful, statistical juxtaposition of risk factors to diseases—are the raison d'être of the kind of research typified by the DES study. They can *hint* at a causal relationship between one and the other, but they can never prove it. In the case of the early DES research, the data might have indicated that there was something about these particular women (say, a genetic defect) and that the DES use might merely have been a substitute for this hidden abnormality. Perhaps, given that all the women were from Massachusetts, the reason lay in some hidden environmental factor and the DES use was merely a coincidence.

To be clear, my goal here isn't to suggest that DES isn't causally linked to clear cell cancer: so much quality research has been done since that first paper that such a claim would stretch credulity. (Likewise, for those intrigued by the notion that a great biostatistician would doubt that smoking isn't linked to lung cancer, stay tuned until the Appendix.) Instead, I'm trying to point out that the process by which researchers stumbled across this tragic side effect is subject to limitations. Correlations do not equal causations. The fact that they occasionally *seem* to can be a trap—sometimes a multibillion dollar trap, as we'll soon see.

The DES study was successful for a number of reasons. First, the cancers were, in the medical parlance, "zebras"—that is, they stood out for their unusualness. Young women simply weren't known to have this kind of cancer before the mid-1960s. That helped in the search for potential causes because if a risk factor could be identified that was peculiar to the patients, it would make a strong circumstantial argument that the risk factor might be the cause itself.

Second, the questionnaire that the researchers prepared for the "DES mothers" focused on their pregnancies. That's a relatively short period for the women to recall, during a time when they were more likely than usual to be aware of what medications they were taking. Even then, one of the seven mothers who took DES wasn't certain that she had, in fact, taken it, and her obstetrician was consulted to confirm its use. The lack of reliability in retrospective recall, as I'll discuss in a moment, can have a profound impact on studies that look for correlations.

Third, DES was a relatively new drug. It had been around for not much more than twenty years and had a very narrow usage. Obviously, it had no indication for men, and even in women it was indicated for a fairly small group. That meant that tracking its effects was a much simpler task than looking at, say, the effects of common chemicals in the environment.

All of these factors made DES an ideal candidate to study in relation to a rare cancer, where a strongly positive correlation might be reasonably assumed to suggest a causal link. Even so, sorting out genuine risks from mere incidental associations in rare diseases is still a challenge. When AIDS first came on to the medical scene, all of the patients described in the literature were young gay men. Much of the early epidemiology focused on their sexual behavior, and one of the risk factors that was strongly associated with the disease were drugs known as "poppers." Belonging to a chemical class named alkyl nitrites, poppers created brief but intense highs and were considered to be aphrodisiacs. Essentially all of the first patients with AIDS* reported using poppers: if a case-control study were performed on these men in the same way the DES study was done, with heterosexual men as controls, the data on popper use would look no different from that of DES.

Of course, we know now that poppers had nothing at all to do with AIDS and was simply a marker—that is, it was a risk factor that tracked with the disease. AIDS was caused by a virus that could spread only through sex and blood. Young gay men who had multiple sexual partners took poppers as part of the party culture where the virus was spreading, and they were being used deliberately to augment the sexual experience. Poppers, then, were merely a marker for having sex—the very activity that

---

* These first patients in 1981 and 1982 were not diagnosed with "AIDS" as there was no name for the disease initially, which may seem difficult to believe in an age where routine blizzards are now heralded with names on the Weather Channel even before they strike. The first well-known name for AIDS was GRID, or Gay Related Immune Deficiency. "AIDS" was proposed as a name in August 1982 to account for patients, among them Haitians and hemophiliacs, who had similar presentations but were not gay. More than anything else, it was the presence of AIDS in nongay populations that led most scientists to suspect that the disease was caused by a virus rather than recreational drugs then in use among gay men.

was leading to the transmission of the virus—but that was a reflection of that particular subculture and played no direct part in causing AIDS. (To this day, in AIDS-denialist circles, poppers are still sometimes invoked as the cause of AIDS-related diseases such as Kaposi's sarcoma.) This association, however, seemed plausible in the early days of the epidemic such that papers like "Toxicity, Immunosuppressive Effects and Carcinogenic Potential of Volatile Nitrites: Possible Relationship to Kaposi's Sarcoma" could be found in mainstream scientific journals as late as 1984, one year after the announcement of the discovery of HIV.

The "poppers theory" wasn't bad science. In fact, it was essentially of the same scientific quality as the DES / clear cell cancer theory. What the poppers theory does demonstrate is how carefully one must approach even strong correlations between risk factors and disease. The theory that poppers caused AIDS was wrong, while the theory that DES use in a mother caused her daughter's cancer was right. The only reason we know this to be true is the many subsequent studies. As more information poured in on AIDS patients, the notion that poppers was involved became less and less plausible; as more information poured in on young women with clear cell adenocarcinoma, the notion that DES was involved became stronger and stronger.

Both clear cell adenocarcinoma and AIDS, at the time of their initial descriptions when researchers were trying to understand their causes, were rare diseases. Moreover, both were found to have risk factors strongly associated with the disease, in the forms of DES and poppers. Very few people who did *not* have these diseases used either drug, but nearly all of those who were afflicted did use them. That provided very strong circumstantial evidence of causation, and despite this only one of them turned out to be truly important to understanding the disease, while the other was a red herring.

Coffee, Heart Attacks, and Correlation

Those are, in effect, the simple situations. When we try to understand the causes of much more common diseases, the kind that most of us are likely to die from, the correlation/causation problem is much more difficult to tease apart. Because many people suffer from common diseases like heart disease, various cancers, and dementia, it's very challenging to find common denominators particular to one group of patients when comparing it to healthy controls.

At the same time, the blurring of correlation with causation is even more likely to occur when the news media is eager for a catchy story. If the purported risk on which the news bit is based is something common, that's even better, because it has a greater chance of grabbing the attention of the red-meat eater, or television watcher, or booze consumer, or whatever else is being discussed. Here, for instance, is a typical example where researchers are trying to learn about the possible causes of heart attacks and looking at a common risk factor: coffee consumption. The following is a portion of an article from the Internet health website *Medscape:*

Coffee May Trigger Heart Attack
Attacks After Single Cup, Light Drinkers Most at Risk

That cup of coffee you're craving might not be such a good idea.

Research in the September issue of *Epidemiology* suggests coffee can trigger a heart attack within an hour in some people. Java junkies can take some comfort from the finding that the risk was highest among light coffee drinkers (those who consumed up to one cup a day). *For those people, the risk of heart attack increased fourfold when they indulged.* Couch potatoes and those with other risk factors for heart disease were also at greater risk of having a heart attack after drinking a cup of coffee, the study showed. As a result of these findings, "people at high risk for a heart attack who are occasional or regular coffee drinkers might consider quitting coffee altogether," [say the researchers].

The new study was based on 503 cases of nonfatal heart attacks in Costa Rica. *The researchers asked participants about their coffee consumption in the hours and days before their heart attack.* Although the study was conducted in Costa Rica, the researchers say the results are relevant to the U.S. because Americans and Costa Ricans have similar caffeine habits. (my emphasis)

This is a special kind of a case-control study, where the people who had the heart attacks themselves serve as their own controls:* they do this

---

* Technically, it's called a case-crossover design.

by reporting how much coffee they've consumed roughly over the past month, and then the statisticians look for an uptick in any of the factors immediately prior to having the heart attack. It's a common study design to identify risk factors for "acute events" like heart attacks, and these researchers carefully tried to "control for confounders"—that is, they did their best to make sure that it was really the coffee that was associated temporally with the heart attack and not, say, having a cigarette *with* the morning cup of joe. They also asked about other risk factors besides coffee and cigarettes. Although it's a very well-done study, it's still subject to the limitations of case-control studies in general, which I'll discuss forthwith, and in failing to point out those limitations, the article oversells its conclusions. Dramatically.

Leave aside the issue of whether it's absolutely safe for Americans to extrapolate data obtained from a study of Costa Ricans—although they may have similar caffeine habits, they probably don't have similar dietary, drinking, and exercise habits, among several other factors. First, the story falls into the classic trap of confusing correlation and causation: at most what can be said is that coffee consumption is *associated with* having a heart attack, which is not quite the same thing as saying that it's the *cause of* heart attacks. The researchers present a rationale in both their paper and in the article as to *how* coffee could cause a heart attack and why occasional drinkers might be at the highest risk. But they didn't prove it to be the cause of the heart attacks because, as I've discussed, that's not possible to do in a case-control study.

Second, the study results are very much influenced by the problem of recall bias. Imagine yourself, lying in a hospital bed in Costa Rica, mulling over the major change that just took place in your life, and suddenly a researcher comes to you and starts asking questions about how much coffee you drank *just before you had the heart attack.* It's a leading question, as are all of the questions about all of the risk factors. It's not the fault of the researchers; it's just the normal process of recovering from some devastating medical event. Patients commonly review their lifestyle decisions after such illnesses and theorize no less than scientists as to why they became sick. They can be heavily influenced by guilt and many other emotions, which warps their reports to researchers. The question isn't whether a case-control study like this can avoid recall bias because it can't; the question is how much confidence one can have in the conclusions.

Finally, imagine being given a questionnaire that asked you to recall everything you've consumed—all the different foods and drinks, how much alcohol, how many cigarettes—during the past twenty-four days. In addition, you need to give a reasonable estimate of what *time* you had those things: the heart attacks in this study happened more often in the mornings: Was that because of the time of day or the coffee? Plus you need to report your level of physical activity, your emotional state, and a few other factors to boot. Could you recollect the details of the past month of your life accurately enough to be of use to a scientist? It's difficult under optimal circumstances; I can barely remember what I ate yesterday, let alone report how much coffee I had a week ago.

For all these reasons, identifying genuine risk factors commonly used in the general population is notoriously difficult and subject to all manner of uncertainty. A risk factor like coffee, if it is a risk for cardiovascular disease at all, is almost certainly small in its effects. We know there are millions of non–coffee drinkers who have heart attacks and millions of java fiends who do not. As a consequence, the number of people researchers need to recruit for a study looking for a slightly higher prevalence of coffee consumption in a heart-disease cohort is large. Risk factors with small effects are much more sensitive to random sampling issues: if you happen to recruit, just as a matter of chance, ten or twenty extra non–coffee drinkers into your cohort of 2,000 subjects with heart disease, you might find no effect where in fact there really was one; if you include the same number into the healthy control group, you might conclude the opposite. Plus, there is the issue of recall bias, as well as the problems introduced by standardization—if the questionnaire asks about cups of coffee per day, not all people are drinking the same size cups, to say nothing of the difference in caffeine between a mega mocha grande with an espresso chaser and the local donut shop's sixteen-ounce standard brew. Finally, after all of these obstacles, there is the irreducible problem of correlation and causation.

In short, studies such as these, which involve identifying some common risk factor of some common disease and asking whether they are associated, almost by default find themselves in the dead middle of the spectrum of certainty. They seek to find causations where at best only correlations may exist, and high levels of uncertainty are inherent in their structural design because they introduce recall bias as well as lump together people who had different degrees of exposure to the risk factor, good or bad.

Sweet Dreams: Does Eating Chocolate Lower Your Risk of Heart Failure?

Over the past several years, one such risk factor has become a media darling: dark chocolate. However, unlike the coffee described above, which is a "negative" risk factor, dark chocolate has—mercifully—been studied mainly with respect to its beneficial properties. (Coffee, actually, is something of a mixed bag, with some studies associating harms, but others with benefits.) Chocolate is actually a complex amalgam of compounds, but starting in the early 2000s a small number of research papers began focusing on one category called flavonoids. These are chemicals found in high levels in chocolates, especially in the more pure form of dark chocolate. Some early studies in test tubes showed that flavonoids have a variety of effects that might be favorably linked to reducing heart disease risk. They have antioxidant effects, alter the endothelium (the cells that line the inside of blood vessels), and possibly inhibit platelets from clumping, which is a particularly beneficial side effect because platelet clumping is one of the initial processes in the cascade of events that causes heart attacks. The research looked genuinely promising, and for that matter it still does.

Whether medical science has definitively demonstrated that regularly ingesting dark chocolate really reduces one's risk of heart failure is another matter entirely. A variety of studies have been performed over the past decade, and there has been a steady drumbeat in the popular press about its ambrosial effects. Take a paper from the *Journal of Internal Medicine* in 2009. It is slightly different in structure from the DES paper in that it is prospective rather than retrospective in nature; that is, patients were recruited at a given point in time and then *followed into the future*—in the case of this study, for eight years. More than a thousand Swedish people who had experienced their first heart attack were given questionnaires looking at dozens of risk factors, then followed in Swedish national registries for hospitalizations and deaths. They concluded that the more chocolate the people consumed, the more likely they were to survive. This received a cheerful review in the *New York Times,* among many other news outlets, and is but one example in dark chocolate's fawning press coverage that was at full steam by the time the story was published.

The highest-quality prospective studies follow patients *before* they develop disease and then look for risk factors by comparing who goes on to develop disease versus who doesn't. The great Framingham Heart Study—which deserves more than this small detour, alas—is one of the classic examples of prospective cohort research. The study began in 1948 in Framingham, then a small town about an hour west of Boston. They enrolled just over 5,000 men and women and met with them year after year, having the subjects fill out questionnaires and undergo physical exams and blood tests. Eventually, some subjects in this cohort had heart attacks or strokes or developed some other form of cardiovascular disease, while others didn't. Researchers and statisticians could then start finding factors that were associated with disease. And find them they have: more than 1,200 research papers have come out of FHS. Nearly every major risk factor for cardiovascular disease familiar to even moderately informed laypeople—like smoking, diabetes, a sedentary lifestyle, high blood pressure, obesity, and high "bad" cholesterol—has either been discovered or confirmed by research in Framingham.

By contrast, the Swedish chocolate study is a variant where the cohort is formed by people who've *already* been diagnosed with heart disease and then are followed to see who died sooner. This unusual study design should leave one far more circumspect about its conclusions than if a similar effect were found as part of the Framingham research.

A large number of the dark chocolate studies, like the Swedish study, suffer from this blending of correlation with causation—both in the research itself and especially in its media coverage. Maybe the reason chocolate eaters were less likely to die in this time span is that they were simply healthier people to begin with and eating chocolate was merely a cultural marker associated with happiness and healthiness. There is the further problem of standardization: Especially when there are multiple purported mechanisms that could be due to a number of different compounds found in chocolate, it is difficult in a study like this to know *how much* of *which kind* of chocolate might be physiologically beneficial. None of these people were taking doses standardized to their weight, height, or body mass. And chocolate itself is a product that is cultivated in different parts of the world, leading to the question of whether it's a particular flavonoid unique to African chocolate that might have benefits compared to chocolate processed in Honduras. For all of these reasons, one can overinterpret the findings in myriad ways, and conclude that dark chocolate is a life-giving elixir when in fact it is nothing more than a much-loved confectionary.

I am not a member of the anti–dark chocolate or antiflavonoids lobby: there is always a bowl of chocolate in my office for my residents and students to snack on to make the day more pleasant. Rather, I'm pointing out why I believe we're living in an age of uncertainty about its effects, and why you should read news reports such as those on dark chocolate with a certain amount of caution. In this particular case, the *New York Times* piece helpfully includes such a caveat. "Before concluding that a box of Godiva truffles is health food, chocolate lovers may want to consider some of the study's weaknesses," the author writes. "It is an observational study, not a randomized trial, so cause and effect cannot be definitively established." Such warnings are often left out; I practically wept for joy when I read these sentences.

So how *do* researchers manage to learn whether strong correlations are equivalent to the causes of a given disease? The ideal answer is to do a prospective clinical trial, the randomized double-blind placebo-controlled study discussed in the previous chapter, exclusively focused on the one single variable of interest. These studies are expensive and time-consuming, so there has to be a pretty big incentive to tackle such a project when there's already circumstantial evidence that some *thing*— environmental chemical, drug, radiation exposure—really does cause, or protect people from, disease. In one instance, just such a prospective clinical trial led to the mother of all correlation/causation confusions, causing billions of dollars of losses for several drug companies, but one in particular: Wyeth Pharmaceuticals.

Correlation/Causation and Hormone Replacement Therapy

That story begins in 1966 when a gynecologist named Robert Wilson wrote a book that stands as one of the watershed moments in what we might call the medicalization of everyday life—that is, turning natural processes into "diseases" for which doctors, and by extension the pharmaceutical industry, can offer "cures." Titled *Feminine Forever,* Wilson argued that menopausal women could enhance nearly all aspects of their lives by taking estrogen therapy. "Many women simply refuse to recognize menopause for what it is—a serious, painful, and often crippling disease," he wrote. In a line that practically defies belief today, he claimed that estrogen would counteract this by ensuring that her "breasts and genital organs will not shrivel. She will be much more pleasant to live with and will not become dull and unattractive." Simply to peruse Dr. Wilson's thoughts today is an exercise in trying to keep one's lower jaw attached to the rest of one's face. It is difficult now to conceive that a book of such unadorned paternalism—both in the sense of physician paternalism as well as male paternalism—could be the best seller that *Feminine Forever* was, influencing millions of women for nearly a generation.

Dr. Wilson's financial relationships with several pharmaceutical companies who had a stake in expanding the hormone market have since been well documented, and even adjusted to the social mores of the 1960s it wasn't pretty. Not long after *Feminine Forever* debuted, questions were being raised about its objectivity; an article in the *New Republic* documented that Wilson was effectively paid to write the book by Wyeth Pharmaceuticals. A large volume of commentary has since been generated on the marketing and business aspects of hormone replacement therapy. In effect, critics have charged that books like *Feminine Forever* are representative examples of what happens when physicians hitch their wagons to the star of Big Pharma: whole disease categories are invented to create new markets, and physicians like Wilson become highly compensated dupes, wittingly or not, to the whole enterprise.

Regardless of the financially symbiotic relationship between Dr. Wilson and his corporate masters, in terms of the correlation/causation story, the relevance of *Feminine Forever* is that, because it was so influential, it

effectively began an enormous natural experiment on the risks and benefits of hormone therapy in women. Of course, all freely marketed drugs
create natural experiments. For the most part these go unmeasured, but
following the boom in hormone replacement therapy, researchers started
taking a careful look at whether the benefits touted by Dr. Wilson had any
basis in reality.

For the most part, they did indeed appear to. There were some cautionary tales: research published in the *New England Journal of Medicine*
in 1975 showed that estrogen-only therapy increased the risk of developing uterine cancer. Typically, such a negative study in the world's pre-
miere medical journal causes a massive freeze in prescriptions. But
pharmaceutical companies argued that the problem observed in the *New
England Journal* study was caused by "unopposed estrogen"—which was
in hormonal terms something akin to all accelerator and no brake. In its
place, they offered the newly developed combination of estrogen and
progesterone. By including the "break" hormone of progesterone, the
combination restored the natural balance that unopposed estrogen dis-
rupted. Therefore, the risks highlighted by the study were claimed to be
no longer valid. It was a savvy corporate reply, and although it was pure
theory because no clinical trials were performed to test this hypothesis,
hormone replacement sales continued nearly unabated.

At any rate, despite the occasional study such as this, an increasing
amount of research was being published indicating that hormone replacement therapy really *could* reap substantial health benefits beyond controlling menopausal symptoms and leaving one feeling youthful. Some
studies showed that women who took hormone replacement had a lower
incidence of cardiovascular disease—that is, they had fewer heart attacks
and strokes. Other studies showed that they had stronger bones and fewer
fractures when compared to nonusers, indicating that hormone replacement might prevent osteoporosis.

One concern was that all of these studies were either observational (the
researchers just followed women who chose to take hormones and compared
them to those who didn't, but weren't randomized into a treatment versus
placebo trial) or case control (where women who suffered heart attacks or
broken hips were then asked whether they had taken hormone replacement,

and then their hormone use was compared to healthy controls). Still, the gathering pile of evidence seemed ever more convincing, so by the late 1980s the vast majority of physicians had become sufficiently sold on the many benefits of hormone replacement therapy. Eventually, hormone replacement therapy became part of national primary care guidelines.

Why, then, would a pharmaceutical company wish to interfere with a juggernaut like hormone replacement therapy by performing a costly randomized trial to prove what everyone knew to be true in the first place? The answer lies in the federal legal structure concerning drug approval and drug marketing. Although physicians have a fairly wide latitude in prescribing drugs in whatever way they see fit, drug makers are given approval to *market* their drugs only with very specific indications. Suppose that a company seeks approval by the FDA for its antihypertensive drug, and following approval a group of neurologists use the drug experimentally to treat migraine headaches and discover it is quite effective. The trials are well designed, and they publish their results in respected journals. Despite this unanticipated additional beneficial use of the drug, the company cannot advertise this use unless it returns to the FDA and submits documents seeking approval for the new indication of treating migraine.

Most companies don't bother, as additional approvals for marketing are costly and time-consuming. Usually, they are content with the medical system finding "off-label" uses for their approved drugs, informally touting these soft indications through a variety of means. In some cases the off-label use becomes more important than the use for which it was approved, and drug companies try to massage those situations to their benefit.* Most often, however, the off-label market isn't sufficiently

---

* The most notorious example of the abuse of the off-label system involves the marketing of the drug Neurontin, which was informally pushed as a panacea for any number of ills, including bipolar disorder, chronic pain, alcohol withdrawal, and migraine headaches, among other problems. According to a 2009 article from *Bloomberg,* US federal prosecutors asserted that $2.12 of $2.27 billion—or *94 percent*—of Neurontin's revenues came from off-label use. Neurontin's initial FDA indication in 1994 was as an adjunct (that is, not even first-line) treatment for seizures; in 2002 a second approval was given for treatment of a condition called post-herpetic neuralgia, which is the sometimes severe pain that can follow an episode of shingles.

lucrative to justify the expense of seeking additional approvals for drugs that are already available.

Hormone replacement therapies, however, represented an exception, because an FDA-approved indication for prevention of heart disease could take a drug with a *big* market and turn it into one with a *huge* market. Thus the Wyeth-sponsored HERS Study (Heart and Estrogen/ Progestin Replacement Study) was born. Wyeth initially sought FDA approval without having to perform such a study, but various patients' rights advocates, such as Cynthia Pearson of the National Women's Health Network quoted at the beginning of the chapter, objected. "You couldn't approve a drug for healthy men without a randomized clinical trial. Even aspirin had to have a randomized controlled trial with healthy men," Pearson told *New York Times* writer Gina Kolata in 2002. By contrast, some doctors were concerned about whether it was even ethical to undertake such a study given how strongly the evidence suggested hormone replacement saved lives. *Since we know it works,* the reasoning went, *why would we give placebos to thousands of women and knowingly consign some of them to an early death?*

Because Wyeth's goal was FDA approval for an expanded use of hormone therapy, the HERS research didn't try to demonstrate every purported benefit that had been reported over the past two decades, but was narrowly focused on a question that could be easily defined and answered in a reasonably short time frame. The goal was to demonstrate that hormones were useful in so-called secondary prevention of heart disease—that is, they wanted to show that the estrogen/progesterone combination, when given to women who were already known to have heart disease, would prevent further heart-related complications.

The HERS investigators ran a trial similar to the kind that I discussed in the previous chapter with respect to statins, enrolling under 3,000 women who had known heart disease and following them for four years. In effect, the investigators were proposing that the estrogen/progesterone combination might be as beneficial as statins had been shown to be. Assuming that trial was successful, it was only a short step to prove that hormone replacement could be used for preventing disease in healthy women (what is known as "primary prevention"; secondary prevention decreases the complications of people who already have a disease*) and should be indicated for preventing heart disease in *all* menopausal women. This represented an enormous, and as yet not fully tapped, market.

The results were published in 1998, and they were not encouraging. HERS failed to show any benefit for women: almost exactly the same number of women had major cardiac events (fatal or nonfatal) whether they took hormones or not. Yet although the trial was clearly bad news for Wyeth and the other makers of estrogen and progesterone, it did not completely alter the notion that hormone replacement should remain the standard of care. Even in the conclusion to the study, the authors suggest that although this indicated that women who have heart disease should not *start* taking hormones, if they already happen to be taking hormones for *other* reasons—that is, the benefits that had been attributed to them through observational trials—then they should probably be continued. There were, after all, many such benefits that had been observed.

But HERS was not the final word, for, in addition to it, the National Institutes of Health sponsored a trial known as the Women's Health Initiative. WHI was much a more ambitious study. The researchers were interested in evaluating not only hormones but also diet, as well as the effects of calcium and vitamins, and they were looking at many outcomes besides heart disease, such as fractures, breast cancer, and endometrial cancers. Compared to HERS, the WHI hormone study enrolled ten times the number of women, with the goal of following them for up to twelve years. Moreover, WHI enrolled women whether or not they had heart disease and whether or not they had hysterectomies (in order to avoid problems in interpreting the data, women with hysterectomies were excluded from HERS). The sheer size of the research project could have been underwritten only by the federal government. It was a mammoth undertaking.

The trial was originally designed to last until 2005, but by 2002 a steady accumulation of data suggested that not only were hormones not beneficial but they were harmful. Such harms included an increased risk of breast cancer, heart disease, stroke, and blood clots; we'll look at the

---

* The successful statin trials I discussed in the previous chapter were secondary prevention studies, although there is research on primary prevention with statins as well.

magnitude of those harms below. In the summer of that year, the researchers made a decision to halt the trial, sending a letter to the participants advising them to discontinue taking the estrogen/progesterone combination† The letter was issued in early July, and the bottom fell out for hormone replacement therapy. An estimated 6 million women had been taking hormones before the announcement, and although nobody knows precisely how many women abruptly halted the medications, it was almost surely a substantial proportion of that number.

The consequent media frenzy was predictable if lamentable: hormone replacement was portrayed to be the equivalent of ingesting poison. "It was like an abrupt hit in the solar plexus—with a message that was loud and clear: If you value your life, don't even be in the same room as a bottle of hormones," noted doctor Steven Goldstein, a board member of the North American Menopause Society.

One hesitates to use the word "hysteria" to describe the news coverage, but the majority of the stories dealing with the sudden end to the WHI trial had failed to make explicit the magnitude of the threat. Hormones had been shown to be of no benefit, that much was clear. But how great was the harm? The behavior of tens of thousands of women and their doctors indicated that they believed taking hormones sentenced a woman to endometrial cancer or a heart attack. Many news stories encouraged this view of matters. The bottom line was simply to *stop*. Even though the HERS trial should have given everyone reason to become more skeptical of the elixir-like properties of hormones, the termination of the WHI trial caused an overnight shift in the emotional attitude about them. What was once healthy had become not only useless but menacing, even terrifying.

Yet the harms posed by prolonged hormone use were in fact relatively small. Compared to an equal number of women who were not taking replacement therapy, if 10,000 women took the combination of hormones for one year, 41 additional women would develop complications (8 cases of breast cancer, 7 heart attacks, 8 strokes, and 18 blood clots). Now this

---

† Only part of the WHI hormone trial, which had involved 16,000 women who had not had hysterectomies and were taking the estrogen/progesterone combination, was stopped in 2002. The remaining 11,000 women who did have hysterectomies and were taking estrogen alone continued to be followed, until that arm of the trial was halted in 2004 for similar reasons.

is just one year and those numbers add up over time, but there were also quantifiable benefits as well: for the cost of those problems, there would also be 6 fewer cases of colon cancer and 5 fewer broken hips.

The more nuanced picture, then, was a portrait of uncertainty, allowing clinicians to quantify the risk of a medical approach that certainly didn't live up to its billing, but whose problems were sufficiently minor that one could make a case for its use, particularly in women experiencing debilitating symptoms in the setting of menopause. That would definitely represent a much smaller group of patients than the market that Wyeth and other drug manufacturers had envisioned only years earlier, but in the wake of the news stories in the summer of 2002, the notion that these drugs might still have a place was difficult to imagine. Slowly, however, a reconsideration of their role has occurred, and some patients are having conversations with their doctors about the risks versus benefits of hormone replacement. These are not completely safe drugs, but neither are they without use in particular instances.

The story of hormone replacement therapy is one of weak effects: like statins, thousands of people needed to be followed for years before one could definitively state whether they were helpful (and, unlike statins, they weren't). The answers could be found only through statistics using large samples. Most researchers would have guessed that there was a small benefit to hormones. That turned out not to be true, but the harms that were observed were sufficiently small that the researchers shouldn't have been completely surprised.

Yet the change in *public perception* of hormone replacement therapy pre- and post-WHI couldn't have been more fundamental; one day the sun rose in the east, the next in the west. What could arguably be inferred from this is that because we underappreciate uncertainty, we are left with having to conceive of modern medicine as an either/or proposition of amazingly lifesaving or irredeemably toxic. So when evidence filters in that we might need to reconsider the *magnitude* of a treatment's value, we don't have a conceptual system that allows for a graded adjustment. Instead, we can only flip the treatment from one category to the other.

The fact that hormones had been associated with all that is good in medicine and then were almost immediately associated with its polar opposite indicates that they were wildly oversold. But why was this? Public health officials and doctors could have provided caveats about the kind of correlation-based research that had been performed, and mostly they didn't. It's not that scientists and statisticians weren't aware of the correlation/causation problems in the 1970s and 1980s, when hormone replacement therapy really began to take off. Many drugs are sent to trials and ultimately fail, so skepticism of hormone replacement should have been the norm, yet so many doctors were taken completely by surprise.

There are many reasons for this, but I would suggest that one critical factor may have been that everyone *wanted* hormones to be successful, so the warning signs were largely ignored. What that means is that as we near the center of the spectrum of certainty, where we become less and less confident in the unimpeachable nature of the evidence, our own hopes for a treatment—or our fear of a particular disease—can have a dramatic impact on our approach to that treatment or disease, even if that means we embrace a treatment or a technology that ultimately ends up doing more harm than good. Instead of being thought of as drugs that may or may not have benefits that had not as yet been proven through trials, hormones carried an emotional resonance for women who wanted to demonstrate their commitment to their health, and their doctors shared in this enthusiasm.

Recall the language that one pundit used to describe the cultural importance of screening mammograms: "screening is what responsible and health-conscious women do . . . those are commendable and powerful virtues." Indeed they are. But such charged rhetoric can make it harder to appraise research in as levelheaded a manner as possible and can lead us to think we are more certain than in fact we should be. The tension inherent in the correlation/causation conundrum leaves us, doctor and patient alike, susceptible to overinterpreting the data, and it makes us captives of our own desires.

One well-known cognitive bias from which a doctor—or for that matter anyone—can suffer is called anchoring. Anchoring means that people become so invested in their diagnosis that they actively dismiss information that should lead to a reconsideration of that diagnosis, tossing aside clues that in retrospect make perfectly clear that the original diagnosis should have been reconsidered. Ultimately, the correlation/causation problem teaches us to be aware of where we find ourselves on the spectrum of certainty and, as we near its middle, that we should be conscious of our own motivations, as those motivations may cloud our judgment. We should be especially alert of our tendency to anchor when we encounter such fuzzy data. And *anyone* is capable of doing this: doctors have no special corner on the market of self-awareness of their biases, or lack thereof.

How can nonspecialists raise their antennae when hearing news about some study linking, say, dark chocolate consumption with longer life? To consider that question, we first have to think about how mass media tends to portray medical research. I'll try to provide some specific answers in the conclusion, but, in the meantime, it is worth investigating how our health news copes with uncertainty.

"HEALTH WATCH": HYPE, HYSTERIA, AND THE MEDIA'S OVERCONFIDENT MARCH OF PROGRESS

> To deal with the broader problem of anecdotes, what you need is a framework that tells you which anecdotes are almost surely wrong.
>
> —PAUL KRUGMAN

The previous two chapters have looked explicitly at how uncertainty and our understanding of a treatment's effectiveness are inextricably and irrevocably linked. Before that, we looked at uncertainty's impact on diagnosis, as well as how uncertainty can make experts square off against one another, leaving not only laypeople but even ordinary practicing doctors scratching their heads, trying to understand what the right approach should be to some problem.

Yet whether the uncertainty involves the latest technology allowing a surgeon in San Francisco to use a robot to take out a patient's gallbladder in Longmont, Colorado, or a cutting-edge drug that may revolutionize the treatment of spinal cord injuries, or a revised guideline on the treatment of emphysema, the vast majority of people learn of these advances through some form of mainstream media, whether the *New York Times,* network television news, National Public Radio, or links supplied by their friends on Facebook. (This is even true for most doctors, where all but the most specialized of specialists—who stay up to date at conferences and in journals—get their news from the same sources as most other people.) We swim in an endless stream of media, able to sample from dozens of stories about health each day. In this final stop on our tour of uncertainty, we'll take a cursory look at how the media shapes our understanding of medicine, often by downplaying uncertainty's importance. We'll think about how it adjusts our perceptions of risk, lulling us into a false sense of security about things that are genuinely (if only subtly) dangerous in our lives, but encouraging us to become preoccupied with threats unlikely to ever do us harm.

As we complete this survey of uncertainty, we'll finally consider in a formal way how all this awareness of uncertainty can be *enabling,* rather than making us feel depressed about how deeply flawed some of our medical practices truly can be. But, before we get there, we must understand how media can, even if only inadvertently, manipulate us while trying to inform us—and how we actively participate in that process. To start, we'll consider how the media chose to portray a singularly remarkable event when some German doctors made an announcement that shook the world of infectious disease to its core.

The Berlin Patient

December 15, 2010, was just another day for HIV-infected patients and the people who care for them. Across the world, more than 6,000 people became infected, and although nearly all of these people would not realize it that particular day, they had joined the growing ranks of people around the world living with HIV, which numbered some 30 million. That same day, at the other end of the HIV continuum, nearly the same number (about 5,000), who had been infected for years, succumbed to the disease.

The scourge marched on.

Yet December 15, 2010, was a very different day for anyone *outside* the world of HIV. People casually paying attention to the news that day would have heard a report of something almost astonishing from the scientific community: the complete eradication of the AIDS virus in a patient. "German doctors declare 'cure' in HIV patient," read the Reuters headline, and within twenty-four hours the world media began trumpeting the story. The major television networks devoted several minutes of airtime to announce the news with great fanfare. Tens of thousands of people read the article and shared it online. Doctors' offices were flooded with calls. Had you not read the news story at the time, this may come as a surprise to you because you've probably heard nothing about it since—and a cure for HIV seems like the kind of thing you'd continue to hear about.

The reason you haven't heard any follow-up is because there was one small problem: it wasn't really true.

Now, the *facts* of the story were correct: there was a patient who did have HIV and subsequently had all traces of the virus eliminated from his body. However, the virus was eradicated due to a bizarre twist of cell biology and transplant medicine; the *truth* of the matter was that one patient became improbably, almost impossibly, lucky. More than 70 million people have been infected with HIV since the epidemic began, while no more than maybe a half dozen have managed to clear the HIV virus from their bodies. Of these incredibly rare cases, so far as we know only *one* adult—Timothy Ray Brown, who became known as the "Berlin patient"—has been cured of HIV.* Moreover, his cure came at a very high cost and could have killed him. But this crucial background information played a negligible part in the news stories pinging around the electronic ether in late November and early December of that year.

The health news of December 15, 2010, probably shouldn't have mentioned this item at all, but if it did, organizations might have included a blurb on their websites with the title "One Person in 70 Million Cured." But that is hardly news at all. For this story to have legs, the title had to be "Cure!" With that headline, the viewers and their online readers came by the millions. And, unless they were approaching such a story with skepticism, they would have come away with almost the opposite understanding of the reality of HIV in the early twenty-first century. First, they would have thought a cure was a realistic possibility for those people living with HIV, which it wasn't. Second, they would have walked away

---

* Mr. Brown is actually the *second* person dubbed "the Berlin patient," the first being a man who became able to "control" his HIV infection (meaning the virus replicated at only very low levels) after experimental therapy he received in Germany in the late 1990s, although this was not technically a cure. This anonymous patient likewise became the object of media interest, although the increase in popularity of the Internet has made the second Berlin patient much more famous. Nothing is simple in medicine.

unaware that we *already* have the functional equivalent of a cure for HIV, and that most HIV-infected people can now live basically normal lives and can expect to see old age like anyone else. We call this functional cure "pills." That story, however, isn't very sexy and didn't happen all at once, so it never got sent to health reporters as a press release from some pharmaceutical company or university seeking publicity.

The story of the Berlin patient is emblematic of the professional news media's all-too-frequent obsession with glitzy but largely vapid headlines. It demonstrates a key feature of health news: namely, that stories can often burst with facts, but, much like the Western diet, such facts serve as sugary calories for the brain to gorge upon but lack the context to serve as genuine intellectual nutrition. Thus, we tend to know more but understand less; we drown in news bytes rather than swim in knowledge. The effect is corrosive because, by making a fetish of technology, it undermines popular confidence in medicine when that technology can't deliver. By focusing on the space-age wizardry, it makes some of the genuinely amazing things that modern medicine *can* do seem dull by comparison.

Recall our seven words of advice for maintaining good health from the introduction: *exercise more*, *eat less,* and *do not smoke.* If one lives by those tenets, the likelihood of long life is by no means guaranteed, but faithful adherence to those precepts is more important than anything else in health, by far. Yet, by watching the health news, it's actually pretty difficult to appreciate this message in its glorious simplicity. You are much more likely to become preoccupied with trivial threats to your health, underappreciate the enormous impact that smoking can have on your quality of life, and become fascinated by scientific developments that appear to be just around the corner from the marketplace but in reality have little chance of ever finding their way to hospitals or clinics. Much of this misperception will be caused by the fact that health reporters ignore uncertainty like the proverbial elephant in the newsroom. To discuss uncertainty requires nuance, and a nuanced presentation needs time and makes demands on news consumers. In the news organizations with the largest audiences, health reporters aren't really interested in making any demands on their audience if the bulk of their stories are to be judged, and they don't like devoting more than a minute or two to a story. It's the intellectual equivalent of eating Wonder Bread as one's only source of food.

By "health news" I mean something very particular. A generation ago, when one spoke of media, it was much clearer what one was referring to: the local paper or TV station, the national networks, and the news weeklies were all good examples, and readers could figure out which of these was being discussed by context. In the age of the Internet and hundred-channel cable television, however, "media" and "news" could refer to any number of wildly different organizations, ranging from simple online equivalents of the daily newspapers that struggle to stay afloat in the current marketplace to websites with editorial views well outside the mainstream. We consume news today in a very different way than our parents did, with many more opportunities for finding alternative viewpoints and unusual perspectives.

Yet, despite this evolution of a new media bazaar, where one can shop for all manner of stories, local TV "health watch" stories retain a powerful grip on how people perceive modern health care and the developments going on in medical research. Likewise, national TV health news and the website news stories produced by those networks are still a principal route for many people to learn about what's going on in the world of medicine. They still command a level of trust across a broad swath of the nation; their stories get "shared" on Facebook and passed on in e-mails between friends. These organizations were the outlets that ran with the story of the Berlin patient, that became titillated by the promise of the HIV cure, that excitedly chirped about this "development" without attaching the caveats so necessary to understanding the true meaning of the story.* It is these media groups that utilize television, and to a smaller but ever-increasing extent the Internet, as their principal means to reach consumers on which I will focus my attention in this chapter, and it is the main group to which I refer when I say "media."

---

* I note that the *New York Times* never ran a story on the Berlin patient of 2010 (they did actually feature a longer piece on the *first* Berlin patient more than ten years before). They briefly included a link to a Reuters new piece reporting the HIV cure, but within a day the link had vanished. Apparently some health editor at the *NYT* understood this development for the nonstory that it was: an item of scientific curiosity for physicians and scientists who study and treat HIV, but one that didn't translate to anything useful for the public to know. One day I would like to meet that editor and hug them.

Before I proceed with itemizing some of the methods by which the media fails to incorporate uncertainty, let me explain the story of the Berlin patient. The physiology of it is quite remarkable, and Brown's team in Germany performed a very nifty scientific trick for which they deserve only praise. But, in addition to the science, I also want to describe the *medicine* of Brown's cure. That was hardly commented on during the media deluge of late 2010, and it's just as important as the science to understand his medical odyssey.

Like all viruses, HIV needs to enter human cells, where it uses the cell's machinery to produce many copies of itself and thus spread to another host. Each virus is specific for the kind of cell it will infect: hepatitis viruses infect liver cells, the rabies virus infects neurons, and so on. The HIV virus infects a special kind of immune cell known as the CD4 cell. The CD4 cell can be thought of as a "central commander" for the immune system; without it to send signals to other cells, the overall organization of the immune system collapses to a great extent. People who die from AIDS don't die from the direct effects of the virus, but rather from the infections that result from a nonfunctional immune system.

The molecular biology of how and why these viruses are matched with specific cells is complicated, but one essential point is that cells are coated with large molecules known as receptors, and different cells have different receptors based on their function as well as their need to communicate with other cells by sending and receiving molecular messages that utilize these receptors. The surfaces of viruses are likewise coated with proteins matching these cell-specific receptors. Think of it as a lock-and-key way of gaining entry inside a cell: if you want to communicate with a particular cell, you must have the key to gain access. Through evolution, viruses have "stolen" a key to gain entry to cells.

In the case of HIV, *two* keys to two different cell receptors are required for entrance: the CD4 protein itself and a second protein known as CCR5. It turns out that a very small number of people have a mutation in their DNA that changes the shape of the CCR5 protein. Thus, the lock no longer fits the key held by HIV, and HIV cannot enter CD4 cells, so these people are immune to HIV infection. Therefore, if HIV-infected people could have all of their infected CD4 cells removed and be replaced by

CD4 cells with the mutation that prevents infection, they could in theory become virus-free altogether.

Normally, this opportunity doesn't present itself. The only way to remove someone's CD4 cells and replace them with a different set is by doing a bone marrow transplant. In the case of Timothy Ray Brown, he had developed leukemia, the treatment for which *is* a bone marrow transplant. His doctors in Germany thought that he would be an ideal person to test the theory that infusing someone with another's immune system containing HIV-resistant CD4 cells might result in a cure, not only for the leukemia but for the HIV as well. Thus far, they have been right, and Mr. Brown has shown no traces of the virus following his successful transplant.

It's a pretty amazing story, and the biology used to make it happen is awe inspiring. For Mr. Brown, it has unquestionably been a life-altering event. But there are some details about the process that make its relevance highly unlikely for almost all other HIV-infected patients. These details were almost completely ignored in the tempest that accompanied the publicity surrounding his cure.

First, a bone marrow transplant is a *very* risky procedure with a high mortality rate. The survival data for these kinds of procedures vary based on the age of the patient, the type of disease being treated, how closely genetically related the donor is, as well as other factors, but a reasonable estimate is that a patient has a 15–30 percent chance of dying within the first year of a bone marrow transplant. The only reason we resort to such a brutal procedure is because the alternative—chemotherapy, usually, or perhaps holy water—is much less successful. These transplants typically require weeks of hospitalization during which the patient becomes extremely ill while the new immune system orients itself.

Second, even if one survives, a bone marrow transplant almost always comes with some kind of treatment complication. Among the most feared is something known as the "graft versus host disease," where the transplanted immune system "sees" its new home as a completely foreign landscape, in effect assuming that it is surrounded by infectious organisms, and therefore reacts by mounting a massive inflammatory response. People suffering from graft versus host can develop skin rashes, mouth ulcers, severe abdominal pain, and liver failure. To counter this, patients must take immune suppressants, which have their own side effects often as unpleasant as graft versus host disease. Some patients do well, but it's by no means a guarantee.

Third, even if a bone marrow transplant were a simple matter, there really are very few people in the world who have this genetic mutation to serve as donors for HIV patients. Northern Europeans appear to have the mutation in greatest proportion, but even then it's only about 10 percent of that population. Fewer still have the mutations in *both* genes (one mutation from the mother's chromosome and one from the father's), and this small group constitutes the only people who can be acceptable donors for this attempted cure.

If an HIV patient was willing to run the gauntlet of a bone marrow transplant, and happened to be lucky enough to find a more-or-less genetically matched donor who had the mutation preventing HIV attachment through the CCR5 receptor, it *still* might not be enough to be cured of the infection. Some strains of HIV don't even use the CCR5 receptor but gain entry using a different surface molecule, which means that patients might have their HIV come roaring back even *if* all the technical and medical obstacles were easily surmountable. Amazingly, Brown carried both types of virus. In theory, the second type of virus should have been able to start a new chain of reinfection, but, for reasons poorly understood, it didn't. Unfortunately, that's no guarantee that it wouldn't happen to the next person.

Thus, in short, Timothy Ray Brown was a medical arrow hitting a bull's eye shot by doctors hundreds of meters from the target in the midst of a windstorm. He was amazingly lucky. It's not likely to work for more than a few people in the coming decade or two; in the meantime, there are 30 *million* people infected, some of whom weren't given this additional explanation when the story came to light. If they feel cheated, they have a right to.

The Medical Manufactroversy

The story of Timothy Ray Brown's HIV cure highlights the problems that arise when the media uses one person's story to exemplify a much larger medical issue. The enormous publicity over his medical odyssey illustrates how medicine can become oversold, where the story of the one (he was cured) fails to stand in for the many (there is no cure for HIV right now). It doesn't have to be this way, of course, as there are millions of people living with HIV whose stories *could* represent the current reality of the disease—a reality that is a complicated amalgam of tremendous scientific achievement and the daily grind of dealing with taking meds and living with their side effects. When Timothy Ray Brown was morphed into The Berlin Patient by starry-eyed reporters, the media made medicine look *too* good as part of its insatiable need for eye-grabbing headlines. Reporters wanted to pretend uncertainty was utterly absent in his story—*of course* he was going to want this treatment; wouldn't *everyone?* Why, what could possibly be the downsides?

This is what an acknowledgment of uncertainty brings: that there might in fact be legitimate downsides, and that a happy outcome is in doubt. Such information might have allowed consumers of the story of The Berlin Patient to navigate themselves to a different place on the spectrum of certainty—that is, closer to the middle—than where the reporters wanted to believe it to be.

That same principle can be applied by the media to make medicine seem *worse* than it is as well. One person's medical nightmare may or may not indicate a troubling flaw in the medical system, and although an individual's story is a valuable tool in drawing readers and viewers into a news piece, the proof of the trouble relies upon journalism that is thorough in its research and careful in its explanations. When those explanations are absent, the horror story can be ginned up to hint at a grave problem in medicine, implying a raging debate among physicians and researchers about the proper course of action, when in fact no real debate exists and there is almost total consensus by the medical community about the right thing to do.

This deliberate construction of a controversy that does not, in fact, exist—brilliantly dubbed "manufactroversy" by Professor Leah Ceccarelli of the University of Washington—can of course apply to any story. (We have already seen one such noncontroversy in the form of the pseudodebate about Lyme disease.) The quality that defines medical manufactroversies is the heavy reliance on this medical synecdoche, where one person's travails serve as a stand-in for the larger picture, and viewers are encouraged to conclude that the singular story represents a common state of affairs with respect to a treatment, a public health policy, and so on.

No subject better defines the medical manufactroversy than the question of vaccine safety and effectiveness. As explained by journalist Seth Mnookin in his excellent book *The Panic Virus,* the public discourse about vaccines has been so dominated by fringe opinions, even highly sophisticated news consumers believe there is sharp disagreement among experts about the dangers of vaccines, when in reality vaccines are one of the few areas in medicine in which there is almost universal consensus with respect to its considerable benefits at the cost of vanishingly low side effects. No serious doctor or nurse, epidemiologist, or public health official who has studied the subject of vaccines thinks they are a source of grave caution.

How has the value of vaccines become so misunderstood by the public? The scare story is one of the principal mechanisms, and one of the finest—or worst, one supposes—examples can be found in a recent TV show devoted to the controversies surrounding one vaccine. The vaccine in question was one of the newest on the block: Gardasil, the vaccine against particular strains of the human papilloma virus. Ironically, the show was hosted by Katie Couric, one of the most well-respected mainstream journalists in the United States, especially when the subject of health care is concerned. There is even a double heaping of irony here, because Gardasil's value comes from preventing cancer, and Couric as a journalist has a special relationship to that disease.

Couric's history with cancer coverage began with the heartbreaking loss of her husband to colon cancer at age forty-two. Following his death, she assumed an activist stance toward colon cancer, using her considerable journalistic muscle at the *Today* show to promote cancer screening awareness. She underwent an on-air colonoscopy in 2000, and the number of colonoscopies in the United States was estimated to have increased by 20 percent the rest of that year following the episode. In 2005 she underwent a mammogram as part of Breast Cancer Awareness Month. She cofounded the group Stand Up to Cancer, whose aim is to provide grants to mainstream scientists focused on innovative research and has thus far raised more than $200 million. Her advocacy for cancer research and public health measures such as screening—no controversies were in evidence as part of this journalism—won her the Award for Distinguished Public Service by the American Association for Cancer Research in 2013. It was harder to find a journalist friendlier to the cause of cancer eradication than Couric. So it must have come as a surprise to the cancer research establishment later that year when Couric, who by then had become the host of an afternoon talk show called *Katie,* decided to air a segment titled "The HPV Vaccine Controversy."

It was surprising principally because there *was* no controversy, at least among public health officials. HPV is a sexually transmitted virus with dozens of strains. Four of these strains are associated with the majority of cases of cervical cancer; having immunity to these cancer-causing strains should reduce the total number of cervical cancer cases, and Gardasil works by providing this immunity. HPV is also associated with other genital cancers as well as genital warts, and a vaccine rollout should reduce the incidence of these diseases as well. Gardasil is well tolerated; a study of nearly 300,000 young women from Sweden published in the *British Medical Journal* in 2013 found no serious adverse events associated with its administration. So there was fairly strong consensus that this was a big step forward in the field of cervical cancer. There simply wasn't a raging debate going on among specialists.

What *is* controversial, however, is teen sex, and the recommendations are to provide vaccination for HPV at age eleven or twelve, prior to the onset of presumed sexual activity in mid- to late teen years by many or even most kids. That recommendation has angered socially conservative groups who believe premarital sex is morally abhorrent, and further believe the recommendation for HPV vaccination *encourages* such behavior. (No evidence has ever supported this claim.) These groups have found allies with antivaxxers, and the rollout of the vaccine has generated a backlash against Gardasil and its maker, Merck, as well as GlaxoSmithKline, the maker of another HPV vaccine called Cervarix, which is likewise accepted by the CDC and other professional groups as part of the recommended vaccinations. Regardless of the social policy discussion, in terms of the risk-to-benefit analysis, the HPV vaccine was a slam dunk.

Because there was no actual scientific controversy, Couric was obligated to spin a tale of an indifferent scientific medical establishment that was paying no attention to the bodies accumulating outside the clinic door. The centerpiece of the *Katie* episode featured Lauren Mathis, who claimed that Gardasil nearly killed her. Her story is the mirror image of Timothy Ray Brown's: a medical dystopia in which ignorant doctors push her, jab by jab, toward death. Lauren's story, and that of another girl named Christina Tarsell whose mother claimed Gardasil *had* killed her, were given the lion's share of time. Toward the end, about three minutes were set aside for a pediatrician from Massachusetts General Hospital, Dr. Mallika Marshall, to try to counter the claims that the *Katie* episode had so clearly accepted at face value. Dr. Marshall's eloquence and poise notwithstanding, it was largely a failure because the millions of viewers who had tuned in throughout the segment would no doubt have already concluded that Gardisil unleashes horrors aplenty. Indeed, given the over-all tenor of *Katie*'s teach-the-controversy approach, Marshall's presence simply allowed the producers of the show to provide window dressing to the notion that the show was somehow being objective and representing "both sides of the debate."

Why can we be so certain that HPV vaccination is safe, and that Katie Couric not only misrepresented all the reliable evidence about its effectiveness, but essentially thrust a set of nonsensical claims at a credulous public, aimed directly at her afternoon TV-watching demographic group, with the apparent intent to stop moms from vaccinating their kids for HPV? Why should we think that her skepticism should have been applied at least with equal, if not more, force to the claims of these two mothers than to the vaccine manufacturers and the public health officials who work with them?* What evidence allows us to conclude that she used the

---

* In asking this question, I don't mean to imply that skepticism *isn't* warranted for public health officials or drug manufacturers or doctors at prestigious academic institutions. The problem with the *Katie* episode on HPV vaccines, and other report-age in this vein, is that the skepticism being applied to "the establishment" is totally out of proportion to the existing data indicating that "the establishment" got this one right. She allowed the accusations of HPV harm by her guests to stand without even the slightest inclination to signal to her audience that they might want to treat those accusations with some caution. Therefore, in the unspoken logic of the show, if these claims are good enough for Katie, why shouldn't they be good enough to persuade a member of the audience?

uncertainty inherent in claims of vaccine safety into a counterproductive exercise in sophistry?

Before I answer those questions, I should return to the idea of the spectrum of certainty. As I will show, HPV vaccination is a practice whose value is not completely at the far, positive end of the spectrum of certainty, but that's mainly because we have yet to count in reality how many lives have been saved from preventing cervical cancer, which will take some time to do, as cervical cancer takes decades to manifest itself. Yet, as we will see, the risks of HPV vaccination are negligible, so even *potential* but not quite fully proven benefits, at the cost of vanishingly small risk, move us away from the absolute middle of the spectrum.

The answers to the questions above can be found in a variety of places, but a good example of how data is misunderstood by people who have already reached their desired conclusion can be found in a national database known as the Vaccine Adverse Events Reporting System, or VAERS. Some of the key claims made by HPV antivax groups rely heavily on data from VAERS, and, at first blush, the evidence they marshal would appear to be damning, especially because VAERS is a database not run by some antiestablishment alternative medicine group, but by the US federal government itself, in a joint effort of the CDC and the FDA. In the case of HPV, those hostile to the vaccine cite VAERS data indicating that, by the end of 2013, nearly *25,000* adverse events were associated with the vaccine, which included an even more shocking number of approximately *one hundred* deaths (the number can vary depending on the source). Why won't public health authorities sound the alarm, or even recognize the threat, of a vaccine that kills so many?

To appreciate the answer, one must have a nodding familiarity not only with the guts of the VAERS system, but also with the process by which a drug or vaccine receives approval from the FDA. In the vast majority of cases, a so-called Phase III study is required of manufacturers to demonstrate that whatever they propose to bring to market is not only reasonably safe but also that it is effective at doing whatever the manufacturer claims it can do. In the case of Gardasil, that meant that Merck had to enroll nearly 12,000 young women, provide the vaccine, and follow them for three full years, during which time Merck repeatedly evaluated them to see what side effects they might have suffered from and whether the vaccine prevented the condition of cervical intraepithelial neoplasia—the forerunner to cervical cancer. Those results, which did indeed show that the vaccine prevented a significant number of cases of this protocancer, were published in the *New England Journal of Medicine* in 2007.

The safety of Gardasil was also studied in this paper, and the results have direct bearing on how one can interpret the VAERS data. Of the roughly 6,000 women in the vaccine arm of the trial, there were forty-five "serious adverse events"—the kind that would reflect the sort of data seen in VAERS. But because a Phase III study performed for FDA approval is very carefully controlled, there is an *equal* arm of subjects who *don't* get the actual vaccine (they receive a dose of fluid lacking the virus-like particle that produces immunity, essentially getting saltwater). Therefore the researchers were able to look at the number of serious adverse events in *that* group as well. Because unusual and serious illnesses can occur in a small number of people at random, and because Merck was following 12,000 women for three full years, the placebo arm allowed them to compare the total number of serious adverse events between the groups.

Similar to the vaccine group, the number of serious adverse events in the placebo group was fifty-four. In raw numbers, this amounted to a *higher* percentage of cases, but in terms of statistical analysis, it was well within the range that one would expect random variation if a small number of serious medical problems were randomly distributed between two groups—that is, forty-five versus fifty-four is different, but not *so* different when the total number of each group is 12,000, and is probably due to pure chance. The lack of significant difference meant two things: first, because there was no evidence of *additional* harm in the vaccine arm, it almost certainly meant it was a very safe vaccine; second, not only were there an equal number of serious adverse events in both groups, it was also a *very* small number of people who had such problems. That is what one would expect when following a cohort of thousands of young women for three years. The vast majority of them will be fine, but a very small percentage will have something terrible—and even inexplicable—happen to them, whether they received a vaccine, took a pill, worked a particular kind of job, lived in a certain place, or any number of other factors that could in theory be measured.

The Phase III trial is about as carefully constructed a scientific experiment as can be done on large numbers of humans, and the data that is produced is significantly more reliable than that produced by other ways of investigating the benefits and harms of a drug or vaccine. We saw this in the previous chapter when we looked at how hormone replacement therapy *seemed* to be a wonder drug when analyzed through the lens of other kinds of studies; when various Phase III–type trials were done and the numbers between those treated and those not were compared, those medications not only didn't achieve the benefits everyone was so certain would be there, but they actually came with a small amount of harm. Viewed in this light, the evidence of the overall safety of Gardasil and Cervarix (whose Phase III trial included 18,000 subjects followed over the same time) was about as good as it could get.

Compared to the data generated in a Phase III trial, the VAERS database so frequently invoked in the pseudodebate about HPV vaccination is a different beast altogether. VAERS is a component of the regulatory oversight of medications and vaccines *after* they have been approved, known as postmarketing surveillance. The means by which data gets entered into VAERS bears no resemblance to the strict rules of evidence required of drug companies performing Phase III trials. *Anyone* can file a report to the VAERS database, at *any* time, regardless of when the vaccine was administered.* The database makes no judgment as to which claims might raise genuine concern for vaccine safety because no supporting evidence is required to link the timing of the vaccine to the reported symptoms. Moreover, there is no control group that can be used for purposes of comparison. In the words of one medical scientist who blogs under the name of Orac, VAERS is the medical database equivalent of an unmoderated Internet discussion board, where pretty much anything goes. The hope, as the VAERS website itself notes, is that the system can be used to enable "the early detection of signals that can then be more rigorously investigated." In other words,

---

* More than two-thirds of VAERS reports are entered by vaccine manufacturers themselves as well as health-care providers. The remainder come from a variety of sources including state immunization programs and the vaccine recipients themselves, the latter group accounting for about 10 percent of total reports.

the CDC and FDA do *not* believe that it should be used as a source of reliable information *in its pure, raw form.*

Reviewing a specific report in VAERS allows us to see how it actually works. Let's look at the brief story of case number 29281 from the 2013 VAERS report, which is freely available to anyone wishing to download it, because it serves as a reasonably good example of the difficulties interpreting this database. Because this is already public information, and because we do not know who this person is, I haven't altered any details here. The report, submitted in late December of that year, describes a young woman whose life had gone awry in the back half of her high school years, and whoever wrote the report—the use of "we" below could indicate a parent was the author—overtly links this decline to Gardasil:

> Patient got the first Gardasil shot 7-25-12, the second 9/26/12, and the third shot 1/28/13. Im not sure the exact onset date except to say she got the second and third shot during her junior year in high school and she was continually telling me how fatigued, tired, dizzy, light headed and tired she was. She also had continued to complain about her heart racing, short of breath, heart pains, sleeping difficulty, chest pain, rib pain under her breast, brain fog, headaches, back aches, stomach pain, limb heaviness, neck pain random pains everywhere, seeing different shapes and colors in her vision, severe hip pain, electrical shock pain, and numerous other pains. In Aug 2013 (the beginning of her Senior year in high school) she was walking slowly like she had rode a horse to long, Sept 2013 she needed a walker because she was starting to trip and had trouble standing, Oct 2013 she had to use a wheelchair and unable to walk by herself. We have had MRI, bone scans, CT scans, xrays and numerous bloodwork [*sic*].

What's going on here? It's very difficult to know. We can make a reasonable guess that this young woman has become the victim of a tragic neurologic disorder, but the precise diagnosis cannot be divined from this snippet. Whether this is due to an oversight on the part of an evaluating physician or the manner in which the patient has attempted to obtain a diagnosis (are all these tests from the emergency room, for instance?), we have no idea. Could this be multiple sclerosis, a rare but not unheard-of condition in teenage girls? If it is—in fact, *regardless* of what it is—there is no way to know from the report whether her condition is a *consequence* of receiving the vaccine. This is another version of the correlation/causation problem we saw in the previous chapter.

We also cannot know whether this report is an instance in cognitive bias, because perhaps the author has been psychologically primed to link the two events in a similar manner to that of the psychiatrists of the Rosenhan experiment we witnessed in the first chapter, who themselves linked harmless neurologic phenomena to deep psychiatric illness. Had the author just watched the *Katie* episode, and under the power of the dark suggestions from the show, or even by encouragement from friends who had seen the show and planted the idea, suddenly and belatedly "realized" that the patient had received Gardasil a few months before the onset of her symptoms?* If so, can this really be considered reliable data?

At the time case number 29281 was entered in the database, more than *10 million* girls and boys had received the vaccine. Whenever you do *anything* to 10 million people—just give them a glass of water—*some* of those people will develop strange medical symptoms, and an even smaller subset will develop serious medical problems. That's because they were going to develop them anyway, so the default assumption that a report like 29281's implies causation indicates a deeply naïve view of the VAERS data.

Despite this, virtually all of the literature put out by groups opposed to the HPV vaccine, whether online or on paper, trumpets the number of serious adverse events, and deaths, in the VAERS database as proof of the giant cover-up perpetrated on an unsuspecting public.

None of this was discussed in the *Katie* episode. There simply wasn't enough time for it because all the oxygen available was devoted to two horror stories by mothers who are convinced of the vaccine's evils, data analysis be damned. Given her powerful platform, and the fact that she brought major credibility to the subject of cancer reporting, Couric could have taken a chance to use her program to ask a simple question on her audience's behalf: *How do we know when a vaccine is associated with*

---

* The episode aired December 4, and the report was filed December 29.

harms? Surely she and her producers were aware of the rumors about HPV vaccination that were circulating among the kinds of people likely to tune into her show. They were probably likewise aware that this demographic was increasingly suspicious of the HPV vaccine, a fact that Katie Couric herself in all likelihood realized was due to pseudoscientific misinformation of the kind illustrated by the VAERS story. She *could* have used the opportunity to explain why the theory that HPV vaccination is dangerous is almost certainly nonsense, but she didn't, going all in for an approach celebrating credulousness and making a virtue of misrepresentation, an exercise in Kool-Aid consumption that had all the appearance of a desperate grab for the approval of a viewing audience different in nature from those who so admired her during her stint at *Today.*

Backlash

As a testament to the perceived influence of a show like *Katie,* an eruption of criticism ensued within hours of the show's airing, and the episode itself became a news story in its own right. Whether it was the kind of publicity the producers of *Katie* were seeking is unclear, but the mainstream media coverage wasn't favorable, as the (entirely justifiable) story line became "Couric does irresponsible journalism." A CBS news story written the following day documented the consensus opinion that Couric had engaged in innuendo of the worst sort. It quoted bioethicist Arthur Caplan, whose thoughts were representative: "The show was kind of inexcusable in terms of damage done. . . . [T]he problem in TV and all media, [is that] human interest drives the story. In science and public health, it doesn't."

Indeed, this CBS article serves as a decent template for what media stories about health *should* be. Anyone unfamiliar with the kerfuffle over HPV vaccination would read the article and conclude that it was, at least, safe, and at most, safe *and* effective. Moreover, the reader would be aware that there is a database that tracks adverse events from vaccination, but that most of these adverse events are minor. It never mentions deaths reported in the VAERS system because such reports cannot be trusted to indicate that the death is attributable to the vaccine, because that isn't what VAERS is designed to do. The five minutes it takes to read the CBS news piece was considerably more valuable to an uneducated consumer than the thirty minutes that were devoted to the topic on *Katie*.

A mildly chastened Couric issued a not-quite-apology the following week in an online editorial for the *Huffington Post*. In the editorial, she acknowledged that she might have been more careful in exploring the subject. "Following the show . . . there was criticism that the program was too anti-vaccine and anti-science, and in retrospect, some of that criticism was valid," she wrote. This had the appearance of contrition, but like everything else attached to the *Katie* HPV episode, it was mere show, not least because essentially *all* of the criticism levied at her following the show was valid. After backtracking for a few paragraphs with almost mea culpas, she plunged back into the pseudoscience that got her into trouble in the first place, even invoking the very VAERS data that serves as a primary weapon in the antivax arsenal of misrepresentation.

Couric, in fact, was so untroubled by the whole dustup that she let the video segment that was the object of much of the criticism stand on the *Katie* website. Because this would be a strange action to take for someone who was earnest in trying to create a more "balanced" picture of the safety of HPV vaccines, it is hard not to conclude that Couric was trying to have her cake and eat it, too, by pacifying critics with theoretical apologies at the *Huffington Post* website while simultaneously perpetuating the anti-intellectual claims on her own. "IS THE HPV VACCINE SAFE?" her web page asked in large all-caps lettering. The logic implicit in asking such a question is that the answer is in doubt, because if it really *was* a remarkably safe vaccine, it wouldn't make any sense to ask the question at all. During the remainder of *Katie*'s TV run, none of this was retracted or even altered. The *Katie* website did include the CDC recommendations, as well as the segment where Dr. Marshall "defends" the vaccine, but by leaving all the misdirection to stand at her website, Couric effectively conceded that she had no real interest in doing anything other than pandering on this topic.*

---

* The final *Katie* episode aired on June 9, 2014. The show's website, as I complete revisions in mid-2015, is no longer available on a basic Internet search. Clips of this *Katie* episode are still available on YouTube as of June 2015, and in Orac's blog posts on the matter, the links for which can be found in the bibliography.

Fear, by the Numbers

The *Katie* "HPV Controversy" episode is only a highly egregious instance of a broader motif at work in health-care coverage. If the story of a single person is carefully selected and really does highlight some kind of broader trend in medicine, then of course such an illness narrative is a powerful tool; when a narrative is pulled out of context and thrust on a frequently distracted public, as exemplified by the guests on *Katie,* there is a potential for real harm. Yet one doesn't have to watch a poorly executed half-hour segment bordering on propaganda to get a distorted view of the real threats one faces and what one should do about it. All one has do to is watch the nightly health segments on television or look at their online equivalents.

Death, of course, is scary, and in a world of 7 billion people there is *always* someone dying somewhere of something particularly scary. Infectious disease doctors and epidemiologists have a website known as ProMED that takes advantage of the instantaneous worldwide communication provided by the Internet, and it is used to monitor various worldwide outbreaks at any given moment in time so that appropriate public health resources can be brought to bear to contain serious outbreaks. Dozens of reports of deaths at the hands of the witches' brew of the world's microorganisms come filtering in every day: brucellosis, avian influenza, Rocky Mountain spotted fever, Hantavirus, dengue, and a host of other maladies make routine appearances on the ProMED list. Reading it, especially for the first time, requires a certain steeliness of spirit. If you knew all of the ways you could die from exotic infections on a daily basis, you'd stay in bed all day with the sheets over your head and only come out for an occasional cup of soup.

But as a matter of statistics, you *aren't* going to die from these infections, and the reason ProMED is an important tool for doctors looking at disease patterns but not for ordinary people living their lives is because there is an absolute lack of context with respect to these reports. The steady stream of death that flicks across the ProMED page does not ruin the lives of the professionals reviewing that data because they traffic in such matters on a daily basis and can read these reports with the much-needed context already hardwired into their brains. Yet mainstream media news reports of rare deaths from unusual viruses and bacteria almost never are accompanied by such context to help laypeople make sense of it. The consequence of that lack of context is fear, and because of that fear people overestimate remote threats and vastly underestimate real ones.

As I write this book in 2014, there is a low rumble about a nasty infection that has been given the tongue-swallowing name of Middle Eastern respiratory syndrome coronavirus—MERS-CoV, or just MERS.* From its discovery in 2012 to the early months of 2014, MERS has killed about sixty people. A lot of press has been devoted to MERS, and many of these reports have dutifully noted that it bears a close relationship to another notorious virus, SARS, which had captured the world's attention in 2003 as part of a global outbreak that killed as many as eight hundred people, perhaps more. SARS became part of an elite group of viruses that are well known to laypeople despite being remarkably rare. In addition to SARS, people who have only a passing knowledge of health topics are aware of avian influenza, the Marburg virus, Eastern equine encephalitis, and probably the all-time scary virus champ, Ebola—whose notoriety likely not only derives from its high mortality rate, but from the fact that it comes from deep within sub-Saharan Africa, a region over which people from developed nations still have considerable anxiety and guilt.†

Could MERS become a real-life Andromeda strain? Yes, it's certainly possible. Of all the scary viruses that have become objects of media fixation in the past few decades, only SARS has all the necessary ingredients to cripple the health infrastructure of every country on earth: it is lethal, it moves quickly, and it is airborne, easily passed from person to

---

* I wrote most of this chapter in the spring of 2014, before the largest Ebola outbreak in history had truly erupted and dominated world health news stories. I am willing to wager that MERS has largely been forgotten by most people who expressed deep reservations about allowing flights from Saudi Arabia to enter US airspace only a few months ago.

† And I finish the *revisions* on this chapter as the Ebola epidemic is winding down (but not yet extinguished) in summer 2015 while MERS has erupted in Southeast Asia and is once again dominating health news headlines. So I leave these bookend footnotes in place because who knows what will be the Terrifying Virus of early 2016.

person and therefore able to outstrip even the best quarantine procedures.* MERS exhibits the same basic biological features as SARS and indeed is a member of the same phylogenetic group, the Coronaviruses, so it's plausible to assume that it could wreak havoc on civilization.

Yet one could just as easily endlessly fret over equally catastrophic threats to the world. We could include monthly news stories about how close we periodically come to nuclear annihilation (or at least what would happen if a rogue political group got hold of just one); we could publish stories of asteroid strikes, noting that, had some been just a little bigger and in a more metropolitan area, hundreds of thousands of lives might have been threatened. These are very real dangers that we face, but they are equally difficult to quantify. The media obsession with magnifying these threats on a constant basis leads to what Marc Siegel, a physician and writer, has dubbed "the epidemic of fear."†

The downstream effect of medical panic is that, because we can't really do anything at all to prevent a cataclysm like a MERS pandemic, we become more passive about the kind of *actual* threats that can be found in our everyday existence. "Influenza" is a word, when it is shorn of its terror-inducing modifiers "avian" or "swine," that people often assume is the equivalent of a bad cold. Yet influenza is a *killer*: since 1976, when the CDC began systematically tallying influenza mortality, the estimated number of annual deaths from the flu has ranged from about 3,000 to 50,000, with a typical year resulting in about 25,000 deaths. One can actually *do* something to prevent influenza in the form of getting the annual flu vaccine. The flu vaccine doesn't provide 100 percent protection (estimates hover in the 60 percent range), but it is effective and

---

* For instance, Ebola and Marburg, which are passed through blood and other body fluids, have thus far not developed into lethal airborne mutants. The Ebola Reston virus *is* airborne but lethal only to nonhuman primates. It was the subject of Richard Preston's bestseller *The Hot Zone* and formed the basis of the movie *Outbreak*, starring Dustin Hoffman. Although it was not "news" by any literal definition, movies such as *Outbreak* and their nonfiction counterparts like *The Hot Zone* become the narrative backdrop against which real outbreak stories such as the current MERS-CoV reports are interpreted by laypeople, or even specialists for that matter.

† The irony of Siegel's professional life is that he serves as a senior medical contributor at *Fox News,* given that Fox has arguably done more than any other powerful media outlet at exploiting fear.

unquestionably prevents morbidity and mortality. Yet our national vaccination rate among adults runs about 40–45 percent. The only good news is that nearly two-thirds of adults most at risk for the worst ravages of influenza, those over sixty-five, are vaccinated annually; the very bad news is that among equally at-risk "near-seniors" in the fifty to sixty-four age range, fewer than half get vaccinated. Given that the only effective action one can take in the face of the rare but lethal MERS agent is to buy Depends undergarments and pee one's pants, it seems a waste not to get a vaccination for something that can legitimately be prevented.

The overemphasis on reporting rare and scary diseases also has the effect of inuring the public to the real threats that we face every day. A death toll of 25,000 from influenza in one year is big, but it doesn't hold a candle to the true killers in an industrialized country like the United States. In any given year for the past generation or so, about 2.5 million people die. One of every four of those deaths is due to heart disease. When diseases such as diabetes and strokes are taken into account, about one in three Americans dies from such pathology. Similar figures hold for other developed countries. Although the causes of these diseases are multifactorial, the science is well established that a low-fat, low-calorie diet, along with routine, vigorous exercise, have a dramatic effect on lowering the incidence of vascular disease. Would you like a news story about an epidemic? Would there be nonstop coverage if a new virus killed even a fraction of the percentage of people who die from cardiovascular disease in one year?

Yet this *is* an epidemic. Call it a virus, too—the "too much fat, not enough exercise virus" if you wish. But a casual observer of the news would be forgiven for failing to appreciate the gravity of the danger, that signal being buried in the noise of reports of frightening but trivial threats.

Indeed, it is even possible that some people might conclude that exercise *itself* could be dangerous, taking a bad problem and making it even worse. In the summer of 2013—at the precise time of year when people should be maximally motivated to get outside and put their muscles to aerobic activity—the *New York Times* published an article about a health study of Swedish cross-country skiers with the remarkable headline "Can You Get Too Much Exercise?" The article went on to describe a study indicating that these Swedish marvels of aerobic activity, who participated in an annual fifty-six-mile cross-country ski event, were *slightly* more likely to be hospitalized if they participated in more of these races. It was, in fact, a very small effect. Moreover, the comparison group wasn't a cohort of people who sat around munching Cheetos or their Swedish equivalent while living a sedentary life; it was the other racers themselves, making exercise-versus-lack-of-exercise comparisons useless.

Normally an excellent source of news for health issues, the *Times* tried to be a little too cute by asking this question and by reporting on the results, even with a fairly long, detailed discussion that followed the explanation of the study. Because one would normally assume that the answer to the question *Can you get too much exercise?* would be no, people who perused the Health section's titles without diving into the particulars might be forgiven for concluding that exercise wasn't all that it was cracked up to be. Perhaps for Swedes pushing themselves to the absolute limit of endurance, that could be true, but, for the rest of us, there is simply no question that we exercise far too little. That mainstream media health news does not treat cardiovascular disease as the single most important, most lethal, and yes, *scariest* epidemic of our time is evidence of the skewed perceptions of what constitutes danger in our lives. Can you be certain that you will die of a heart attack? No, but you can be as certain as one can that if you eat and laze yourself into diabetes, you stand a much higher risk of it than if you exercise and lay off the Big Macs with large fries washed down with thirty-ounce sodas.

Caveats and Silence

What I've tried to demonstrate thus far are three major mechanisms by which the media obscures the importance of this simple health advice, and each of these mechanisms is related to either discounting or overemphasizing uncertainty, often doing so through inappropriate anecdotes. The case of the Berlin patient demonstrates a situation in which there is *too much* certainty of a new therapy's promise; the vast majority of experimental therapies of the kind that Timothy Ray Brown endured never pan out, and, by not attaching this critical qualification, news consumers (especially casual ones) overestimate the genuine promise of cutting-edge medicine. The *Katie* HPV vaccine debacle is an instance of portraying medicine as being far more *uncertain* than it really is, using a single person's story to trump a large amount of data that all points toward the benefits of a given therapy, all the while hiding behind the fig leaf of logic that one can't prove a negative. And the stories about the respiratory virus known MERS display how the media can lead people to do what former President Bush called "misunderestimation" in this case of the real risks that we face in life.

There is a fourth path by which uncertainty gets warped in far too many media articles. This relates to the language used by journalists when they describe medical research, and the impression that can be created by such language. For instance, perhaps the two most pernicious phrases in medical journalism are "researchers have found" and "doctors have discovered." Those words "found" and "discovered" give the impression that whatever they found or discovered was unassailably, incontrovertibly *there,* like a new species of Amazonian bird or a new set of hominid bones unearthed in Olduvai Gorge. They imply that physicians and human researchers are looking at the world *exactly as it exists.* A more precise analogy is that we are looking at the world through cracked, warped, and foggy glass: there is some external reality out there, but getting at that reality is sometimes difficult, and all of our speculations should be regarded with skepticism.

How do articles utilize the wrong language, besides applying these two blanket phrases? In many cases, the wrong language is simply no language at all. By failing to mention caveats to research—and all research has caveats—too many of the health news stories create misperceptions among their readers. Medical scientific research is, in fact, a daily exercise in uncertainty. Investigators make their living by staring at streaked gels, trying to divine whether those streaks indicate an underlying reality. Bench research routinely leads scientists into blind alleys, and clinical research often is accompanied by about-faces where one study will show something to be beneficial, only to have that study contradicted by a trial a year or two later. This portrayal of smart people walking around laboratories with large question marks above their heads is often absent in health reporting. Every new paper that a medical center trumpets with a press release is accompanied by the aura of inevitable certainty, researchers being portrayed as a Bringers of Truth to the world rather than people who think they might be on to something, with a partial shrug of the shoulder.

Gary Schwitzer, as a website devoted to his work notes, has specialized in health-care journalism involving radio, television, and the Internet in a career spanning four decades. Perhaps more than any other person in the United States, Gary thinks about the lack of caveats in health news reporting, the silent gaps in health stories that lead people to the wrong conclusions about the current state of health care. He should be as famous as Sanjay Gupta; instead, he is little known outside a small group of health-care professionals and media types. He is the embodiment of media skepticism, coming at his work from an insider's perspective, arguing about what *could be* instead of what currently *is,* and doing so by knowing intimately what changes really are possible and offering concrete solutions for doing so.

In 2006, Schwitzer founded HealthNewsReview.org, a website devoted to, as it says, "improving the dialogue about health care by helping consumers critically analyze claims about health care interventions and by promoting the principles of shared decision-making reinforced by accurate, balanced, and complete information about the tradeoffs involved in health care decisions." Led by Schwitzer, *HealthNewsReview* pooled the talents of nearly thirty health-care professionals ranging from doctors and researchers to writers and reporters and was designed with one basic idea in mind: grade health news stories from one to five stars based on overall quality. The reviewers analyze news stories focusing on ten principal qualities, among them whether it quantifies benefits, explains harms and quantifies those as well, reviews the quality of the evidence, and establishes the novelty of the idea on which the report is based. In a way, those categories can be thought of as an elaboration of the question *How certain can we be that what the story claims to be saying really is true?*

What the reviewers found is that these critical ingredients for context were often missing. A representative sample can be found in a review of an article published in *US News & World Report* in 2007. Titled "To Build a Knee," the article is a poetic paean to the magic of the computerized "motion analysis laboratory" and the role it plays in helping orthopedists decide on what measures to take, up to and including knee replacement, which the article highlights in the best possible terms. "Knee replacement can bring an end to years of crippling pain. 'Ninety-five percent of the people I treat feel much better after having surgery. How great is that?'"

asked Dr. Stephen Haas, the chief of the knee service at the Hospital for Special Surgery in New York City.

This is a classic entry in the category of "good story" on health care, one in which doctors appear to be miracle makers, and their work, the work of angels. *How great is that?* On the one hand, it *is* great, and knee replacement really *can* bring an end to years of crippling pain. But the job of a health news piece is to give context: *When* can surgery have that miraculous effect? Moreover, its job is to include caveats: *How often* do things go wrong? Is Dr. Haas's claim of major improvement in 95 percent of his patients really accurate? Can someone else out there verify that claim? And what happens to the 5 percent who *don't* improve? Do they just not improve, or do they have complications, and if so, what are they? And, by the way, how much does a knee replacement cost?

Answering *those* questions is what good health reports do on a daily basis rather than making medicine sound like an advertisement, and *HealthNewsReview* found this particular news piece wanting. "Total knee replacement is but one treatment that . . . yields often remarkable results," the review noted, echoing the sentiments of the article. Then came the caveat: "Despite its good reputation though, there's more to the operation than this article's glancing overview suggests. For starters, knee replacement is a major surgery with potentially important complications, including blood clots in a leg or lung, infections, and (rarely) death." Of the ten criteria that *HealthNewsReview* uses, one—whether the story appeared to be a rewritten version of a press release—was not considered applicable. Of the remaining nine that were graded, seven were considered to be unsatisfactory and reflect the kinds of concerns raised by my questions above. The reviewers thought that the story did establish the general availability of the procedure and explained its novelty, which is not altogether surprising because the inclusion of these items in the story serves only to portray knee replacement in a good light.

It's not that what *US News & World Report* published was false, but the silence on the caveats ultimately lead to a false impression: *It's safe! It's great! Look at the neat computer lab! Everyone's doing it!* Should patients do due diligence when researching options for chronic knee pain, which includes finding out the answers to the kinds of questions that I've posed? Why yes, of course they should. But isn't that the reason we *have* news organizations like *US News & World Report?* Shouldn't *they* be the first line in helping patients understand the risks and benefits of a treatment? And if the reporters who write puff pieces like "To Build a Knee" *don't* think it's their obligation to include this level of cautionary detail, then whom precisely do they think they're working for?

Not only did Schwitzer and his colleagues take this message to the masses at the website, but he communicated this information to the very professionals being covered by this news. Writing in the scientific journal *PLoS Medicine* in 2008, Schwitzer analyzed five hundred stories that *HealthNewsReview* had evaluated. Using the ten categories, Schwitzer presented data that should be considered alarming by anyone who thinks that patients aren't getting the proper context in health news, well before they've ever stepped foot in a doctor's office to have a discussion. What were the categories most consistently missed? Several of them are those that, when excluded from a news story, can give people warped perceptions about how much uncertainty surrounds the subject, similar to what I have illustrated in this chapter. Only about a third of these articles quantified either benefits or harms, and only a very slightly higher percentage (35 percent) discussed the *quality* of evidence in a medical news story. Only half of the news stories sought independent sources or explored whether the people touting some medical treatment technology had a financial conflict of interest. The categories where news stories did best was exactly the categories the "To Build a Knee" story nailed, and they were also not uncoincidentally the most self-serving: 70 percent of stories highlighted the availability of new medical approaches, and 85 percent of stories established the true novelty of the new approach.

But perhaps the most chilling statistic is that 65 percent of news stories went "beyond a news release." That means that *one out of every three* news stories is just the regurgitated offerings of a public relations department from some university, doctors' office, or drug or device company. It is safe to say that lightly amended versions of press releases generated by these groups aren't going to give consumers critical information that might paint a more nuanced picture of their promise, yet every third story to be found on the major media websites as of the mid-2000s did just this.

When *HealthNewsReview* came bounding onto the scene, it was greeted by the medical and the media establishment in two very different ways.* The first was overwhelming praise. The year the website was launched, it received the Knight-Batten Award for innovations in journalism from the group J-Lab, a center of American University's School of Communication. The following year it received a Mirror Award from Syracuse University's Newhouse School of Public Communications, and a few years later it won the title of Best Medical Blog from the website Medgadget.com. The *Columbia Journalism Review* lauded its mission in a news item in 2011. Among medical scientists, the journal *PLoS Medicine* published Schwitzer's analysis with an editorial praising his work, saying that his "alarming report card of the trouble with medical news stories is thus a wake-up call for all of us involved in disseminating health research . . . to work collaboratively to improve the standards of health reporting."

The second reaction was, it appears, more important to the lifeblood of *HealthNewsReview*. That reaction was *not* one, as one might think, of overt hostility. Rather, it was one of indifference: the multibillion dollar media conglomerates that were, consciously or not, complicit with Big Medicine in foisting fluff on a less-than-ideally educated public did not respond in defensive outrage. For the most part, they didn't respond at all, acting as if none of this critique was actually taking place. Whether they were even aware of *HealthNewsReview*'s mission—which ultimately was not to throw spitballs at the media but rather to provide feedback to enable the media to do its job better—is not completely clear. The media tool kit provided by the website, which includes a set of tips for journalists to interpret how studies are done and how to understand the impact of their findings, in addition to a list of independent experts to help journalists with their stories, wasn't apparently useful enough to the major organizations to figure out a mechanism to keep a resource like this sustained. For in July 2013, after about seven years inhabiting cyberspace, *HealthNewsReview,* like the Australian

---

* HealthNewsReview.org was modeled after a website in Australia called *Media Doctor,* the true trailblazer in the field.

website *Media Doctor* on which it was based, lost its funding—though read on to the next chapter for an update.

Meanwhile, the band keeps playing a happy tune.

Full Circle

This may seem like a particularly unpleasant note on which to complete our survey before we draw final conclusions. The message that the media ignores its own best advisors, and routinely misrepresents health stories by avoiding discussing how much uncertainty exists on a given topic, leaves one wondering how it might be possible to change such a nonresponsive structure. After all, we can't all become reporters, to say nothing of statisticians or scientists, and simply perform the research on all of these topics firsthand. We *need* media to supply us with accurate and contextualized information. Short of becoming a chief of a health news division, how do we change the system?

We don't, of course, because almost no single person is capable of doing this, even with all the best training in the world. Instead, we do something much more profound and empowering: *we change ourselves.* Simply by understanding uncertainty, *we* become more able to find the gaps and overstatements in a news story. The more we focus on the "how" of uncertainty, the better we become at carrying around a little, internalized *HealthNewsReview* in our brains. That allows us to change the dynamic from a monologue, where we passively receive the news, into a dialogue, where we actively engage with it. In short, we turn news consumption into a two-way street.

Changing ourselves, and changing how we interact with the medical system, is the basis for a healthier and more fulfilling experience as a patient. Understanding uncertainty is liberating rather than oppressive, and it allows us to utilize the dialogue model not only when we read a health news tidbit, but when we sit in the office and face a doctor with decades of training. How to incorporate this powerful tool is how I'll conclude the book.

CONCLUSION: THE CONVERSATION

Everybody talks, but there is no conversation.

—DEJAN STOJANOVIĆ

Just Trust Us

Where does one go from here? Or, to phrase the question some-what differently: What is the practical value of investigating the limits of what we know in medicine? One cannot, for instance, assume that patients and their families will become experts on the topics covered thus far, sifting through the technical literature so that specialist advice becomes unnecessary. We can't expect people to become steeped in the data and commentary on mammography recommendations, the guidelines for cholesterol management, the limitations of Lyme testing, and so on for every conceivable medical issue that they or their loved ones might encounter. There are simply too many issues, each with its own particular oddities and refinements, for one person to assimilate. Of course, this is the *point* of having physicians in the room. They are a structural short-circuit for patients: trained professionals who are there precisely to relieve patients and families of the burden of mastering all the relevant studies in order to make reasoned decisions.

One of the implicit goals of this book has been to offer a new vision of medicine, one where the roles of doctor and patient are significantly redefined. At least in my model of medicine, patients should be the masters of their care, and doctors should be advisors—trusted advisors, one hopes, but advisors nonetheless. Yet doctors should not be expected to simply decree the major elements of a medical plan for a patient.*Along with many other colleagues, I conceive of the role of physician as a guide to the perplexed instead of a general commanding troops in a war against disease. Part of the reason sometimes there is a disconnect between patients and their doctors is that each party may be operating under different assumptions about which of these two different patient/doctor models is the more appropriate one.

Yet if patients should be the captains on their own ships of life, as it were, then what do we expect them to do in the kinds of situations I have outlined in this book, where often even experts disagree? Wouldn't this justify an older, more paternalistic model in which doctors decided and patients "complied" with their judgment? That model, whose boiled-down message could be summarized as *just trust us,* may be the most useful because it can alleviate most of the anxieties surrounding patient decision making.

I think not. I think that the older style infantilizes patients and leaves doctors feeling as if they are engaged in some supernatural process, far beyond the talents of mere mortals. I think it reinforces the kind of hubris that we have seen over and over again in example after example in this book, where doctors place too much confidence in their judgment and in the technology they utilize. As I tried to show, the results of that system can on occasion be disastrous.

Thus, we need to imagine a new model, one based on the strengths that *both* the doctor and the patient possess when they encounter one another, for the clinical proficiency of the physician is only one kind of strength in medical decision making, yet we have taken it to represent the

---

* The philosophy underpinning this model of medicine is beyond the scope of this book (note to publisher: I have more material for another book!), but it is worth emphasizing that supporting patient autonomy doesn't mean that one expects patients to decide on every minor adjustment to a medical plan. In discussing these meaty matters with colleagues and students, occasionally someone defending an older, more paternalistic model will get a bit too cute and wonder aloud the wisdom of letting a patient decide whether to adjust the potassium level during an inpatient hospitalization, for instance. That's not the kind of decision making to which I am referring. But paternalism still has its defenders: Sandeep Jauhar, a physician and sometime essayist for the *New York Times* whom I admire, wrote about the case for what he called "hard paternalism" in an op-ed in 2014 titled "When Doctors Need to Lie," which was a piece that I didn't admire so much.

whole. I would submit that a much more powerful model is that of a *conversation* between the two parties, on equal footing but each with a special area of expertise without which any medical plan is incomplete.

How can such a conversation take place? And what should be expected of each party in this conversation vis-à-vis uncertainty? Let's break down each role separately.

For doctors, the most important adjustment that is required is to acknowledge the potentially lifesaving benefits of *humility*. This means that doctors should nearly always be circumspect when talking about their judgment, either with respect to a diagnosis, a prognosis, or a treatment plan. It doesn't mean *not* having an opinion, but it does mean that such opinions are constrained by the limitations of what is known about a particular subject, and how those constraints affect the risks of taking action versus doing nothing.

For instance, in the Introduction to the book, we looked at cancer prognosis: once upon a time, oncologists used to offer prognoses to patients. They had developed a variety of scales that predicted how many years or months a patient might have to live. These scales were built in part on complex staging information of the cancer, combined with various laboratory values that indicated how advanced a patient's disease was. They would tailor their treatment recommendations based on how long they thought a patient with a terminal cancer would have to live.

But, as I discussed, once researchers started studying this in detail, they found that oncologists were unable to make accurate prognoses. When their ability to predict was put to the test, they failed fairly profoundly. So, instead of burying their heads in the sand and retreating from the implications of this fairly humbling revelation, oncologists made two important adjustments. First, and most important, they got out of the prognosis business. That's not to say they stopped talking about survival *odds* and the data on groups of patients with a particular stage of cancer, for indeed a patient with a glioblastoma multiforme (a highly aggressive brain cancer) is much more likely to have a shorter time to live than a patient with a hormone-responsive prostate cancer caught at an early stage. But they stopped offering *specific guesses* for how long a given individual had to live.

Second, they created a much more simplistic scoring system to guide their recommendations for therapy. This four-point score doesn't take into account the dozens of variables used in staging a cancer, but instead looks at patients' general state of health and their ability to perform the kinds of daily tasks that healthy individuals do as a matter of course (like brushing their hair, bathing, and dressing themselves).* On these basic criteria alone, oncologists can make recommendations to their patients about treatment, precisely *because* they do not know with complete certainty which patients are likely to respond to chemotherapy or radiation and which are not. Therefore, they simply look at who is functionally strong enough to tolerate the side effects—one might use the word "ravages"—of these treatments. It is a much better and more useful model, one that incorporates uncertainty into its bones. And it rests on the premise that doctors simply cannot provide the kind of confident predictions that are often expected of them or that they may expect of themselves.

Humility is the cornerstone of this approach. It requires saying the words *I don't know* without moving immediately into a defensive crouch— indeed, it requires the acknowledgment that *I don't know* often reflects the status of some medical topic, even though much may be known about it. It calls for not *talking at* but *listening to* patients and families, and making a real attempt to understand their goals, especially in the setting of long-term or terminal disease. To do this, physicians have to ask questions, gently probing to make sure that both parties are on the same page, and locating themselves in roughly the same portion of the spectrum of certainty.

For patients, the conversation requires asking questions, lots of questions, about not only the benefits but the risks of treatment, and the consequences of declining to be treated for something. Sometimes those consequences are quite profound, and patients should develop a framework for understanding when a doctor's recommendation is strong and not so strong. And if the doctor's recommendations about *everything* is strong, and no explanations are offered about why this is so, it's probably time to find another doctor. If you're feeling bullied, you're being bullied.

Patients should also ask about the difference between *relative* and *absolute* risks and benefits. When possible, try to have your doctor put

---

* Technically, five: the fifth "score" is death.

numbers to these ideas. *How many people like me need to take this drug before one life is saved?* is but one question that can be asked of a physician. At present, many physicians do not automatically incorporate relative versus absolute benefits into their medical decision making, so this process may take some time and so "the" conversation may require several discussions at more than one office visit. Furthermore, patients are better served in the conversation by knowing more about statistics and probability, so that if their doctors are able to rattle off data from the latest large, randomized trial, they will have a working idea about what's impressive and what isn't. Needless to say, familiarizing oneself with all of these concepts takes some time. The more you read about these matters, the more adept you will become at grasping what's really at stake in a medical recommendation. In that way you will become a more equal partner with your physician, able to formulate a plan based on your goals, rather than follow a plan handed to you by fiat.

Let's look at two specific examples of how I think this type of conversation can play out. The first case is hypothetical, and I will talk about it from my perch as a doctor. The second case, however, really did happen, and it happened to me, but as someone on the *receiving* end of the medical system, as a family member of a patient.

Earlier in the book I wrote about the complicated issue concerning blood pressure management in a select, but large, group of seniors: those age sixty to eighty with blood pressures above 140 but below 150 without diabetes or kidney disease. What would I do if I were evaluating a new patient who fit this demographic and presented a pressure of 146, which was then confirmed after repeated checks at several early visits? How would I go about discussing the controversy with such a patient?

I am not a specialist in blood pressure management, and I have only a nodding familiarity with the studies that have formed the basis of the guidelines published by the JNC8 group and the dissenting minority. In this respect, I'm not much different from typical primary care physicians who must grapple with such matters for their patients, although as an infectious disease physician, I do much less blood pressure management than a primary care doctor. What this means is that I do not have a definitive, expert opinion about whether I should follow the older JNC7 guideline and recommend that the patient start treatment to take him below

140. That said, I think I could have a reasonable conversation with the patient about how uncertainty is crucial to understanding why there is disagreement, and in doing so help him make a fairly informed decision about his goals with respect to his blood pressure.

The first point I would make in such a conversation is that, despite much heated rhetoric surrounding this process, there is actually a significant overlap between the JNC8 and minority groups about *most* blood pressure targets in *most* people. "Although there was *almost unanimous agreement on nearly all recommendations,* a minority of the panel disagreed with the recommendations to increase the target blood pressure . . . in persons 60 years or older without diabetes or chronic kidney disease," stated the authors of the minority report (my emphasis). In other words, the current dispute about the applicability of JNC8 applies to just one type of patient. Granted, there are about 30 *million* of these patients, but anyone who has diabetes or chronic kidney disease, or is over the age of eighty, need not worry about ambiguous messages. For these patients, all of the experts weighed the evidence and arrived at precisely the same conclusions. This is important because it emphasizes to the patient that the experts are hardly in overall disarray, so one just shouldn't throw up one's hands and say "nobody knows anything," and walk out of the office.

If the patient in front of me *was* among those 30 million who might be affected by the new guidelines, our conversation would be aimed at exploring how uncertainty led to the dispute. I would explain that the difference of opinion boiled down not so much to a quarrel about the numbers, but the attitudes we have toward evidence and the goals of guidelines in the first place. For although it may be true that it is easy to memorize a target pressure of 140 or 150, nobody really believes that, all of a sudden, the totality of lifesaving benefits of blood pressure control kick in if someone drops from 141 to 139. Consequently, some of the disagreement can be explained by the intellectual and emotional response to data as much as the data itself.

I would also explain what we observed in various instances in this book: that there are big benefits to treatment if your problem is severe, but as you approach "normal" the risk-to-benefit ratio changes, such that the risks become greater and the benefits correspondingly smaller. So if my patient was skittish about taking medications, as many patients are for perfectly justifiable reasons, I would explain that one option is to hold off. But I'd also emphasize that it's critically important to continue to receive evaluation, because if that patient's pressure gradually moves up to the 170s or 180s, those bigger benefits kick in, and my recommendation to start treatment would become much stronger. In other words, the severity of this patient's hypertension influences where my advice to take medication can be found on the spectrum of certainty: the higher it is, the more leftward it moves.

Some patients, however, can't stand the idea that they are at risk for some complication of their disease, and will want to do everything they can to minimize those risks. For such patients I would explain the controversy in a slightly different way by emphasizing the potential *downsides* of treatment, and emphasizing what I noted in that chapter, that lowering one's pressure *too* far can lead to its own set of problems. Still, if this were the kind of patient I was facing, I wouldn't actively discourage him from trying to aim for a goal below 140, for the JNC8 guidelines merely noted that there wasn't evidence to indicate that such a goal was unambiguously beneficial—but neither did they indicate that it put one in danger of complications.

From my vantage as a physician, this conversation depends upon a patient's aims, concerns, willingness to live with the risks of medications, and attitudes about the disease. The conversation also depends on an honest assessment of what constitutes a small amount of risk versus a big amount of risk. These form all the essential ingredients of the process we call informed consent.

Now let me pivot to relate a different story where I was on the flip side of the equation.

Several years ago a much-loved family member went out one winter's day to collect the mail and collapsed. A neighbor happened to see him fall to the ground and called 911. If it had not been for that chance event, he would have died in all likelihood, but because of the call and the rapid response of the emergency medical technicians, who were on the scene in a matter of minutes, he was revived, intubated, and taken to the nearest hospital. The family was summoned from various corners of the country to support one another and review the doctors' recommendations.

One vital problem was that, unbeknownst to the EMTs, our relative had a "do not resuscitate" order in place. He was seventy-six and had various medical problems, including diabetes, heart disease, and high blood pressure. He directly expressed to his primary care doctor that he had no interest in lingering in a hospital bed for months on end if he should have some terrible medical calamity befall him. Once he was brought to the hospital, where this could be sorted out, it should have been a simple matter of "reversing" his status, taking him off the ventilator and letting him pass away (or live, if that should be the case). His primary care physician was well aware of his DNR status, and there is no ethical dilemma in extubating a patient who never wanted to be intubated in the first place. A few phone calls could have taken care of the issue, and although tragic, it would have been consistent with my relative's clearly stated wishes.

As I made my way across the country I thought it would end there, but the team of doctors, which included an intensive care physician, a neurologist, a cardiologist, and the primary care physician, never even hinted they were considering withdrawing care. When we as a family pointed out the advanced directive, they responded that he was on a new treatment known as a "hypothermia protocol," and that this required time to see how he would fare. The family turned to me, as the lone physician in the bunch, waiting for an explanation.

Only I hadn't *heard* of a hypothermia protocol. It had been more than five years since I had last worked in an intensive care unit, and I wasn't familiar with this new practice, which had very rapidly been adopted by the neurology community. This meant that, although I had a more sophisticated grasp of the technical matters in play, I was not much different from any nonmedical family member speaking with the doctors about the plan. I learned that the hypothermia protocol was designed to preserve the brain function of patients who were "found down" and that it involved lowering the patient's central body temperature from the high nineties to the low eighties Fahrenheit through the use of cooling blankets and other means. The protocol lasted for seventy-two hours. By the time I had arrived, the first twenty-four hours of the protocol had already passed, and before I could even formulate questions about the process, another twenty-four had flown by. We were given status updates, but never at any point was there a conversation about whether it made sense to take this course of action given our relative's wishes.

Eventually, I decided to call some of my own colleagues back in Massachusetts—first a few neurologists to learn more about prolonged hypothermia, and then a palliative care doctor familiar with the ethics of situations such as these. What I learned from the neurologists was a case study in uncertainty. For, far from bringing *all* or even *most* patients back to resuming anything close to their previous lives, patients who survived events like these through hypothermia protocols were assessed in terms of their ability, for example, to hold a *toothbrush* six months after the event. It sounded like this kind of life was exactly the fate our relative was trying to avoid. Moreover, while the trials performed on patients with these hypothermia protocols showed a reasonable relative benefit, the absolute benefit was (as we have seen many times in this book) much smaller.

Not one physician with whom our family spoke during this time ever made this clear; all of them assumed that this was something that we should simply *want* by dint of the fact that, well, it just worked. There was no individual or collective recognition that "worked" was a term that might need some further explanation, and that, because our relative had made explicit that he didn't want the kind of things done to him that currently were being done to him, there absolutely should have been someone making some attempt to do so. They were behaving as if this protocol belonged at the far left of the spectrum of certainty, so clearly beneficial it hardly merited a second thought. Once I got my head around the concept and took a cursory glance at the studies on this new technology, I thought it just a hair to the left of dead center. It's entirely reasonable that some patients and families should want such treatment without question, but it also seemed clear to me that this isn't what our relative would want.

Eventually, after many long and painful family discussions, we became more assertive with the physicians about these matters, finally convincing them to extubate our relative, which they grudgingly did a few days after he completed the hypothermia protocol. He survived that event but passed away several days later, never having awakened after the initial event, his brain simply having taken too much of a hit during those minutes after he collapsed.

That relative was my father.

Looking back, what astonished me most about my own role in the saga of my father's final days is how much *I* was intimidated by the process. After all, I *know* medicine; I know how to talk to doctors, I know how they think. I also knew without any doubt what my father wanted out of the medical system, and it was plain to see as I watched him lie in a bed with a tube stuck down his throat, with a machine doing his breathing for him, that this wasn't what he wanted. But faced with a new set of variables (he had inadvertently been intubated by people who weren't aware of his wishes, here's this fancy new technology that we use leading to better outcomes) I hesitated. The consequences of that hesitation included a great deal of tension within our family about how to proceed. We were fortunate to resume, after a time, our loving and caring relationships with one another. Other families who find themselves in a similar bind may not be so lucky.

You might conclude from all of this that I've just given you another example of doctors lacking in humility about the value of their medical plan—which it most certainly is—but I am providing this as an example about what can be done when speaking *to* doctors because eventually I *did* assert myself, and, along with my family, we *did* ask the right questions, explained our goals, and repeatedly drew their attention to what my father wanted. I wish that they had listened better and understood us sooner, or even had been proactive in seeking our thoughts once they realized that his advanced directive was in conflict with what was taking place in his care.* Yet, with polite but firm insistence, we got them to understand (if perhaps only dimly) that this was not about *their* plan but *his.* From a patient standpoint, that is the essential point to grasp when you begin a conversation with a doctor. Your medical plan is *yours:* you own it, and your doctor should be your guide, not your director.

---

* One doctor "got it" right from the start: the palliative care physician. For me in particular, he was critically important because early on I thought I was losing my mind for even bringing up the issue of whether he should be extubated, given the subtle but unpleasant response from the other physicians, as if I was a cruel and heartless son for wishing such a thing.

The Spectrum of Certainty, Redux

As we think about how to have a conversation with physicians and deal with uncertainty, it's important to emphasize the altered perception of certainty among people both inside and outside medicine. I hope to have shown that our treatments and technologies are sometimes given far too much credit for their effectiveness once one carefully considers the data. This is one of the reasons why about-faces like that seen in the changing evidence on the benefits of hormone replacement therapy seem so embarrassing, and why physicians a century hence might view the rhetoric from today's leading doctors as ridiculously and sometimes lethally smug, as we sometimes view what passed for common knowledge among physicians who came one hundred years before us.

As I've tried to persuade you to see, the level of certainty in many of the topics I have covered in this book resemble those of the JNC8 guidelines mentioned above, falling somewhere toward the middle part of the spectrum. The evidence supporting the proposition that screening mammograms save lives in women over fifty is mixed, but on the whole many or perhaps even most experts still favor some form of screening—although as discussed previously, the popular perception about the scientific certainty of mammography's benefits is profoundly different from this mild statement.

In women younger than fifty, there is much, much less certainty. Does the evidence from scientific trials suggest that screening mammograms in women under fifty belong on the *other* side of the certainty spectrum, and move toward some level of evidence of harm? It's hard to say at the moment, in part because it's extremely difficult to quantify and measure harms of mammography in such a trial, and the expense in conducting such a trial is enormous at the very time when the US government (and a good many other governments) is cutting back on its support of scientific and medical research. After spending time doing the research to write this book, I now believe in general that screening mammograms for women under fifty does indeed provide net harms without a clear corresponding net benefit. It's not *far* to the right, but I'm fairly confident that, barring some additional technology that will help separate false positives from true positives, it doesn't belong to the left of the center on certainty's spectrum.

Of course, nothing magic occurs in the biology of a woman when she turns fifty, so the precise moment when the risks of the false-positive mammogram are outweighed by the benefits of early detection may range from anywhere in the late forties to the early fifties (if they exist at all) and could be influenced by any number of factors that can really only be measured in theory. That is, one *could,* for instance, perform a screening mammogram trial on women aged forty-seven to fifty-three who are positive for the *BRCA1* gene mutation, which predisposes women to a higher risk of breast cancer, but the logistical hurdles required to address such a narrow question make such a study impossible in reality.

(As an aside, as this book is finishing its final revisions in mid-2015, the US Preventive Services Task Force is seeking public comment on a draft form of its newest iteration of screening mammography guidelines. It does not appear to be a dramatic departure from the 2009 document for the three major items. Screening for women under fifty has retained a C grade, while every-other-year mammograms for women fifty to seventy-four continues to be given a B grade, and mammograms for women seventy-five and over are still given an I grade.*

It is hard to predict what the reception will be like, but an early indicator might be found in a press release by the American College of Radiology. Recall that the ACR had taken the USPSTF to task in 2009, and that stance has not changed. "They ignored more modern studies that have shown much greater benefit," said Dr. Barbara Monsees, the chair of the ACR Breast Imaging Commission. "These limitations result in the misrepresentation of the real trade-offs that women and health care providers need to know about in order to make good decisions about screening. They also ignored the demonstrated views of American women on screening. Unfortunately, these recommendations will only add to confusion that is placing women at risk," she noted. Why the ACR's opposition doesn't *also* appear to add to the confusion is not made clear by Dr. Monsees. And again the USPSTF continues to be charged with having been tone deaf to the "views of American women," as if somehow that were one unified, monolithic view, and as if the view should forever be fixed without ever reconsidering the strength of the data.

---

* I'll explain the I grade a little later in the chapter.

Thus, my impression remains that even with new guidelines about to be issued, not much has changed, and this book's consideration of a report that was issued nearly a decade ago is still very topical. For which I suspect my publisher is breathing a sigh of relief. End of aside.)

Prolonged antibiotics (that is, months and months) for so-called chronic Lyme disease occupy that part of the spectrum where we become more certain of the harms of treatment. As to what causes the symptoms that are given the label of chronic Lyme, it is a true unknown unknown— it is even unclear whether Lyme itself plays a role at all. A variety of theories have been proposed to explain chronic fatigue syndrome, many of which involve various infections and all of which are highly speculative. The simple truth at this point in time is that nobody really has any idea why this happens to people or even how to measure it. Nevertheless, we *do* know with much higher certainty that more antibiotics aren't helpful and are highly likely to be harmful. Long courses of antibiotics for chronic Lyme is out at the right end of the spectrum of certainty, and we've known this for well over a decade.

On this very brief tour of the certainty spectrum, we should finish by coming full circle. As I've indicated, in medicine there are very few absolutes, few points at which we really can look a patient in the eye and say, "just trust us," and mean every syllable. Part of this is that all treatments come with risks. The conversation must deal with the balancing of these risks and benefits. But there is one area of medicine in which the benefits are so enormous, and the risks so minimal, that it occupies a spot on the far left of the certainty spectrum and represents the single greatest triumph of modern medicine. Not altogether surprisingly, the public perception is that this medical miracle is actually a highly controversial topic. But it's not, and the reason it's not is due to the overwhelming scientific evidence that it saves lives and is associated with almost no harm.

I am referring to the practice of vaccination. From their origins, when the practice of protecting against smallpox through variation (a forerunner to true vaccination) was introduced to Europe via the Ottoman Empire in the early eighteenth century, vaccines have always engendered a certain level of paranoia. Over these three centuries, some of the arguments against the practice remain more or less the same: one of the complaints that the clergy levied against smallpox prevention when Lady

Wortley Montague was among the first to not only engage in the practice but publicize it as well, was that the practice defied God's will, for if one was meant to get smallpox and die, that was fate and fate should not be circumvented. Today's antivaxxers, with their zeal for what they fancy are "natural" remedies, sometimes organize "measles parties" so that their children can be exposed to the virus in one happy group. Whether one wants to let God sort them out or let Mother Nature take her course (two different but equally powerful kinds of narratives driving these attitudes), the hostility to vaccination in part rests on a fatalism that made only a small amount of sense at the advent of the Enlightenment, and makes considerably less sense today.

It is impossible to assess with any accuracy the total number of lives that vaccines have saved since Edward Jenner began the practice of vaccination in earnest in 1796, but that hasn't stopped researchers from making some decent attempts at estimating the effect where the epidemiological data are more reliable. Recently, the CDC engaged in just such an exercise. In order to make reasonably solid conclusions, it focused narrowly on childhood immunizations over the twenty years between 1994 and 2013. In this brief span of the vaccination age, the estimates are mind-boggling: 322 million overall illnesses along with 21 million hospitalizations were prevented, and more than 700,000 lives were saved. The estimated cost savings was more than $1 trillion.

The biggest lifesaver came from preventing diphtheria, a disease that is almost never talked about today but was an absolute terror in the early twentieth century. The vaccines that were estimated to have saved large numbers of lives included vaccines against measles, pneumococcus, Hepatitis B,* and to a smaller extent pertussis, polio, and a relatively new vaccine against the bacteria known as *Haemophilus influenzae B*. The remainder of the vaccines proportionally saved a smaller number of lives but often had big impacts on morbidity. For instance, the vaccine for varicella (the virus that causes chickenpox) was estimated to have saved

---

* The estimated lives saved for Hep B run into the future because Hep B causes chronic liver disease that can lead to liver cancer. Because this happens decades later, children vaccinated against Hep B (especially children of Asian and African immigrants, where the prevalence of the disease is very high) will reap the benefits later in life.

perhaps one thousand lives over these twenty years—a still not inconsequential sum—but prevented nearly *70 million* illnesses.

That's just over twenty years of work in just *one* country. Suffice it to say that the burden of disease in many other countries is much higher, and therefore the benefits of vaccines in places like Ulan Bator or Kinshasa are that much more profound. Keep in mind that these are lives saved—tragedies averted—usually with a one-time clinic visit. Moreover, most vaccines, especially those given in childhood, provide extremely high levels of protection for the recipient. Tetanus, measles, polio, and diphtheria are almost totally unheard of among those who have been vaccinated. Contrast this with the impact of statins I discussed in Chapter 6, which are clearly lifesaving drugs but only reduce the mortality from heart disease by a modest portion, require lifelong adherence, and carry a small number of risks.

It's safe to say that, assuming we continue to develop an ever more sophisticated understanding of the human body and how to keep it healthy, doctors two hundred years hence will look back at our statins and our antidepressants, our mammograms and our CAT scans, our chemotherapy and our blood pressure management, and think that we were only really a step or two beyond butchery. But they will look at what we did with vaccines, and they will see real accomplishment in precisely the same way that we regard Newton and his laws of motion, or Harvey describing the circulation of the blood. The success of vaccination is truly the one matter on which we can bring near certainty to the discussion, and it is a heartbreak to see such an easy topic so terribly muddled in the public discourse. There are books that elegantly explain this principle in much greater detail than I have in these meager paragraphs, of which volumes such as Paul Offit's *Autism's False Prophets,* Seth Mnookin's *The Panic Virus,* and Arthur Allen's *Vaccine* are but a few.

Media

Exercise more. Eat less. Don't smoke. *Everything else is commentary.* This *should* be the beginning and ending of every single health news story. It is the most important message the media could convey about health, and yet most people don't understand just how important this message is because it is obscured in a dust cloud of largely irrelevant material. Of course, educated people are *aware* that there are health benefits to be had by a moderate diet and regular exercise, and certainly the news media doesn't try to oppose that message at a conscious level. However, the media's fascination with the latest bauble of technology and its obsession with improbable threats ends up producing the same effect.

The essentials of Western (and particularly American) health—or lack thereof—can be boiled down to these few basic points: we eat too much, and too much of that consists of crap; we don't exercise anywhere near enough because we spend far too much time either sitting in front of televisions or getting to and fro in our cars; and a smaller subset of us smoke cigarettes, a practice that wreaks disproportionate havoc on the body. Of the many news stories on lifestyle research—what types of food and drink are associated with healthy outcomes, whether trans fats are healthier than saturated fats, the healing powers of the açaí berry, and so on—those that fail to place such stories in the context of those basic points aren't really making any genuine contribution to health education. Readers of such articles invariably walk away with wildly skewed notions of what they need to do to improve their health, which accounts in part for the repeated waves of fad diets or trendy foods that dominate the health consumer market.

The conversation about uncertainty is not merely between patient and doctor, for both patients and doctors enter the clinic doors having shaped their opinions by watching the evening news, or reading online articles sent by friends or colleagues, or just soaking in popular culture where some health story is related in a movie or TV drama. It may be too tall an order to hope for all forms of media to highlight the challenges that uncertainty brings to the practice of medicine, but it seems reasonable to expect at least health reporters to understand something of it. In the news media, the state of affairs is so sorry that really the only direction to go, in terms of quality and sophistication, is up.

How can health news stories achieve this? Simply put, they can acknowledge that uncertainty happens, and, in putting it out there for all to see, they can explain where on the spectrum of certainty a given story belongs. Let's suppose that some group of researchers has found a drug known as K29-X that can reverse multiple sclerosis in rats. They publish their results in a prestigious medical journal, and a press release is generated by the medical center where the researchers work. Some local TV stations pick up the story and devote three minutes to the promise of K29-X. Various viewers afflicted by the disease then happen to watch the feature on K29-X and soon are called by friends who have seen the pieces as well. Should they call their doctors' offices asking for a prescription?

In reality, the better question to ask is whether K29-X has even been *tested* in humans—which it almost certainly hasn't—but after such a story lands on the local 6 p.m. newscast, one can rest assured that, the following day, the administrators of local neurologists' offices across the viewing area will be deluged with calls. I'm making the K29-X scenario up, although the phenomenon I'm describing is very real. The "HIV cure" story of the Berlin patient happened to have been a nationwide example of the same, and HIV providers spent much of those weeks in December 2010 tamping down expectations for their patients (most of whom were healthy anyway through the magic of antiretrovirals) who thought they could be free of the virus henceforth.

So the starting point here is to couch a story like this in a chain-link fence of caveats so that viewers might catch the message of "enter at your own risk." Or *believe* at your own risk. K29-X was used in an experimental model for MS that was not MS itself—uncertainty—was studied by looking at animals rather than humans—uncertainty—animals that are only distantly related to humans—uncertainty—nobody has any idea whether or not K29-X is even safe in humans—uncertainty—and even if it turns out to be safe, nobody has any idea whether it's *effective* in humans—*uncertainty.*

Is this a *lot* of uncertainty? Is this in that part of the spectrum of uncertainty that includes the unknown unknowns, where really just a bunch of clever scientists have been messing around with some interesting ideas, none of which may have direct applications for multiple sclerosis, and even if it does are almost definitely not going to happen anytime soon? Pretty much. Of course, local newscasters may not be interested in hearing this critical appraisal, as it may interfere with their business model. So, until this changes, the only reasonable solution in the interim may be to turn the television off—or to construct that mental chain-link fence on one's own. There is a value in actively identifying the limitations of health news stories, and although it takes some practice, one can get pretty adept at doing so after a time.

Health news would also better serve its consumers by explaining the quality of research and the level of evidence that supports a given claim. So many of the items that purport to show odd or counterintuitive health information are based on small observational studies, which are subsequently extrapolated and inflated into sweeping statements that bear little relation to reality. The *New York Times* article that considered the health benefits of dark chocolate was careful to note the relatively weak level of evidence supporting the claims of the researchers, specifically noting that the research was observational in nature, akin to the kind of research that was performed on the benefits of hormone replacement therapy before a properly constructed drug trial showed that hormones didn't lead to greater health. I see no reason why *all* health news can't similarly do this, even if one is talking only about a televised "health minute." It takes but a moment to say that the quality of a given type of research is high, medium, or low; no matter how cleverly a researcher designs an observational study, it's still an observational study, and reporters would serve their readers and viewers well by explaining the differences among these types of research as part of every single report.* Again, readers can't change what news organizations do, but what they *can* do is identify whether a useful assessment of a study's quality is present, and, in the age of the Internet, it is possible to find legitimate sources that will discuss these studies, especially those of interest to the general community.

Another simple change media outlets could make is to attach a grade to a given health claim by noting that it is based on strong or moderate or weak evidence. Even for readers and viewers who do not wish to trouble themselves with the fine print, news media can intimate the level of

---

* Throughout the West African Ebola epidemic, for example, the BBC articles covering Ebola included a few bullet points on the virus—how the virus spreads, how long it takes a person once infected to become sick, what options there are for treatment, and so on. These were the same few bullet points, in *every single article,* so that lay readers may always have some contextual information in the background (like the fact that the current strain isn't airborne, an important issue that needed to be addressed constantly in the early months of the outbreak). I don't see why we couldn't do the same for every health article with "strength of evidence" bullet points.

confidence one should have in a given health news item. Indeed, this is the approach taken by the US Preventive Services Task Force in issuing its various recommendations, not only for screening mammography but for prevention of falls in the elderly, the use of aspirin to stave off heart attacks, and much else besides. In all of these cases, the recommendations are given grades that are easily comprehensible to anyone who has survived public school: Grade A evidence represents a recommendation toward the left, "fairly certain" end of the spectrum, while Grade B indicates less certainty, and Grade C much less certainty.[†] However, all three of these grades still do recommend *for* something, while Grade D recommends *against* a practice because the evidence tilts against it on the whole, and so it is on the right side of the spectrum.

The USPSTF assigns the grade of I to its true unknowns, where the evidence is so scant that to take any stand, however meek, would be an exercise in shooting in the dark. Looking through the USPSTF website, "I" statements aren't found at every turn, but neither are they so rare as to stand out. Incidentally, that's not a bad thing—not only is it an honest admission of uncertainty, but it is also an identification of the areas where quality research must be done.

It's not *that* hard to see the intuitive appeal of such a grading scheme. Like sportscasters who explain the meaning of some clever maneuver to an audience that may include viewers new to a sport, health news reporters could gradually ease their audience into the levels of uncertainty in medical research by attaching such grades to every article they write or every TV segment they air. The additional benefit of this approach is that all the various items of health news then become linked by analysis about the quality of evidence; news consumers can suddenly see the common theme of uncertainty in a diversity of stories, which applies equally to the latest newspaper report on a new test for Alzheimer's disease, to a TV

[†] Recall that the recommendation for biennial mammography in women fifty to seventy-four was given a grade of B, while the recommendation for *particular* women aged forty to forty-nine for any kind of mammography was given a grade of C, implying that there was a moderate to significant amount of uncertainty as to whether there was any benefit at all for any woman in that age range, but it *might* be indicated for women at especially high risk, such as those carrying gene mutations that are known to increase the risk of breast cancer, such as the *BRCA1* mutation.

piece on the link between saturated fats and depression, and to an Internet webinar on new techniques for estimating cancer risks. This book has simply been an extended exercise in illustrating that point. In all of these topics, our state of knowledge is at varying levels, and making this matter explicit can only help people make better judgments and avoid the problems associated with the Just Trust Us model.

One small ray of hope has started to shine again on the media, for as of the summer of 2014, Gary Schwitzer has resurrected the *HealthNews-Review* and resumed his advocacy for measured reporting. One early review from the rebooted website centers on the news surrounding the latest entry in mammogram technology, so-called tomosynthesis imaging, and the glowing reviews that accompanied an important article published in the *Journal of the American Medical Association.* "The list of stories that resorted to sensational language—breakthrough, game-changer, best way of detection, any woman should have this—was long," Schwitzer noted. He proceeded to itemize the ways in which caution was thrown to the wind: one story featured only one single patient anecdote, another interviewed the lead study author but sought no other expert voices, another made no mention of limitations, and so on.

But so, too, did he point out the stories that at least got *part* of the story right, which was that this undeniably big technological leap may *not* translate to a clinical benefit, and may simply exacerbate the underlying problem of false positives and the harm that may result from them, especially in women younger than fifty. Those organizations called out for varying levels of praise included *USA Today,* the *New York Times,* the *Boston Globe,* and the *Wall Street Journal.* Whether the work of Schwitzer and the many experts that comprise *HealthNewsReview* in its reincarnated state will be appreciated for its value is unclear, but at least they are back at it.

The End

Through efforts like the grading scheme introduced by the USPSTF or the publication of guidelines that emphasize the limitations of evidence such as those seen in the JNC8 hypertension recommendations, we're beginning to see the conversation about uncertainty take place between specialists and laypeople. Yet these documents are still fairly technical and, although they are eminently readable, are mostly accessed by professionals rather than the general public. Still, the fact that these items are becoming ever more explicit in stressing the uncertainty attached to current medical knowledge and practice is representative of a growing awareness among medical researchers and public health authorities that we must have this conversation as medicine becomes ever more complex and intimidating.

The media has far to go in terms of enabling this conversation, although as noted above, some reporters and news organizations get it right. Among doctors, nurses, social workers, psychologists, and everyone else who can claim the title of health-care worker, the conversation is not yet happening in a systematic way, although those guidelines may offer a picture of things to come. Currently medical schools, as a rule, still encourage a model in which students are appraised by knowing right answers, choosing them among a field of wrong answers. That measures a certain type of knowledge essential to medical practice, but it consequently engenders a conception of medicine best described as overly certain, and residency and fellowship directors must spend part of their energies remolding their trainees to be aware of the pitfalls of this approach. Most nascent doctors are not judged on being able to express uncertainty to their patients, but, given the changing nature of guidelines and the many examples of uncertainty that we have seen in this book, some medical school deans may begin to incorporate those concepts at an earlier phase in physician training than we do at this time.

There *is* a place where a direct conversation about uncertainty is taking form. Health-care workers, alongside patients and families, are starting to wrestle openly with the challenges and opportunities that uncertainty brings to a medical problem. This place is not in a simulator at an academic center, nor is it in an experimental holistic-healing alternative medicine nationwide movement. In fact, the conversation is taking place in what at first glance might seem the least hospitable of environments, where the stakes could not be higher and the tension and anxiety experienced by patients and their families take them to the breaking point. As the Foreword described, the conversation about uncertainty— and a formal analysis of its promise and perils—is happening in intensive care units.

An ICU is about the most intimidating environment possible for a layperson. The activity is frenetic, and the advanced technology is omnipresent. The pinging and beeping of every conceivable machine can paralyze family members with fear. *Don't look at the monitors, and ignore the alarms* is almost always among the first things I say to family members when I am involved in the care of an ICU patient, as they anxiously glance at cycling blood pressures or react to a drop in their loved one's heart rate by nearly fainting themselves. By definition, if you are in the ICU, you are there because you are potentially facing the end of your life, and you require the lifesaving equipment and personnel that ICUs provide. Patients are, it goes without saying, almost always quite ill. Their family members wear their tensions on their sleeve, and if they aren't exhausted initially, they often become that way, and with each passing day, their nerves fray bit by bit. As I noted above, even I experienced it as a son when my father was critically ill. I was intimately familiar with the rhythms and noise of the place, so I felt only a fraction of the anxiety that others must normally feel, and even for me it was a brutal assault on the senses. It's a very tough setting.

So it comes as something of a surprise that the ICU has become a testing ground for transparency about uncertainty. After all, in the midst of the chaos and tension, having frank discussions with families about what may be moderate or even high levels of uncertainty at the very moment their loved one is at their most vulnerable could seem like sheer folly. But a small cadre of professionals from various disciplines have posited that the ICU may be the *optimal* environment to test the theory that more openness from medical professionals—including honest assessments about uncertainty—leads patients and family members to believe they have *greater* control over their decisions, not less. Transparency in the ICU offers readers a living, positive proof of the potential we have to experience and improve medicine though *embracing* uncertainty.

It is still very much a new approach, but it is spreading and gradually gaining acceptance. The origins of what is now increasingly called ICU family rounds lay in observations from the late 1990s that lack of communication from medical professionals was a much greater source of frustration to families than perceptions about competency or dedication of the staff or even the overall care of the patients themselves. There isn't an overwhelming amount of research devoted to the topic, but what work has been done highlights a classic flaw of the modern medical machine: patients can be cared for with the finest technology and be saved from what would otherwise be almost certain death, and yet, because scant attention is paid to keeping the lines of communication open, patients and family members can nevertheless emerge from such experiences feeling sullied and violated.

Thus, the original concept of ICU family rounds was meant to overcome the problem of communication, and wasn't thought of as a chance to hold a seminar on epistemology. Not altogether surprisingly, the early literature discussing the potential benefits of family rounds could be found in the pages of nursing journals, because nurses are on the front lines of patient care and are much more likely to be aware of the vibes of frustration emanating from families as they try to comprehend the complexities involved in an ICU stay. Among physicians, many of the initial forays that considered how to incorporate families into ICU rounds occurred in pediatric intensive care journals. But the idea has spread, and although I am an outsider to the daily practice of intensive care medicine, it seems to me to be gaining some traction.

ICU family rounds may have been conceived as a tool to improve communication, but all physicians who have done some training in intensive care medicine know that it is exceedingly rare to find a case where one can interpret the avalanche of information into a coherent whole for which there is one single treatment devoid of any downsides—so uncertainty as a topic simply can't be avoided if one chooses to adopt this model. Uncertainty of varying levels rules the scene: Do we give blood thinners for what may be a serious heart attack and in doing so risk a life-threatening colonic bleed? Do we subject a patient with a tenuous respiratory status to a bronchoscopy if it means that we may worsen the problem and end up causing the very intubation and dependence on the respirator that we are trying to avoid? Such kinds of questions are part and parcel of the treatment of critically ill patients, and the consequence of being transparent with families, and sometimes the patients themselves, is that these questions have to be addressed openly.

In keeping with the experimentation of this new method, not all ICU family rounds are the same. Some ICUs still tend toward a more

traditional model and have simply organized the daily schedule to opti-
mize communication, performing staff rounds separately but setting aside
an hour—say, in the late morning—when the nurses and physicians are
available primarily to discuss the patients' plans of care with families.
Such an approach allows family members to know precisely when they
can find the team and avoids one of the major hassles associated with
communication. But there are more aggressive approaches, the most profound of which is to simply bring families right to the patient's bedside
and let them not only observe but to an extent participate in daily rounds.

In a medium-sized community hospital in Salem, Massachusetts, a
group of intensive care nurses and physicians chose the latter strategy.
Writing in a newsletter published by the Massachusetts Board of Registration in Medicine in early 2014, Dr. Barrett Kitch of the North Shore
Medical Center discussed his group's experience with this more radical
form of ICU family rounds. It reads like a primer on how doctors and
nurses can have the conversation about uncertainty and in doing so enable
rather than exasperate patients and families. "The initial reaction to the
proposal was one of skepticism," Kitch wrote. "Patients' families would
become worried about information that shouldn't worry them. They
would become distrustful because they would hear us (physicians, nurses,
respiratory therapists) second guessing ourselves. They would get lost in
the details and miss the important message."*

After convincing some of these skeptics to allow a pilot trial, the results were impressive: "[The medical staff] reported that the families were
extraordinarily appreciative," Kitch noted. And in a phrase that couldn't
be better suited to this book's thesis, he added, "[The families] shared that
transparency *paradoxically seemed to increase trust despite more openness*

---

* I can't help but be amused by this last objection because, as part of my work in an
  academic medical center, with multiple specialists coming and going on a daily basis,
  I have firsthand witnessed the more traditional model in which attending physicians
  hurriedly sweep into a room, make a bunch of pronouncements about a patient's
  problems that could be spoken just as easily in Sumerian as in English because one
  could hardly tell the difference, and proceed to sweep back out with no less alacrity,
  leaving patients and families behind in a cloud of mystified dust. It's certainly possible that exposing families to medical or surgical ICU rounds in its raw state might
  cause people to get lost in the details, but from where I stand that's probably nothing
  worse than the current situation.

about our uncertainty, our second-guessing, or our lack of consensus as to the treatments needed for their loved ones" (my emphasis). The pilot program did overcome the more skeptical members of the staff, and this rather remarkable form of specialist/layperson interaction has been the standard of care there ever since.

Notably, rounds are not intended to be a form of participatory decision making. Despite this, they have allowed family members to feel some comfort by understanding the process, and they have enabled situations where family meetings can take place to discuss the weighty goals of care, which often involve questions of life and death. These family meetings, of course, take place in all ICUs across the world, but one gets the impression that the families in Salem might be better prepared and less mystified.

Because the ICU family rounds as practiced at North Shore Hospital is not a rolling family meeting, it is not a perfect model for how to conduct the conversation about uncertainty. The staff don't trouble themselves to explain their jargon (Dr. Kitch wrote that "rounds were not simplified so that they could be understood by the layperson. . . . [W]e spoke in the language of the healthcare worker."), and they make no real attempt to modify their rounding structure. Yet the fact that their form of rounding has succeeded demonstrates that families—and, by extension, patients—are able on the whole to live with uncertainty without regarding the staff as a bunch of dunderheads, and without being paralyzed by fear. They have shown that we need not pretend uncertainty doesn't exist at the edge of life. How much more can be gained when, in other, less anxious environments, the specialists *do* explain in plain language the conundrums that they face in making treatment decisions?

Our age is one where there appears to be little time for reflection about what we know and what we do not, not only in medicine but in almost any aspect of our lives. The gradual process by which we have squeezed out that area where we can ponder the limits of our knowledge has come via the ever-increasing yowls of the overly certain, who as a rule have something profitable to peddle. Part of the point of having the conversation about uncertainty at all is to reclaim that space where we can contemplate our goals—for our health, our jobs, and our sense of meaning.

We are capable of achieving it.

Acknowledgments

I had been thinking in a vague way about writing a book dealing with the ambiguities inherent in medical knowledge since I was in residency many years ago. Those thoughts crystallized during a series of seminars led by Robert Goldberg, an epidemiological researcher at the University of Massachusetts Medical School. Rob is a source of much insight on the subject of trial design, interpretation of medical literature, and biostatistics, all of which he serves up with a dash of dry wit. He also introduced me to the remarkable story of diethylstilbestrol and how it revolutionized obstetrics. Much thanks to him.

As part of those seminars, I was lucky enough to work with a small group of physicians and scientists at the junior faculty level, all of whom were starting careers in clinical research, and their perspicacity and energy was an early inspiration to write this book. In particular, Wendy Marsh's research on the effects of menopause on mood disorders in women fascinated me from the moment she explained it. Many of the topics that I write about here were initially stimulated from my thinking about the challenges of doing the kind of research that Wendy does, and I'm grateful for her willingness to discuss her work with me, as well as the pick-me-up lunch talks we have from time to time as we keep tabs on each other's careers.

In my home of internal medicine, I deeply appreciate the advice and encouragement of Oscar Starobin, who has since retired and whose presence will be sorely missed by his UMass colleagues. Thanks to him, Naomi Botkin, and Nancy Skehan for reviewing portions of the manuscript; thanks also to Brad Switzer and Glenn Kershaw for providing their insights from their respective areas of expertise in oncology and nephrology. An abbreviated list of other folks from UMass who have been aware of my work and have offered helpful thoughts and moral support include Kimberly Cullen, Rebecca Lumsden, Mary Philbin, David Clive, Trish McQuilkin, Allen Chang, Mary Hawthorne, Sara Jacques, Rick Forster, Linda Paszkowski, Mary Roberts, and Jackie St. Martin.

All of my colleagues in infectious diseases have played a part in shaping my thinking on these matters, and I'm appreciative of their carefully considered opinions, even including the sometimes gladiatorial manner in which they are delivered. Of these, I'd especially like to thank Mireya Wessolossky, Sonia Chimienti, Jennifer Daly, and Doug Golenbock for maintaining faith in me during some tough stretches—why they did so is a separate matter—as well as Gail Scully for our ongoing discussions about overdiagnosis and the general state of modern health care, and David Bebinger for all of the above and being my ID homeboy. Special thanks also goes to Kathy Scalley and Ann Carroll for all of their support, to say nothing of their saintly tolerance of the more eccentric aspects of my personality, over the many years I've been at UMass.

Judy Ockene was always gracious in offering her insights on mammography and her work on the USPSTF. My former mentor Linden Hu of Tufts University kindly provided help by reviewing the chapter on Lyme. Further afield, thanks to Sasha Retana for thoughtful critiques both substantive and grammatical, Sid Pazol for helping me track down the Bertrand Russell quote that had been rattling around in my brain for twenty-five years, William Krieger for serving as a general sounding board of ideas, Vitaly Belyshev for introducing me to *London Hospital,* Noam Shoresh and Doris Damian for insights and feedback on statistical matters, and Beth Giladi for all her encouragement and allowing me to read early drafts to her.

Of my many professional influences, Alan Rothman deserves special mention. Although Alan did not make any direct contribution to this book, his intellectual footprints can be found all over it. My philosophy of the social aspects of medicine was in place long before I met Alan, but he has had an enormous impact on my understanding of how to think about data, and I suspect I'm not only a better doctor but a better human being as a result of being exposed to his cautious, rigorous approach to knowledge.

Thanks to the Basic Books family, T. J. Kelleher, Ben Platt, and Quynh Do, for their helpful feedback. Their insights have made this a better book. Likewise, I very much appreciate the postmanuscript help from Melissa Veronesi, as well as the amazeballs copyediting skills, to say nothing of the exceptionally kind words, of Carrie Watterson. A *big* thanks to Andy Ross, my agent, for taking me off the slush pile and for providing three years of fruitful and thoroughly enjoyable collaboration.

Three people have stood by me offering encouragement since well before I began to conceive of this work. They have known more than anyone the importance that writing has held in my life, and they have come to see how important medicine is in it. They have been tireless readers whose frequently irrational optimism has buoyed my spirits over long stretches. I can't really convey the gratitude I feel toward Lee Hatch, Mark Meyers, and Miriam Tuchman, so I won't try beyond writing this paragraph.

Finally, to Erez and Ariella: thanks for being understanding about the many hours I have sat in the office clattering away on the keyboard. Dad's obsessive in that way. I love you more than anything in the world.

Appendix

*A Very Nonmathematical Description
of Statistical Significance*

I originally envisioned *Snowball in a Blizzard* as a book that would focus on methodological aspects of human-subjects research, mainly the difficulties of study design and the subtleties of statistical interpretation. When, for instance, does a relative risk value diverge from an odds ratio, and why are the two often confused? What is a Type I versus Type II error? How do we "power" studies? A few years ago, as I was struggling with these kinds of issues in my professional work, I thought that they would be ideal subjects to illuminate to a general audience. I can see now that these fairly technical matters were unlikely to help nonspecialists have a more thorough understanding of clinical research, and it is probably why I received fairly tepid responses from literary agents.

Over time, I realized that more was to be gained by telling stories about the *consequences* of these issues, and that I could occasionally sprinkle the text with brief explanations of the more essential methodological points. For instance, I thought it absolutely critical to explain the concept of positive predictive value in order to show why the USPSTF does not universally recommend mammograms for women under age fifty. One can't easily grasp the justification for the task force's reasoning without being acquainted with the notion of positive predictive value; once one understands the concept and sees the truly lousy predictive value of a positive screening mammogram in this age group, it's hard to understand why there was (and is) so much fuss in the first place. However, I shelved the idea of devoting entire chapters, say, to the difference between nested case-control and case-cohort studies or the beauty inherent in the

Mann-Whitney U test. Such subjects, fascinating though they can be to epidemiologists, would probably be valuable to nonspecialists only as a soporific.

Thus, I elected to prioritize narration over technical explanation to describe these points, and whether I have succeeded or failed at that task, I leave for you, the reader, to judge. However, I do believe that there is one statistical concept worth exploring in a little more detail than the structure of this book allowed for because so much of what I have discussed in the previous pages relies on it: significance. I can't speak for the basic research scientists, but for clinicians statistical significance is in many ways the yardstick by which we measure relevance in medical knowledge.

I have hinted at how we use statistical significance throughout, but what follows is a very cursory overview of the concept and an explanation of the two main types of data used in calculating significance: categorical and continuous variables. There is *much* more that could be described, and at a much deeper level of detail. My only goal here is to give readers a sense of what it means to hear that a study "found" something, and when skepticism may be in order. In doing so, I also want to provide readers with a way to understand news about medical breakthroughs *not* mentioned in this book because a moderate portion of the medical "knowledge" discussed here will be out of date by the time it hits bookstore shelves, assuming that any bookstore shelves are left by its publication date.

For those eager readers who have a deeper interest in the details of clinical research or statistics, among the many fine books devoted to the subject, I recommend *Epidemiology,* by Leon Gordis, as well as *Naked Statistics,* by Charles Whelan. The former is actually a textbook, but it is so elegantly written and has such clear examples that it can be easily understood by lay readers, while the latter is intended for a nonspecialist audience and is rollicking good fun, a rare thing to say about a book on statistics.

Statistical significance relies on the idea that some events are random and some are not. *How* we separate the two is through various mathematical calculations, the details of which are unimportant for this discussion, but these calculations allow us to say something to the effect of

"Mathematically, what we have observed in this experiment is so unlikely that it can't just be a matter of chance." Statisticians have numerical measurement (known as a "p value") for statistical significance. With those measurements, they have selected an arbitrary dividing line between randomness and pattern, a bit like an umpire's strike zone, to allow for the process of calling the balls and the strikes of research. Different kinds of research questions call for different strike zones (i.e., there are different thresholds for statistical significance), but in general, in clinical research, the p value for significance is 0.05. What that means is that, in order for something to be considered statistically significant, for whatever observed differences are being assessed, there has to be less than one-in-twenty odds—or 5 percent, thus 0.05—that it could have happened by chance. To explore that further, let's flip some coins.

Flipping a coin is an act with a random outcome. Barring trick flips and trick coins, when a coin is flipped it has an equal chance (or one-in-two odds) of landing heads or tails. Thus, when we consider the mathematical likelihood of flipping two *consecutive* heads, the odds are one in four, or 25 percent. This can be seen by looking at all the actual possibilities of flipping a coin twice:

1.	Head	Head
2.	Tail	Head
3.	Head	Tail
4.	Tail	Tail

In a relative sense, an event that has one-in-four odds of happening is fairly likely: although the *more* likely event is a combination (either #2 or #3), if you were to repeat the "two flip" experiment many times, you would expect to see this happen with some frequency—indeed, assuming the flip of the coin is genuinely random, and if you repeated this two-flip experiment thousands of times, you would expect to see it almost precisely 25 percent of the time! Think also of parents who are planning on having kids: odds are about 50 percent that they'll have one boy and one girl and 50 percent that they'll have two children of the same sex, but only 25 percent that they'll have *either* two girls *or* two boys. And that should match most people's experiences with other friends' siblings. The point is that a one-in-four chance of something happening is pretty common: 25 percent likely things happen all the time randomly, and we don't think much of them.

Now flip the coin *three* times, and there are eight different outcomes.

1.	Head	Head	Head
2.	Tail	Head	Head
3.	Head	Tail	Head
4.	Tail	Tail	Head
5.	Head	Head	Tail
6.	Tail	Head	Tail
7.	Head	Tail	Tail
8.	Tail	Tail	Tail

So the odds of flipping three consecutive heads (or having, say, three girls) is one in eight, or 12.5 percent. It's less likely, but still not *that* uncommon. Most people know of some lovely lady bringing up three very lovely girls, or of a man with three boys of his own, or perhaps even an old-fashioned nuclear family doing the same. We're starting to get close to the boundary of statistical significance, but we're not quite there yet.

Flip the coin four times, and the odds of landing consecutive heads is one in sixteen, or just over 6 percent. Five consecutive heads has about a 3 percent chance (one-in-thirty-two odds) of occurring—or, to put it another way, if you flipped your coin five times in a row one hundred times over, odds are that about three of those hundred five-flip series would be all heads. In other words, that's *very* unlikely: if you had someone randomly flip a coin five times, and in those five flips they got five heads, your first instinct would be that they were incredibly lucky or that it wasn't random: either it's a trick flip or a trick coin.

In most of the scenarios we have discussed in this book, the mathematical threshold that statisticians want to see in order to regard something so unlikely to occur by chance as to be "real" is in this kind of range. The p value for statistical significance requires an event that is a little *more* unlikely than flipping heads four times in a row (i.e., a 6 percent chance of happening randomly) and a little *less* unlikely than flipping heads five times in a row (a 3 percent chance).

So thus far you can see that a statistically significant finding means that researchers observed a difference between two groups of things, and that the observed difference is slightly more unlikely to occur randomly as a person picking up a quarter and flipping heads four times in a row. But people aren't coins, and, besides, not every event that researchers study (like heart attacks or occurrences of cancer) has the same odds as flipping a coin. So how do statisticians ultimately arrive at a p value?

The answer is that although people and the clinical events they experience aren't actually coins, their behavior in a statistical sense is very much like a flipped coin. And although it's true that not every event has the same odds of happening as a flipped coin landing heads, statisticians make adjustments for this. To get at how this can happen without resorting to equations, let's step away from flipped coins for a moment and think about randomly plucking marbles out of a jar.

Recall the story of James Lind's scurvy experiment. Let's re-envision his experiment as observing the differences between two jars filled with marbles. The marbles come in two colors, either blue or red. Blue marbles signify "alive and healthy," and red marbles signify "dead or very close to it." Now, we modern readers happen to know with hindsight that vitamin C is essential to life, so even though Lind investigated *six* different interventions, only one arm of the study contained any appreciable amount of vitamin C. Therefore, for this example we'll pretend he only looked at the one variable of citrus fruit. The sailors who got the oranges and lemons were really getting vitamin C even if he didn't know that, and everyone else was getting nothing at all.

So if Lind had started this trial *before* his sailors went to sea and then followed them over the course of their voyage, we would say that he was going to withdraw *two* marbles out of one jar (the men who got oranges and lemons) and *ten* marbles out of the other "just watch them" (or control) jar. Picture these jars filled with hundreds or even thousands of marbles: this would be the *theoretical* population in the treatment group or the control group. In performing the experiment, the researcher is basically saying, "If I gave everyone in the world this particular treatment, and the treatment succeeds, there would be *more blue marbles in the treatment jar* (i.e., more healthy people because of the beneficial effects of my treatment) than there would be in a control jar that contained an equal number of marbles." The actual trial, then, is just like plucking out a sample from this much larger theoretical pool of people in order to compare results.

But what is the statistical likelihood that, for whichever jar, you will pluck out a blue versus red marble? If you don't know that, you can't actually know the odds of finding two blue marbles in one jar and ten red ones in the other. Let's suppose that dying from scurvy on a long sea voyage really *did* carry the same risk as flipping a coin, that is, you had a one-in-two chance of dying from scurvy when you set sail. For Lind's experiment, that would mean one would have expected equal numbers of red and blue marbles in each jar if the oranges and lemons had no effect on scurvy at all.* (In fact, although I chose the 50 percent mortality of scurvy just to make the example of picking red versus blue marbles to be a 50/50 proposition, at about the time Lind was performing his experiment, the mortality rate from scurvy on long sea voyages probably *was* 50 percent, and perhaps even higher. A famous episode in British naval history known as Anson's voyage took place in the 1740s; a small squadron of ships sailed around the world with the goal of harassing the Spanish navy as part of a geopolitical chess match between the two superpowers. At the end of the four-year journey, as many as *three-quarters* of the original crew had died, most from disease or starvation, a significant portion of which included deaths from scurvy. Almost none of the crew died from actual warfare.)

Therefore, if you had only *two* people in your trial, that is, if you randomly drew only *one* marble from each jar, and retrieved one blue marble from the oranges and lemons (treatment) jar and one red marble from the control jar, you wouldn't know what to conclude because it's basically a coin flip as to whether you draw red or blue. The chances of finding one person surviving scurvy in the treatment arm and one person dying in the control arm are 25 percent—hardly convincing data. That should make it obvious enough why enrolling two patients for a drug trial isn't a recipe

---

* The idea that we wouldn't expect to observe any difference if we assume the intervention (the oranges and lemons in this case) does *not* work is called the "null hypothesis." When a difference is observed, and the observed difference is calculated to be less likely than a one-in-twenty chance, the null hypothesis is rejected.

for success from the standpoint of clinical study design. But how many is enough?

What if the trial had *eight* participants, equally split? Suppose that you randomly drew four marbles from each jar and found three of four healthy-blue marbles in the treatment jar and three of four dead-red marbles in the control jar. Without doing statistics, at first glance most readers wouldn't find this *wildly* improbable, only *slightly* improbable. You'd say that it might *hint* at something but you'd need to see more marbles before you could be confident. That's the intuitive take, and the math backs that up: the likelihood that you would see this pattern if you drew four marbles from each jar is about 15 percent, or just under one-in-seven odds. So if Lind had run a four-person-per-arm experiment today under modern standards, we would say that his results did not support a firm conclusion that citrus fruits prevent scurvy, although he might be set up for the next grant application after this promising pilot study.[†]

As we have said, Lind's *actual* experiment involved six groups of two, but, because of what we know today, we realize that really it was one treatment group of two and a placebo group of ten. If we perform this experiment with our red and blue marbles, the math would bear out his nonmathematical conclusions about the value of oranges and lemons: the likelihood of plucking out, by pure chance, two blue marbles from the oranges and lemons jar and ten red marbles from the control jar, is about 1 in 2,000. *That* is statistically significant, and we would say that he proved that citrus fruits prevent or cure scurvy. And shame on him for not being a citrus fruit convert right away.

Now let's transport ourselves two centuries forward (while staying in Great Britain) to the site of the first truly modern drug trial, where researchers evaluated streptomycin for the treatment of tuberculosis. Unlike the situation with scurvy, the risk of dying from TB in the mid-twentieth century had different odds of happening than a coin landing on heads. Or, to think about this in another way, in a TB treatment experiment, the number of blue and red marbles in the jars is *not* equal: the mortality rate from TB among these study subjects in 1948 was just under 30 percent.

---

† Joke aside, that's actually how most modern "pilot" therapies are studied, in very small trials not geared for statistical significance, but just to see whether the researchers or clinicians are barking up a suitable tree.

That means that if you had two 10,000-marble jars, you would expect about 3,000 red marbles in each jar, and you would adjust your mathematics of the odds of plucking a red marble from each jar accordingly.

For the streptomycin study, fifty-five patients were allocated to the treatment group, and fifty-two to the control group. Of these, four of the fifty-five "marbles" in the streptomycin jar were red (a 7 percent mortality), compared to fourteen red marbles in the control jar (a 27 percent mortality). You can see at once that this is a difference, but it is not quite as dramatic a difference as in Lind's scurvy data. Keep in mind that 30 percent of the marbles in each jar should be red if streptomycin was not effective—that's the null hypothesis. Through some calculations with which we won't currently concern ourselves, the likelihood of this pattern happening by chance (i.e., of randomly plucking this particular pattern of red/blue marbles from each jar) is still very improbable: it is about 1 in 167. That's still statistically significant, and based on that we would reject the null hypothesis and conclude, as the researchers did, that streptomycin saves lives. Streptomycin is still effective against TB today, though we use it only on rare occasion because of highly toxic side effects.

But you can see that the streptomycin trial results are less dramatic than what Lind had seen in treating scurvy. If we had recruited half the number of patients for the trial (that is, about twenty-five each) and observed the same proportions of red and blue marbles, we would not have been able to conclude confidently that streptomycin saves lives, noting that it could purely have been a matter of chance that some of the streptomycin-treated patients had improved, perhaps because some patients in the treatment arm were in a better state of health and thus more likely to recover and, therefore, less likely to die. Because the mortality rate is somewhat lower, it doesn't take much of a difference to make a real effect disappear when sample sizes are small.

The implication for clinical research is that, to observe big effects, researchers don't require many "marbles" (i.e., people to recruit), but, to observe small effects, large trials are required. Most medical innovations—whether medications, new surgical techniques, screening tests, or various other developments—worth studying today have weak effects. Therefore, the kind of clinical research that's required to sort out these small effects can be a massive undertaking and can be very expensive and time-consuming. The Canadian mammography trial mentioned at the end of the chapter on mammograms took nearly three decades to complete and enrolled nearly one hundred *thousand* women. That's a remarkable allocation of resources for one clinical question, and at the end of it they found no difference. The sheer size of previous mammography studies, which recruited similar numbers of women and followed them for equally long stretches, should now indicate to you the relative magnitude of mammography's benefits even if we assume that the most optimistic estimates of their value are accurate.

Small effects can be small for more than one reason. Some interventions may be lifesaving—a saved life is a *big* benefit for a patient—but like mammography may require hundreds or even thousands of people to be treated before one life is saved. The statin drugs discussed midway through the book have a pretty big bang for the buck in patients with heart disease or very high cholesterol, but the patients now considered eligible for treatment by the new American Heart Association guidelines are almost certainly going to benefit less as a group.

Similarly, medications that lower blood pressure are lifesaving, and statistically significant results can be obtained with fairly small numbers of patients when the patients have very high blood pressures. However, many more patients are required to demonstrate that even a few lives are saved as the pressures get closer to "normal." This is the rub in the new JNC8 guidelines discussed toward the beginning of the book. The entire argument about target blood pressure revolves around the problem that, as we get lower and lower pressures, people are healthier, so it is harder to observe statistically significant effects. In other words, the jars are filled with so many *blue* marbles that we must sample from thousands and thousands of marbles to see whether there really are fewer *red* marbles in the treatment jar than in the control jar. Again, we come to the boundary of what we can distinguish, no matter how hard we squint in a statistical sense.

It is also at this edge of resolution that we have to consider that people sometimes *are* different—in their genetics, their lifestyles, and their surroundings—and we may be pulling marbles out of the jar and making conclusions based on statistical significance that cannot be generalized to all the marbles on the planet. If we were to perform statin studies on fifty-year-olds in Botswana, we might miss the value the drug has for people living in industrialized nations because the mortality rates from HIV, tuberculosis, and malaria are so high that any lifesaving effect would be negated by premature death from something else—in other words, there are too many *red* marbles in the jars for this kind of a drug trial. Likewise, if we were to perform statin experiments on a similar cohort in some Scandinavian country where everyone lives to 115 and a 50-year-old is thought of as something like an adolescent, there are too many *blue* marbles in the jars of this experiment to see any effects. As I illustrated in the arguments about blood pressure trials, the so-called FEVER study (cited by advocates of a lower target blood pressure) was performed in China. There are many reasons to suspect that this study can't be generalized to Americans or Europeans or anyone else. Alternately, two studies from Japan that found the opposite (no clear benefits from lowering blood pressure past a certain point) should also be considered with the same level of caution.

Other small effects may come in medications or lifestyles or procedures that don't *save* lives but merely improve the *quality* of life. You can find many people who will swear to you about the benefits of any number of treatments for the common cold. I'm often asked in professional and personal settings about zinc and whether that "helps." The simplest answer is, nobody knows, and that's due to a multiplicity of reasons. To really find out, in a scientifically meaningful way, that zinc can shorten the duration of the common cold, you would have to do a trial that satisfied many criteria. First, you would have to make sure that people who have symptoms that resemble the common cold actually *have* a viral infection and not some other problem like seasonal allergies; otherwise, you wouldn't know whether the fact that zinc failed to show benefit was because it was being given to the wrong population. Then you would have to enroll most patients at about the same time course of their illness because if zinc helps at all, it helps only in shortening the time people are sick, as nobody dies from the common cold. Finally you would have to figure out how you're going to actually *measure* improvement with enough precision that you could be confident that your results really do show a benefit to zinc. Measuring mortality, for instance, is easy: there is generally very little confusion among researchers when a study subject dies. But trying to find a scale for sniffles or blechiness—the kind of symptoms seen with the common cold—is much harder to design and quantify. They are "fuzzy variables," difficult to reproduce, quite subjective, and easy to manipulate, even if unintentionally.

To perform such a study with scientific exactitude, therefore, would be very expensive and probably require thousands of people. Ultimately, it would need to be funded by a group for whom cost either was not the principal concern (i.e., government) or was the overriding concern (a drug company). Because zinc cannot be patent protected, no multibillion-dollar pharmaceutical company will ever be interested in taking on a clinical zinc trial. Likewise, the NIH mercifully does not consider this a research priority, so there the matter rests, assuming nobody at the National Center for Complementary and Alternative Medicine finds the question absorbing enough to allocate funds to study it.

Do I recommend *against* people taking zinc for the common cold? No, not really. Do I take zinc *myself* when I am similarly afflicted? No, not really, unless it will mollify some well-meaning friend who feels impelled to fob said panacea upon me. Zinc for the cold is simply a question that has no answer, and, as an over-the-counter supplement, it's basically harmless—though more on that with respect to similar treatments in a moment.

Virtually all of the elixirs found in "healthy living" aisles and nutrition stores and the like resemble zinc in that if they have any beneficial effects at all, they are sufficiently small that they either *can't* be studied for reasons similar to what we've witnessed with zinc, or they *won't* be studied because there is no profit in it for potentially interested manufacturers. There are the occasional exceptions: Saint John's wort has been studied in the treatment of mild depression, and although the evidence supporting its effectiveness is mixed at best, at least it's been studied. Other over-the-counter herbals that have been evaluated include saw palmetto (prostatic hypertrophy), echinacea (common cold), and ginkgo biloba (memory loss). For the most part, no benefits have been found for any of these herbals, but given the strong likelihood that whatever beneficial effects they have are not only weak but very weak, well-designed trials on these drugs are largely wanting.

The majority of herbals, however, haven't been studied at all—and the special concoctions made by some companies as they vie for customer loyalty have combinations and home-cooked ingredients that are nearly impossible to study in any standardized way. Mostly, they're harmless except to the pocketbook, although some of them can have either interactions with prescription drugs or come with their own dangers. In the early 2000s, for instance, a rash of deaths from the use of an herbal used for weight loss known as *ma huang,* or ephedra, led the Food and Drug Administration to ban its sale in the United States. That would be not so benign.

Weak effects also make it hard to know what really constitutes the healthiest diet, another topic that is covered ad nauseam, as it were, by health reporters. Based on many observational studies, it's very clear that the combination of modest eating and frequent exercise has lifesaving benefits. What *kind* of food is associated with the greatest health is a much more difficult question to assess, although it never stops some commercially driven personality from hawking the latest fad diet or food. While this book has been in preparation, the açaí berry has become ever more revered by a particular slice of the American public bent on maximizing its health. The rapid rise in popularity of this fruit, which grows mainly in Brazil, is causing hardships for locals who had eaten it for subsistence but now cannot due to the commercial demands for this product, which is usually consumed by people who are in turn likely to donate to causes like the loss of traditional living in Amazonian rain forest that their own consumer habits are driving.*

The juice of the açaí is indeed lovely, but any firm claims about its healing properties are as nonsensical as those medieval totems that

---

* See, for instance, Adriana Brasileiro's article, "Superfood Promoted on Oprah's Site Robs Amazon Poor of Staple," on the *Bloomberg* website, May 14, 2009, http://www.bloomberg.com/apps/news?pid=newsarchive&sid=ai8WCgSJrhmY &refer=environment. Dr. Mehmet Oz, in touting the berry during a show in 2008, noted, "It has twice the antioxidant content of a blueberry." The follow-up question should have been, *So what?* There is just so much pseudoscientific nonsense in this one assertion that it's hard to know where to begin, and although it's not a big deal for people to favor açaí to blueberry in the almost certainly mistaken belief that it is somehow healthier because it has twice the antioxidant content, it has become a very big deal for poor families living in the Amazon who have been robbed of a staple crop by their wealthy and fad-susceptible cousins to the north.

pilgrims traveled vast distances to touch for their curative powers. Basically, the deep belief that people have in the benefits of fruits like these, or of herbal remedies, is just a modern expression of those same inner desires. Similarly, as with the priests of old, someone is around to capitalize on this fervor to make a few bucks. At least the medieval clergy left us cathedrals; I have no idea what lasting monuments are being generated by the herbal supplement crowd.

However, medications or approaches that lead to a completely new paradigm for a disease often *don't* require such large numbers of patients to be studied precisely because their effects are so dramatic. The drug Gleevec, mentioned in a footnote earlier in the book, completely changed the landscape for a fairly uncommon cancer known as chronic myelogenous leukemia, or CML. CML is a cancer that can be fairly indolent for years but ends in a deadly "blast crisis," and treatments designed to stave off the blast crisis had only limited benefits and came with toxic side effects. Gleevec didn't rid the body completely of the leukemia but it increased survival by several years—in some sense "curing" the disease, because CML patients are usually older anyway, so those extra years mean that CML patients pass away at around the same age as the average person. One of the famous early trials comparing Gleevec to the then-gold-standard treatment enrolled more than one thousand patients, but you didn't need a PhD in statistics to see how superiorly Gleevec had performed: about 87 percent of patients taking Gleevec had a "major cytogenetic response," compared to about 35 percent in the standard treatment group. One thousand patients weren't needed to show *that* level of benefit. (NB: the "major cytogenetic response" is a commonly accepted indicator of treatment success, but, to be clear, the trial didn't measure actual mortality, which is a more difficult thing to study in CML, owing to its prolonged course.)

In my own field of infectious diseases, Hepatitis C treatment has, like CML, undergone a paradigm shift in the past several years. For years, the backbone of Hep C treatment was a drug called interferon alpha, which like the existing treatment for CML was both toxic and not especially effective. (This is because the backbone of treatment for CML *also* was interferon alpha!) The published cure rates for Hep C using interferon-based regimens were often only 50 percent, and in the real world this almost certainly meant that all patients had a lower chance of cure. Because interferon often caused patients to be very ill, the 50 percent success rate was based on patients enrolled in studies, and these patients are typically much more motivated to complete a treatment course, side effects be damned.

Then in the late 2000s a few new drugs such as boceprevir and telaprevir came out, and suddenly the eradication of Hep C went from 50 to about 80 percent. Interferon was still required, yet real cure seemed a possibility for many more people. But the biggest change came in 2013, when the results of a trial known as COSMOS were presented at a professional meeting of hepatologists and infectious disease physicians. COSMOS involved a treatment regimen that didn't require interferon, and although the trial did not compare these two approaches head to head, the cure rate with this new combination was about *90* percent. The study looked at only about 150 patients, and thousands won't be required to see how profoundly our approach to this disease will be altered. By the time this book comes out, several new Hep C treatments that do not require interferon will be on the market, and most observers expect the cure rates of these to be so high that we are unlikely to know which of these combinations of drugs is the *most* effective, because at that point if drug X is 88 percent effective and drug Y is 92 percent effective, a trial to prove beyond doubt drug Y's superiority would require tens of thousands of patients. So issues like cost, side effects, and raw business negotiations will determine which of these new drugs will be the most commonly used in the years to come.

Much of the research discussed in this book looks at the blue marble / red marble type of studies. Blue versus red marbles in actual statistical language are known as categorical variables—the thing being studied is either this *or* that, either alive or dead, either cured or not. But many studies also look at continuous variables, which are measured in gradations. When we do research that looks at continuous variables, we aren't pulling blue and red marbles from two jars, but rather marbles that are white at one extreme, black at the other, with fifty shades of gray in between.* When we do experiments of this sort, what we're trying to find out is whether one

---

* Couldn't resist.

jar is significantly darker (or lighter) as a matter of statistics, and that the difference in shade we're observing is not due to chance.

For instance, hypertension, diabetes, and depression are all diseases that can be studied by evaluating their severity on a continuum. Suppose we want to know that a new diabetes drug does its job and actually lowers blood sugars. For this experiment we'd have our two jars (treatment and control) filled with thousands of marbles of various gray shades; darker shades represent higher blood sugars, lighter shades represent lower blood sugars. If the drug doesn't work (our null hypothesis), we'd expect the *average* shade of the marbles we pull out of the treatment jar to be more or less the same as the average shade of the marbles from the control jar. By contrast, if the drug really works, we'd expect the average shade in the treatment jar to be lighter, and so *much* lighter that it couldn't have just happened by chance.

To avoid a lengthy departure into a discussion about standard deviation, standard error, and other statistical points, I won't explain *how* the average shades are compared for differences. It's easier to grasp how categorical variables are measured without doing much math beyond talking about coin flips. Suffice it to say that there are equations that enable this comparison making, and that their general outline is reasonably similar to the kinds of math required for evaluating categorical variables. To think about this in a nonmathematical way, it should be clear that if there's a *big* difference in what's being studied, fewer subjects are required to demonstrate the difference. The more subtle the difference, the more marbles must be taken from the jars.

Clinical research on the effectiveness of antidepressants of the kind mentioned in the chapter on drug trials requires analysis of continuous variables like the Hamilton Depression Scale and its ilk. To review, the Hamilton Scale looks at a variety of psychosocial factors, assigns numbers to these factors based on the severity of symptoms, and adds them up to produce a number. Drug trials evaluating antidepressants compare the scores on depression scales of patients receiving the actual drug to those of patients receiving placebos. (They can also compare pretreatment to post-treatment scores, in which patients serve as their own controls.) It's worth recalling that, when all the published studies on antidepressants are pooled together, the drop in depression scales is modest. Like the studies that evaluated high blood pressure, the biggest benefits probably accrue to the most severe patients, where a three- or four-point swing in a depression scale might reflect the difference between being able to get out of bed or not.

The effect of prolonged antibiotics on patients with chronic fatigue syndrome, whether due to Lyme disease or anything else, is another clinical question addressed with continuous variables. In this case various "fatigue scales" are used in place of depression scales. No well-designed trial has ever found any benefit to this approach, although the chronic-Lyme ILADS enthusiasts would say that I have shown that I am a shill for the insurance industry for saying this.* Anyway, that's how the studies would be done—and, indeed, they *have* been done. Chronic fatigue is awful, and most doctors feel helpless in the face of it, precisely because of the fact that we haven't found any effective treatments thus far.

Continuous and categorical variables can be combined as well. One of the early studies on smoking was published in 1952; it looked at 1,357 men who had lung cancer and compared them to an equal group of men who didn't. Then they pulled the marbles from the jar and looked at whether they smoked. If they had looked at smoking *only* as a categorical variable (i.e., black or white marbles), they would have found that smoking was associated with lung cancer: 1,350 of 1,357 men with cancer smoked, while "only" 1296 men who didn't have cancer smoked.† But they also looked at how *much* they smoked, and the results at the time must have been shocking, for smoking more cigarettes was clearly associated with cancer as seen on the next page:

In other words, the average grey shade of the marbles drawn from the cancer jar was distinctly darker than those emerging from the noncancer jar, not unlike the actual lungs these metaphorical marbles represent.

---

* Note to insurance companies: please send money, *lots* of money, for my advocacy. Though, sorry for the Hep C drug costs and all.

† Keep in mind that this is a study of correlation, and that although the study found a significant correlation *between* smoking and lung cancer, as we discussed earlier that does not prove that smoking *causes* lung cancer. Indeed, the father of modern biostatistics, Sir Ronald Fisher, used the "correlation doesn't prove causation" argument to deny the importance of smoking as a risk for lung cancer well past its expiration date, going to his grave in 1962 as a chain smoker, presumably coughing all the way.

Average Daily Cigarettes	Lung Cancer	No Lung Cancer (Control)
0	7	61
1–4	55	129
5–14	489	570
15–24	475	431
25–49	293	154
50+	38	12
Total	1,357	1,357

But what is the use of all this talk of marbles and coins when the headlines come streaming across one's electronic device,[‡] or when a physician is talking about guidelines for screening or treating a disease? I would say that there are a few simple takeaways. One doesn't need to have a PhD in biostatistics to get the basic idea of how relevant or how speculative medical research can be, and whether one should alter one's life just because of the latest journal article or new set of guidelines.

First, know the type of research being done. Clinical research—that is, experiments done involving human beings—is always more relevant than any other form of scientific inquiry when it comes to health news. As I completed the first draft of this manuscript in August 2014, I saw a CNN headline with the title "Venom May Hold Cure for Cancer." The article described the research of a scientist working with bee, snake, and scorpion venom, and how some of the proteins extracted from those fluids appeared to halt the growth of some cancer cell lines in a culture dish.

Intriguing research? Quite possibly. Should patients who have cancer call their oncologists to inquire about experimental venom treatments? No, they shouldn't. Do stories like this with a catchy title encourage those kinds of calls? They do, and, depending on the size of the story and the fantastical nature of the claims, those kinds of calls can occasionally grind a clinic to a halt as the physicians scramble to read about the research so as to give a knowledgeable response. Sometimes, as with this

‡ Or, for the hundred or so people who do not acknowledge the twenty-first century, the newspaper.

"Venom Cures Cancer" story, there isn't any scientific study for a doctor to read *about* because this is preliminary research being presented at a scientific conference and hasn't yet been published in a peer-reviewed journal.

Second, if it is clinical research, understand the *kind* of research that's being done. News articles that don't describe the basic design of the study aren't worth reading. This book didn't go into much detail about the different types of studies, except for emphasizing the difference between studies that identify correlations and those that directly test the effects of a variable (like a drug or vaccine trial). Studies that look at correlation should be viewed with a certain level of healthy skepticism. This is the central problem with the many epidemiologic studies that are fodder for news media: reports about fiber consumption, the link between using electronic devices and various diseases, the environmental causes of autism—these and other studies are all done largely by looking at correlations.

That's not to imply that people should simply dismiss all studies that look at correlations: healthy skepticism is not the same thing as abject disbelief. Still, it's worth keeping in mind the story of hormone replacement therapy, where the correlation data indicating it was beneficial was strong, but, when it was put directly to the test, hormone therapy failed. So *if* there is a clinical question that can be studied directly in a trial (usually, but not always, this applies to drugs), a well-designed trial is always superior.

It's also useful to know whether investigators are studying weak or strong effects, and whether the studies looking at those effects are appropriately large or small. There's always some study looking at the effects of, say, coffee consumption on any number of health questions, such as whether it increases the risk for heart attacks, whether consumption during pregnancy results in low birth weight, of whether it's protective against Alzheimer's disease. Whatever effects routine coffee consumption may have in these situations, they are likely to have a small impact, so studies that assert that something like coffee is linked with certain outcomes, yet enroll a relatively small number of people, should be regarded with caution, and are probably not worth changing your coffee habits immediately.

Finally, it's critically important to understand the *size* of the benefit or harmful effect. Some clinical studies may have findings that meet statistical significance but may nevertheless not be "significant" in anything other than statistics. If a paper or a study merely *says* that there is some benefit, a good question to ask is, *How* big *is the benefit?* If the answer is slow in coming, or never does come, then it could very well be making mountains out of molehills.

For example, male circumcision of infants is sometimes justified in medical terms by studies indicating it may lower one's risk of penile cancer later—*much* later—in life. Supposing these studies are accurate and well designed, circumcision would lower the risk of developing a cancer that, in industrialized nations, affects less than one man per *100,000*. To put it differently, this research shows that circumcision lowers a man's risk of getting penile cancer from almost nothing to *half* of almost nothing. There is just not very much medical benefit to be had, at least in terms of cancer prevention in nations with a high standard of living.* (I hope I am clear here—especially as a member in reasonably good standing of a culture that still practices male circumcision—that I am not opposed to the practice but am using the arguments about its medical benefits to make a point about statistical significance.)

Similarly, a recent set of guidelines has come out about screening smokers for lung cancer with CT scans. The guidelines were based on a large trial comparing smokers who got an annual scan versus those who got an annual chest X-ray. The trial showed that there was a lifesaving benefit to the scans: if you just had an annual chest X-ray, you were more likely to die of lung cancer than if you got an annual CT.

At this point, if I have done a decent job of explaining overdiagnosis, positive predictive value, and uncertainty, your sensors should be on high alert wondering just how *much* more likely death will befall a person who gets annual X-rays instead of CT scans. The answer, as you may not be totally surprised, is *not much,* although the benefits can be framed in very

---

* The situation is different in less industrialized nations. Circumcision at *any* age in sub-Saharan Africa is extremely likely to reduce one's risk of acquiring, and possibly passing along, HIV infection. The data on circumcision lowering the risk of penile cancer is also more robust in Africa, where penile cancer is significantly more common than in Europe or North America.

different ways. The CT scans resulted in a 20 percent reduction in mortality over five years' time. Whether that sounds like a big benefit I will leave for you to judge, but not before I translate that same benefit into a different form. The 20 percent reduction means that, for every one thousand people, three extra lives will be saved during a five-year span.

That statistic, too, might prompt some wondering about the potential harms of CT scanning: Is there any downside to annual screening that might negate this fairly modest benefit? One answer we know in theory (meaning that it has not been studied extensively at a clinical level) is that CTs pack a lot of radiation. That is, CTs *themselves* may increase one's risk of lung cancer, and presumably the risks are going to be higher among younger patients because the radiation has more of an opportunity to create aberrant cells that lead to cancer over decades.

There is at least one other well-understood harm from these CTs, and this, too, should sound familiar, for the chance that just *one* CT will result in a false positive is a staggering 25 percent. After three years, the false-positive rate is nearly *40* percent. Mind you, although a false-positive mammogram may be associated with a more intense form of anxiety, suffering, and loss than a false-positive CT suggestive of lung cancer, a breast biopsy is for the most part a procedure that does not carry significant risk of physical harm. The same cannot be said of lung biopsies no matter how they are done, and moreover their accuracy is much lower than that of breast biopsies.

Lung CT scans for smokers is a different blizzard with its own set of snowballs, but the principles of the storm remain the same, which seems an appropriate place to end.

Bibliography

INTRODUCTION

Glare, P., et al. A systematic review of physicians' survival predictions in terminally ill cancer patients. *BMJ* 2003; 327:195–201.

Kondziolka, D., et al. The accuracy of predicting survival in individual patients with cancer. *J Neurosurg* 2014; 120:24–30.

Pollan, Michael. *In defense of food: An eater's manifesto.* New York: Penguin Press, 2008.

Porter, Roy. *The greatest benefit to mankind: A medical history of humanity.* 1st American ed. New York: W. W. Norton, 1998.

Silver, Nate. *The signal and the noise: Why so many predictions fail—but others don't.* New York: Penguin Press, 2012.

Taleb, Nicholas Nassim. *The black swan: The impact of the highly improbable.* New York: Random House, 2007.

CHAPTER ONE: PRIMUN NON NOCERE

Albertsen P., et al. Prostate cancer and the Will Rogers phenomenon. *J Natl Cancer Inst* 2005; 97(17):1248–1253.

American Cancer Society. *Cancer facts & figures 2013.* Atlanta: American Cancer Society, 2013.

Arkes, H., and Gaissmaier, W. Psychological research and the prostate-cancer screening controversy. *Psychological Science* 2012; 23:547–553.

Berliner, Uri. Tired of gloom and doom? Here's the best good news of 2013. *Morning Edition,* National Public Radio, December 24, 2013.

Berner, E., and Graber, M. Overconfidence as a cause of diagnostic error in medicine. *Am J Med* 2008; 121(5A):S2-S23.

Black, William. Overdiagnosis: An underrecognized cause of confusion and harm in cancer screening. *J Natl Cancer Inst* 2010; 92(16):1280–1282.

Carter, H. B., et al. *Early detection of prostate cancer: AUA guideline.* American Urological Association, 2013.

Harach, H., et al. Occult papillary carcinoma of the thyroid: A "normal" finding in Finland; A systematic autopsy study. *Cancer* 1985; 56(3): 531–538.

Haselton, M., and Buss, D. Biases in social judgment: Design flaws or design features? In *Responding to the social world: Implicit and explicit processes in social judgments and decisions,* ed. J. P. Forgas, K. D. Williams, and W. von Hippel, pp. 23–43. Cambridge: Cambridge University Press, 2013.

Heath, Iona. Overdiagnosis: When good intentions meet vested interests. *BMJ* 2013; 347:f6361–6363.

Ilic, D., et al. Screening for prostate cancer. *Cochrane Database of Syst Rev* 2013, Issue 1.

Kahneman, Daniel. *Thinking fast and slow.* New York: Farrar, Straus, and Giroux, 2011.

Monynihan, R., et al. Preventing overdiagnosis: How to stop harming the healthy. *BMJ* 2012; 344:e3502–e3508.

Moyer, V. A., and the US Preventive Services Task Force. Screening for prostate cancer: US Preventive Services Task Force recommendation statement. *Ann Intern Med* 2012; 157:120–134.

Rosenhan, D. L. On being sane in insane places. *Science* 1973; 179 (4070):250–258.

Soos, G., et al. The prevalence of prostate carcinoma and its precursor in Hungary: An autopsy study. *Eur Urol* 2005; 48(5):739–744.

Spitzer, Robert. On pseudoscience in science, logic in remission, and psychiatric diagnosis: A critique of Rosenhan's "On being sane in insane places." *J of Abnorm Psychol* 1975: 84(5): 442–452.

Spitzer, R., et al. The scientific credibility of Lauren Slater's pseudopatient diagnosis study. *J Nerv Ment Dis* 2005; 193:734–739.

Welch, H. Gilbert. *Overdiagnosed: Making people sick in the pursuit of health.* Boston: Beacon Press, 2011.

Welch, H. G., and Black, W. Overdiagnosis in cancer. *J Natl Cancer Inst* 2010; 102:605–613.

Wiener, R. S., et al. When a test is too good: How CT pulmonary angiograms find pulmonary emboli that do not need to be found. *BMJ* 2013; 347:f3368-f3375.

CHAPTER TWO: VIGNETTE

Mlodinow, Leonard. *The drunkard's walk: How randomness rules our lives.* New York: Pantheon Books, 2008.

CHAPTER THREE: SNOWBALL IN A BLIZZARD

American Cancer Society. *Breast cancer facts & figures 2011–12.* Atlanta: American Cancer Society, 2012.

Bassett, L., and Gold, R. The evolution of mammography. *AJR* 1988; 150; 493–498.

Caplan, Arthur. "Mammogram advice accurate but not 'right.'" *NBCNews .com,* November 19, 2009. http://www.nbcnews.com/id/34040273/ns /health-cancer/t/mammogram-advice-accurate-not-right/#.VZhGllL bJMs, retrieved July 2015.

Elmore, J., et al. Screening mammograms by community radiologists: Variability in false-positive rates. *J Natl Cancer Inst* 2002; 94(18): 1373–1380.

Feld, Ellen. A doctor discovers a patient in the mirror. *New York Times,* July 19, 2010.

———. Finding little comfort in the statistics of survival. *New York Times,* October 17, 2011.

Fletcher, Suzanne. Whither scientific deliberation in health policy recommendations?—Alice in the Wonderland of breast cancer screening. *N Engl J Med* 1997; 336:1180–1183.

Gøtzsche, P. C., and Nielsen, M. Screening for breast cancer with mammography. *Cochrane Database of Syst Rev* 2011, Issue 4.

Jørgensen, K., and Gøtzsche, P. C. Overdiagnosis in publicly organised mammography screening programmes: Systematic review of incidence trends. *BMJ* 2009; 339:b2587-b2595.

Kerlikowske, Karla. Screening mammography in women less than age 50 years. *Curr Opin Obstet Gynecol* 2012; 24:38–43.

Kolata, Gina. Mammogram debate took group by surprise. *New York Times,* November 20, 2009.

————. Vast study casts doubt on value of mammograms. *New York Times,* February 11, 2014.

Lobo, Roger. Where are we 10 years after the Women's Health Initiative? *J Clin Endocrinol Metab* 2013; 98:1771–1780.

Major cancer agencies respond to USPSTF's new mammography guidelines. *Oncology,* December 15, 2009. http://www.cancernetwork.com /oncology-journal/major-cancer-agencies-respond-uspstf%E2%80 %99s-new-mammography-guidelines, retrieved July 2015.

Mandelblatt, J., et al. for the Breast Cancer Working Group of the Cancer Intervention and Surveillance Modeling Network (CISNET). Effects of mammography screening under different screening schedules: Model estimates of potential benefits and harms. *Ann Intern Med* 2009; 151:738–747.

Miller, A., et al. Twenty-five year follow-up for breast cancer incidence and mortality of the Canadian National Breast Screening Study: Randomised screening trial. *BMJ* 2014; 348:g366–g376.

Nyström, L., et al. Long-term effects of mammography screening: Updated overview of the Swedish randomised trials. *Lancet* 2002; 359:909–919.

Pace, L., et al. Trends in mammography screening rates after publication of the 2009 US Preventive Services Task Force recommendations. *Cancer* 2013; 119:2518–2523.

Rabin, Roni Caryn. New guidelines on breast cancer draw opposition. *New York Times,* November 16, 2009.

Saul, Stephanie. Prone to error: Earliest steps to find cancer. *New York Times,* July 19, 2010.

Shapiro, Sam. Evidence on screening for breast cancer from a randomized trial. *Cancer* 1977; 39:2772–2782.

Susan G. Komen for the Cure. *Facts for life: Breast cancer detection.* http://ww5.komen.org/uploadedFiles/_Komen/Content/About _Breast_Cancer/Tools_and_Resources/Fact_Sheets_and_Breast_Self _Awareness_Cards/BreastCancerDetection.pdf. Retrieved July 2014; updated version retrieved July 2015.

US Preventive Services Task Force. Screening for breast cancer: U.S. Preventive Services Task Force recommendation statement. *Ann Intern Med* 2009; 151:716–726.

Zahl, P. H., et al. Incidence of breast cancer in Norway and Sweden during introduction of nationwide screening: Prospective cohort study. *BMJ* 2004; 328:921–924.

CHAPTER FOUR: THE PRESSURES OF
MANAGING PRESSURE

Gibbons, G., et al. Refocusing the agenda on cardiovascular guidelines: An announcement from the National Heart, Lung, and Blood Institute. *Circulation* 2013; 128(15):1713–1715.

Husten, Larry. The heart guidelines are dead: Long live the heart guidelines. *Forbes,* August 9, 2013.

———. Minority report: Five guideline authors reject change in blood pressure goal. *Forbes,* January 13, 2014.

James, P., et al. Evidence-based guideline for the management of high blood pressure in adults: Report from the panel members appointed to the Eighth Joint National Committee (JNC8). *JAMA* 2014; 311(5):507–520.

Moser, M., et al. Report of the Joint National Committee on the detection, evaluation, and treatment of high blood pressure: A cooperative study. *JAMA* 1977; 237(3):255–261.

Myers, M. and Tobe, S. A. Canadian perspective on the Eighth Joint National Committee (JNC8) hypertension guidelines. *J Clin Hypertens* 2014; 16(4):246–248.

Navar-Boggan, A., et al. Proportion of US adults potentially affected by the 2014 hypertension guideline. *JAMA* 2014; 311(14):1424–1429.

Peterson, E., et al. Recommendations for treating hypertension: What are the right goals and purposes? *JAMA* 2014; 311(5):474–476.

SHEP Cooperative Research Group. Prevention of stroke by antihypertensive drug treatment in older persons with isolated systolic hypertension: Final results of the Systolic Hypertension in the Elderly Program (SHEP). *JAMA* 1991; 265:3255–3264.

Wright, J., et al. Evidence supporting a systolic blood pressure goal of less than 150 mm Hg in patients aged 60 years or older: The minority view. *Ann Int Med* 2014; 160(7):499–503.

CHAPTER FIVE: LYME'S FALSE PROPHETS

Asher, Tammy. Unprecedented antitrust investigation into the Lyme disease treatment guidelines development process. *Gonzaga Law Rev* 2011; 46:117–145.

Blumenthal, Richard. Attorney general's investigation reveals flawed Lyme disease guideline process, IDSA agrees to reassess guidelines, install independent arbiter. Office of the Attorney General of the State of Connecticut, press release, May 1, 2008.

Brody, Jane. A threat in a grassy stroll. *New York Times,* July 15, 2008.

cave76. Stricker's alleged scientific misconduct. Lymenet Europe, January 27, 2008. http://www.lymeneteurope.org/forum/viewtopic.php?f=7&t =627&sid=f5c5d5cbd75745be96847bcd6158ce80&start=10.

Centers for Disease Control and Prevention. Other types of laboratory testing. http://www.cdc.gov/lyme/diagnosistesting/labtest/otherlab /index.html, accessed July 2015.

Chang, Kenneth. Paleontology and creationism meet but don't mesh. *New York Times,* June 29, 2009.

Cressey, Daniel. XMRV paper withdrawn. *Nature* (blog), December 22, 2011.

Feder, H., et al. A critical appraisal of chronic Lyme disease. *N Engl J Med* 2007; 357:1422–1430.

International Lyme and Associated Diseases Society (ILADS). Basic information about Lyme disease. http://www.ilads.org/lyme/about -lyme.php, retrieved July 2015.

Klein, Jerome. Danger ahead: Politics intrude in Infectious Diseases Society of America guideline for Lyme disease. *Clin Inf Dis* 2008; 47:1197–1199.

Klempner, M., et al. Two controlled trials of antibiotic treatment in patients with persistent symptoms and a history of Lyme disease. *N Engl J Med* 2001; 345:85–92.

Landers, Susan. Lyme disease debate provokes treatment divide, legal action. *American Medical News,* December 25, 2006.

Lantos, P., et al. Final report of the Lyme Disease Review Panel of the Infectious Diseases Society of America (IDSA). *Clin Inf Dis* 2010; 51(1):1–5.

Levin Becker, Arielle. Blumenthal takes Lyme disease fight to the Senate. *CT Mirror,* July 18, 2011.

National Institutes of Health, Office of Research Integrity. Final findings of scientific misconduct. http://grants.nih.gov/grants/guide/notice -files/not93–177.html, retrieved July 2015.

Stricker, R., and Johnson, L. Chronic Lyme disease and the "Axis of Evil." *Future Microbiol* 2008; 3(6):621–624.

———. Lyme disease: The next decade. *Infect Drug Resist* 2011; 4:1–9.

Whelan, David. Lyme, Inc.: Ticks aren't the only parasites living off patients in borreliosis-prone areas. *Forbes,* February 23, 2007.

Wormser, G., et al. The clinical assessment, treatment, and prevention of Lyme disease, human granulocytic anaplasmosis, and babesiosis: Clinical practice guidelines by the Infectious Diseases Society of America. *Clin Inf Dis* 2006; 43:1089–1134.

———. A limitation of 2-stage serological testing for Lyme disease: Enzyme immunoassay and immunoblot assay are not independent tests. *Clin Infect Dis* 2000; 30(3):545–548.

CHAPTER SIX: THE ORIGINS OF KNOWLEDGE AND THE SEEDS OF UNCERTAINTY

Cholesterol Treatment Trialists' (CTT) Collaboration. Efficacy and safety of more intensive lowering of LDL cholesterol: A meta-analysis of data from 170,000 participants in 26 randomised trials. *Lancet* 2010; 376:1670–1681.

Downs, J., et al. Primary prevention of acute coronary events with lovastatin in men and women with average cholesterol levels. *JAMA* 1998; 279:1615–1622.

Dunn, Peter. James Lind (1716–94) of Edinburgh and the treatment of scurvy. *Arch Dis Child Fetal Neonatal Ed* 1997; 76:F64-F65.

Endo, Akira. The origin of statins. *Atheroscler Suppl* 2004; 5(3):125–130.

Finegold, J., et al. What proportion of symptomatic side effects in patients taking statins are genuinely caused by the drug? Systematic review of randomized placebo-controlled trials to aid individual patient choice. *Eur J Prev Cardiol* 2014; 21(4):464–474.

Frick, M. H., et al. Helsinki Heart Study: Primary-prevention trial with gemfibrozil in middle-aged men with dyslipidemia: Safety of treatment, changes in risk factors, and incidence of coronary heart disease. *N Engl J Med* 1987; 317(20):1237–1245.

General Nutrition Centers, Inc. GNC men's saw palmetto formula. http://www.gnc.com/GNC-Mens-Saw-Palmetto-Formula/product.jsp?productId=13088264, retrieved July 2015.

Gilbody, S. M., House, A. O., and Sheldon, T. A. Psychiatrists in the UK do not use outcomes measures: National survey. *Br J Psychiatry* 2002; 180:101.

Jeger, R., and Dieterle, T. Statins: Have we found the Holy Grail? *Swiss Med Wkly* 2012; 142:w13515.

Johnson, Linda. Against odds, Lipitor became world's top seller. *USA Today,* December 28, 2011.

Kramer, Peter. *Listening to Prozac.* New York: Viking, 1993.

Lipid Clinics Research Program. The Lipid Research Clinics coronary primary prevention trial results. *JAMA* 1984; 251:351–364.

Mark, T. L., et al. Datapoints: Psychotropic drug prescriptions by medical specialty. *Psychiatr Serv* 2009; 60(9):1167.

Maron, D., et al. Current perspectives on statins. *Circulation* 2000; 101(2):207–213.

Mojtabai, R., and Olfson, M. National patterns in antidepressant treatment by psychiatrists and general medical providers: Results from the national comorbidity survey replication. *J Clin Psychiatry* 2008; 69(7):1064–1074.

Pencina, M., et al. Application of new cholesterol guidelines to a population-based sample. *N Engl J Med* 2014; 370:1422–1431.

Pratt, L., et al. Antidepressant use in persons aged 12 and over: United States, 2005–2008. Centers for Disease Control NCHS Data Brief 2011; 76:1–8.

Scandinavian Simvastatin Survival Study Group. Randomised trial of cholesterol lowering in 4444 patients with coronary heart disease. *Lancet* 1994; 344(8934):1383–1389.

Shepherd, J., et al. Prevention of coronary heart disease with pravastatin in men with hypercholesterolemia. *N Engl J Med* 1995; 333: 1301–1307.

Stone, N., et al. 2013 ACC/AHA guideline on the treatment of blood cholesterol to reduce atherosclerotic cardiovascular risk in adults: A report of the American College of Cardiology/American Heart Association Task Force on Practice Guidelines. *Circulation* 2014; 129(25 Supp 2):S1–S45.

Thompson, Warren. Cholesterol: Myth or reality? *Southern Med Jrnl* 1990; 83(4):435–440.

Tobert, Jonathan. Efficacy and long-term adverse effect pattern of lovastatin. *Am J Cardiol* 1988; 62:28J–34J.

Turner, E., et al. Selective publication of antidepressant trials and its influence on apparent efficacy. *N Engl J Med* 2008; 358(3):252–260.

Witzum, J. L. Current approaches to drug therapy for the hypercholesterolemic patient. *Circulation* 1989; 80:1101–1114.

Wong, D., et al. The discovery of fluoxetine hydrochloride (Prozac). *Nat Rev Drug Discov* 2005; 4(9):764–774.

Wurtzel, Elizabeth. *Prozac nation: Young and depressed in America.* Boston: Houghton-Mifflin, 1994.

CHAPTER SEVEN: THE CORRELATION/
CAUSATION PROBLEM

Bakalar, Nicholas. In one study, a heart benefit for chocolate. *New York Times,* September 14, 2009.

Baylin, A., et al. Transient exposure to coffee as a trigger of a first non-fatal myocardial infarction. *Epidemiology* 2006; 17(5):506–511.

Bouchez, C. HRT: Revisiting the hormone decision. *WebMD,* http://www.webmd.com/menopause/features/hrt-revisiting-the-hormone-decision, retrieved July 2015.

Centers for Disease Control and Prevention. Pneumocystis pneumonia—Los Angeles. *MMWR Morb Mortal Wkly Rep* 1981; 30(21):250–252.

Chang, Louise. Coffee may trigger heart attack. *WebMD Health News,* August 15, 2006. http://www.webmd.com/heart-disease/news/20060815/coffee-may-trigger-heart-attack, retrieved July 2015.

Evans, David. Pfizer broke the law by promoting drugs for unapproved uses. *Bloomberg,* November 9, 2009.

Herbst, Arthur. Interview on 40th anniversary of publication of DES paper. The University of Chicago. https://www.youtube.com/watch?v=doSpbfDcJHc, retrieved July 2015.

Herbst, A., et al. Adenocarcinoma of the vagina: Association of maternal stilbestrol therapy with tumor appearance in young women. *N Engl J Med* 1971; 284(16):878–881.

Herbst, A., and Scully, R. Adenocarcinoma of the vagina in adolescence: A report of 7 cases including 6 clear-cell carcinomas (so-called meso-nephromas). *Cancer* 1970; 25(4):745–757.

Hulley, S., et al. Randomized trial of estrogen plus progestin for second-ary prevention of coronary heart disease in postmenopausal women: Heart and Estrogen/Progestin Replacement Study (HERS) Research Group. *JAMA* 1998; 280:605–613.

Janszky, I., et al. Chocolate consumption and mortality following a first acute myocardial infarction: The Stockholm Heart Epidemiology Program. *J Intern Med* 2009; 266(3):248–257.

Kolata, Gina. Citing risks, U.S. will halt study of drugs for hormones. *New York Times,* July 9, 2002.

Kolata, G., and Petersen, M. Hormone replacement study a shock to the system. *New York Times,* July 10, 2002.

Lobo, Roger. Where are we 10 years after the Women's Health Initiative? *J Clin Endocrinol Metab* 2013; 98:1771–1780.

Nelson, H., et al. Menopausal hormone therapy for the primary prevention of chronic conditions: A systematic review to update the U.S. Preventive Services Task Force recommendations. *Ann Intern Med* 2012; 157:104–113.

Newell, G., et al. Toxicity, immunosuppressive effects and carcinogenic potential of volatile nitrites: Possible relationship to Kaposi's sarcoma. *Pharmacotherapy* 1984; 4(5):284–291.

Petersen, Molly. Wyeth stock falls 24% after report. *New York Times,* July 10, 2002.

Smith, D., et al. Association of exogenous estrogen and endometrial carcinoma. *N Engl J Med* 1975; 293(23):1164–1167.

Sommers, N., and Ridgeway, J. Can a woman be feminine forever? *New Republic,* March 19, 1966.

Wilson, Robert. *Feminine forever.* New York: M. Evans, 1966.

CHAPTER EIGHT: "HEALTH WATCH"

Arnheim-Dahlström, L., et al. Autoimmune, neurological, and venous thromboembolic adverse events after immunisation of adolescent girls with quadrivalent human papillomavirus vaccine in Denmark and Sweden: Cohort study. *BMJ* 2013; 347:f5906–f5916.

Brainard, Curtis. Mixed grades for medical coverage. *Columbia Journalism Review,* April 22, 2011, http://www.cjr.org/the_observatory/mixed _grades_for_med_coverage.php, retrieved July 2015.

Ceccarelli, Leah. Manufactroversy: The art of creating controversy where none existed. *Science Progress,* April 11, 2008.

Couric, Katie. Furthering the conversation on the HPV vaccine. *Huffington Post,* December 10, 2013. http://www.huffingtonpost.com /katie-couric/vaccine-hpv-furthering-conversation_b_4418568.html, retrieved July 2015.

———. The HPV vaccine controversy. *Katie,* December 4, 2013. The full episode is now no longer accessible, as the *Katie* website was taken down during the writing of this book. A portion of the show remains on YouTube: https://www.youtube.com/watch?v=DjJd2hK76ZY, retrieved July 2015.

Fox, Maggie. German doctors declare "cure" in HIV patient. *Reuters,* December 15, 2010. http://www.reuters.com/article/2010/12/15/us-aids -transplant-idUSTRE6BE68220101215, retrieved July 2015.

Future II Study Group. Quadrivalent vaccine against human papillo-mavirus to prevent high-grade cervical lesions. *N Engl J Med* 2007; 356:1915–1927.

Jaslow, Ryan. Katie Couric show on HPV vaccine sparks backlash. *CBS News,* December 5, 2013. http://www.cbsnews.com/news/katie-couric -show-on-hpv-vaccine-sparks-backlash/, retrieved July 2015.

Mnookin, Seth. *The panic virus: A true story of medicine, science, and fear.* New York: Simon & Schuster, 2011.

Orac. H1N1 vaccine and miscarriages: More dumpster diving in the VAERS database. *ScienceBlogs,* November 28, 2012. http://science blogs.com/insolence/2012/11/28/h1n1-vaccine-and-miscarriages -more-antivaccine-fear-mongering-about-flu-vaccines/, retrieved July 2015.

———. Katie Couric on the HPV vaccine: Antivaccine or irresponsible journalist? You be the judge! *ScienceBlogs,* December 5, 2013. http:// scienceblogs.com/insolence/2013/12/05/katie-couric-on-the-hpv -vaccine-antivaccine-or-irresponsible-journalist-you-be-the-judge/, retrieved July 2015. Includes links to the *Katie* episode as well as in-terviews with others.

Reynolds, Gretchen. Can you get too much exercise? *New York Times,* July 24, 2013.

Schwitzer, Gary. How do US journalists cover treatments, tests, products, and procedures? *PLoS Med* 2008; 5(5):e95.

Schwitzer, G., et al. *HealthNewsReview: Your health news watchdog.* http:// www.healthnewsreview.org/, retrieved July 2015.

———. To build a knee: Done right, it's fast, safe, and effective. *HealthNewsReview,* http://www.healthnewsreview.org/review/976/, re-trieved July 2015.

Siegel, Marc. *False alarm: The truth about the epidemic of fear.* Hoboken, NJ: John Wiley & Sons, 2005.

US Department of Health and Human Services. Vaccine adverse event reporting system. https://vaers.hhs.gov/index, retrieved July 2015. The database for the 2013 reports can be found at this website.

CHAPTER NINE: CONCLUSION

Allen, Arthur. *Vaccine: The controversial story of medicine's greatest life-saver.* New York: W. W. Norton, 2007.

American College of Radiology. USPSTF breast cancer screening recommendations would cost thousands of lives and could eliminate mammography insurance coverage for millions of women, press release, April 20, 2015. http://www.acr.org/About-Us/Media-Center/Press-Releases/2015-Press-Releases/20150420-Draft-USPSTF-Breast-Cancer-Screening-Recommendations-Would-Cost-Thousands-of-Lives, retrieved July 2015.

Bernard, S., et al. Treatment of comatose survivors of out-of-hospital cardiac arrest with induced hypothermia. *N Engl J Med* 2002, 346:557–563.

Blagden, S. P., et al. Performance status score: Do patients and their oncologists agree? *Brit J Cancer* 2003; 89:1022–1027.

Friedewald, S., et al. Breast cancer screening using tomosynthesis in combination with digital mammography. *JAMA* 2014; 311(24):2499–2507.

Glare, Paul. Clinical predictors of survival in advanced cancer. *J Support Oncol* 2005; 3:331–339.

Harris, Gail. Family-centered rounds in the neonatal intensive care unit. *Nursing for Women's Health* 2014; 18(1):20–27.

Jacobowski, N., et al. Communication in critical care: Family rounds in the intensive care unit. *Am J Crit Care* 2010; 19:421–430.

Jauhar, Sandeep. When doctors need to lie. *New York Times,* February 22, 2014.

Kitch, Barrett. Inviting families to daily ICU work rounds. *Massachusetts Board of Registration in Medicine Newsletter*, January 2014.

Offit, Paul. *Autism's false prophets: Bad science, risky medicine, and the search for a cure.* New York: Columbia University Press, 2008.

Schiller, W., and Anderson, B. Family as a member of the trauma rounds: A strategy for maximized communication. *J Trauma Nurs* 2003; 10(4):93–101.

Schwitzer, Gary. Which journalists reported an extra dimension on the 3-D mammography story? *HealthNewsReview,* June 25, 2014. http://www.healthnewsreview.org/2014/06/who-reported-an-extra-dimension-of-the-3-d-mammography-story/, retrieved July 2015.

Whitney, C., et al. Benefits from immunization during the Vaccines for Children Program era—United States, 1994–2013. *MMWR Morb Mortal Wkly Rep* 2014; 63(16):352–355.

APPENDIX

Christensen, Jen. Bee, scorpion and snake venom may hold cancer cure. CNN, August 12, 2014. http://edition.cnn.com/2014/08/12/health /venom-nanotechnology-cancer/, retrieved July 2015.

Crofton, J. The MRC randomized trial of streptomycin and its legacy: A view from the clinical front line. *J R Soc Med* 2006; 99:531–534.

Doll, R., and Hill, A. B. A study of the aetiology of carcinoma of the lung. *BMJ* 1952; 2:1271–1286.

Gordis, Leon. *Epidemiology,* 4th ed. Philadelphia: Elsevier/Saunders, 2009.

Larke, N., et al. Male circumcision and penile cancer: A systematic review and meta-analysis. *Cancer Causes Control* 2011; 22:1097–1110.

Marshall, G., et al. Streptomycin treatment of pulmonary tuberculosis. *BMJ* 1948; October 30:769–782.

National Lung Screening Trial Research Team. The National Lung Screening Trial: Overview and study design. *Radiology* 2011; 258(1):243–253.

O'Brien, S., et al. Imatinib compared with interferon and low-dose cytarabine for newly diagnosed chronic-phase chronic myeloid leukemia. *N Engl J Med* 2003; 348:994–1004.

Stolley, Paul. When genius errs: R. A. Fisher and the lung cancer controversy. *Am J Epidemiol* 1991; 133(5):416–425.

Whelan, Charles. *Naked statistics: Stripping the dread from the data.* New York: W. W. Norton, 2013.

Index